MW00713818

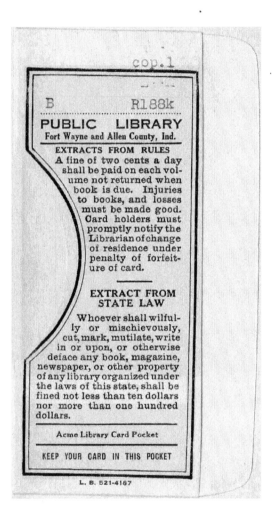

WALTHER RATHENAU

WALTHER RATHENAU IN THE CAR IN WHICH HE WAS ASSASSINATED

Walther Rathenau

HIS LIFE AND WORK

by Count Harry Kessler

HARCOURT, BRACE AND COMPANY

NEW YORK

PRINTED IN THE UNITED STATES OF AMERICA
BY QUINN & BODEN COMPANY, INC., RAHWAY, N. J.

TO

GERHART HAUPTMANN

IN MEMORY OF

OUR COMMON FRIENDSHIP FOR

WALTHER RATHENAU

Walther Rathenau

CONTENTS

ILLUSTRATIONS

WALTHER RATHENAU

INTRODUCTION

N O ESTIMATE of Walther Rathenau, the founder of Germany's new foreign policy and of the post-war rationalization of German industry, can do him justice that is not based on his singular personality. The profoundly Jewish, and yet no less profoundly Prussian, mechanism of his mind and instincts can always be discerned behind his political and social ideas. Scientific proofs for his theories he utterly disdained, appealing for their truth solely to the rightness of his vision and the sureness of his instinct. He propounded them not like a great man of science who proves his point step by step, proceeding from proof to proof, from discovery to discovery, from statistics to statistics, but like an artist who gives you his vision in a flash, as the image of a personal revelation, a thing complete in itself. Thus what in the case of a great economist or practical statesman bears a merely outward relation to his work—the details of his life and character—becomes in the case of Walther Rathenau the very measure of his worth as a teacher and prophet.

But a peculiar difficulty attaches to any presentation of Rathenau's personality. Though he surrounded himself with an atmosphere of impenetrable coolness, not many were able to remain cool in his presence: people were violently attracted or repelled by him—or both simultaneously. That was part of his tragedy: the crystalline coolness for which he laboured recoiled on him in the shape of passionate adoration or passionate hatred. And now that he is dead, this same atmosphere, though it tends to thicken around him into a haze of misunderstandings, yet has also certain advantages; the student who ap-

3

proaches him thus influenced sees him with a distinctness so intensified by excitement or emotion that his figure takes on the sharpness of a vision and grips him like a Golem. I have aimed at eliminating the emotion and preserving only the clearness of the vision. Whether I have succeeded, the reader must be left to decide. But I may perhaps be allowed to set forth tentatively at the outset an explanation why Walther Rathenau had that peculiar effect on those who came within his orbit: he was, and one could not help feeling it, a man who bore Fate within him. One was conscious, when dealing with him, of something in his spiritual structure working mysteriously and blindly after the manner of a physical organism, for which every outward event in his life was merely a rung in a ladder leading inexorably to an end which he darkly foresaw and both welcomed and deeply dreaded. And Fate in this sense belongs to one man in a million.

CHAPTER I

FATHER AND SON

W ALTHER RATHENAU was born in a working-class district of North Berlin, where his father, Emil Rathenau, a middle-class Jew of commanding technical and commercial genius, then still obscure, had invested a small capital of 75,000 thalers (about $55,000) in an iron foundry. Emil Rathenau had served his apprenticeship first as an engineer in Silesia, then as an official with Borsig's in Berlin and finally as an unpaid clerk in England; and now he managed his iron foundry in the Chausseestrasse himself, with a friend to help him as his partner. It was a small affair, and the two friends were rather short of capital, though Emil Rathenau's parents were well-to-do, his father having retired from business as a young man, soon after Emil's birth in 1838, in order to live at leisure on a comfortable income. 'He was,' says Emil in a short autobiographical fragment, 'stern and conscientious, and had made a *mariage de convenance* with my mother, who was clever, alert and ambitious, but whose foible was a hankering after elegance up to the very end of her long life.' In pursuit of this 'elegance,' she set up as a Society leader in Berlin in the forties, first in the square adjoining the pretty little eighteenth-century palace of Monbijou in the city, which was then still a fashionable residential quarter, and afterwards at 3, Victoriastrasse, in the West End near the Tiergarten, where she lived until her death. This lady, *née* Liebermann, whom her portraits represent with a somewhat negroid type of face, was completely wrapped up in Society, and when she died, in the middle nineties, left her children nothing, we are told, but

5

a chest full of forgotten and mostly unpaid milliner's bills. She and her husband being fully engaged in attending to pleasure, and 'their life in Society not leaving them time,' so Emil states, 'for the education of myself and my two brothers,' they entrusted their children entirely to day schools and private tutors, with the result that Emil and his brothers got out of hand, and were finally expelled from school for letting off fireworks in their classroom. Life in Frau Rathenau's circle was gay ('elegant,' as her son Emil puts it), but with a gaiety finely tempered by the highbrow and precious tone of the early fifties in Berlin, when Jewish society, though divided by a sort of mystic chasm from the inaccessible heights of the Court, was yet glorified by genius in the shape of romantic celebrities, such as Ferdinand Lassalle, the great Socialist agitator, and his 'tragic comedian' of a bride, Helene von Dönniges, or Goethe's ward, Bettina von Arnim, and her young friend Franz Liszt, moving like fiery meteors in a frigid world of horsehair furniture, Cashmere shawls, and plaster casts after the antique. Iciness and romanticism were the two main notes of this old middle-class Berlin into which Walther Rathenau's grandmother pushed her way as a leader of Society. Walther himself says of his ancestors: 'My four great-grandfathers were all distinguished. Two were rich; one as a banker to a small prince, the other as a Prussian industrialist. Two were poor. Both my grandfathers lost their fortunes, one by the Hamburg fire [in 1842], the other by the outbreak of the war of 1870.' One of the two, Liebermann, who was also the grandfather of the painter Max Liebermann, was remarkably conceited. Having, under cover of Napoleon's Continental System, introduced into Prussia calico-printing by machinery, which had hitherto been an English monopoly, and being asked by King Frederick William III., to whom he had been presented, which Liebermann he was, he replied, 'the Liebermann who drove the English from the Continent.'

6

FATHER AND SON

Even a small child, such as Walther then was, must have felt the difference between his almost working-class home in the Chausseestrasse and the gay and refined world in which his 'elegant' grandmother moved in the West End. As Emil, Walther's father, says in his autobiography: 'The factory in the Chausseestrasse was very small and employed at the most from forty to fifty men in the construction of steam engines and plant for gas and water works. In addition to this, it made all the apparatus required for the Royal theatres. When I took it over, the most important work in hand was the setting up of the ship for Meyerbeer's opera *Die Afrikanerin*, which was to be performed at the Royal Opera House. . . . There was a charming dwelling-house, with a front garden and a particularly smart façade, once the ornament of the "Bellavista" pleasure gardens. Behind this lay the factory, in what had been the ballroom, which was attached to the dwelling-house by a side wing. Such steam boilers as were allowed at that time in inhabited buildings, and a correspondingly medium-sized steam engine, drove by means of shaftings machinery of the simple sort produced by the factories of Chemnitz and Berlin.' In the rooms that lay over these shaftings Walther Rathenau was born on September 29, 1867, and in them he spent his childhood and early youth. Of these first surroundings he says in his *Apology:* 'For more than a hundred years my paternal ancestors have lived in Berlin, and the [liberal revolutionary] traditions of the 1848 period, as described by my father in his brief notes on the subject, were still active in the home of my childhood. The house, however, was not situated in what was then the quiet West End of Berlin, called the Privy Councillors' quarter, but in the Chausseestrasse, which was in the working-class North of the city. And behind the house, alongside the cemetery, lay the work-shop, surrounded by old trees—the little fitting-up room, the foundry, and the groaning brazier's forge. Those were the engineering works of my father and his friend; and

7

the masters and men of that famous race of old Berlin engineers were kind to the little Jewish boy who toddled about among them, and many a tool and piece of machinery they used to explain to him.'

These reminiscences give a clear and striking outline of the two scenes in which Walther Rathenau passed his childhood. In the house of his grandparents on the Tiergarten (corresponding to Park Lane in London) he witnessed the afterglow of the old aristocratic and romantic Germany, the Germany of Goethe and Humboldt, in which classical culture and good breeding stood for everything; in his father's in the Chausseestrasse, on the other hand, he grew up amidst the first beginnings of the new Germany of Bismarck and Krupp, which, flushed with the victories of Düppel, Königgrätz, and Sedan, sought ever more power and technical progress as the only ends worth striving for, while it deemed art, classical culture, and refinement mere accessories—and rather dull ones at that. Emil Rathenau's remarks about the apparatus he constructed for the Royal theatres are characteristic: 'I felt little interest in this work. Neither the stage nor the chorus, whose groupings were assisted by wrought-iron machinery, had the power to attract me; my attention was wholly absorbed by the progress of the firm, in which principally other people's money was invested.'

Indeed, Emil Rathenau, one of the pioneers and master builders of modern Germany, belonged to a world infinitely remote from that of his gay mother and contemplative, rigid, old father in their fine house on the Tiergarten; and as he not only exerted a decisive influence on his son Walther, but was also an eminent engineer, a great captain of industry and an extraordinary personality, he is worth considering at some length.

His biography by his old and intimate friend, Professor Riedler, together with frequent references in his son's writings, presents us with a vivid picture of his qualities. They are those

8

of a man of great parts, but hampered by a fitful and difficult character, and so absorbed in his own ideas that he often forgot to be considerate. His son writes: 'He was severe both on himself and others, and yet he was a good man, clean and simple-hearted. . . . But his whole nature was absorbed in obtaining tangible results; there was something Napoleonic about him: something powerful, but lacking artifice or routine or diplomacy. Thus may the patriarchs, may Abraham, have been. He thought in things, not in ideas and words. He took for granted the whole traditional structure of the world except where it touched his own work. There he showed daring, imagination, and a rare degree of intuition. . . .' (Letter 584.)

What made him difficult to get on with was the sudden and unexpected way in which he veered from boundless, overflowing confidence and affection to silent, brooding reserve. 'Rathenau,' says Riedler, 'was full of unbounded optimism when planning his ventures, but weighed down with pessimism and the keenest doubt when putting them into practice.' In the optimistic mood he opened his heart to every one, took the whole world into his confidence, 'revealed everything that he had in his mind . . . chatted openly about his plans even with rivals. . . . There is a tale of how a great firm went bankrupt because of St Moritz Bad. The manager of the firm went to St Moritz every year, where he was sure of meeting Rathenau, and wormed out of him his latest ideas; then he hastened to apply them indiscriminately at his own discretion with consistent optimism and steadily disastrous results' (Riedler). In his optimistic phase Rathenau was a visionary, a prophet. 'What he foretold and described,' says Walther Rathenau in his obituary speech, 'was the future, and into this future he saw as clearly as we see in our own time. . . . Thus he saw many things which today are unrealized, but which will one day attain to realization.' He saw them even as Faust saw the unfruitful sea as 'a place for many millions to dwell in, not

9

safe indeed, but free and active.' But then Faust was suddenly changed into Mephistopheles. As his son says in this same passage: 'His thirst for truth made him delve ever deeper into the heart of life and things. . . . And thus he turned on himself; thus in moments of doubt, insufficiency and distress he rent his own work asunder.' Riedler describes this in detail: 'The very opposite, the most intense pessimism, seized Rathenau when the responsible stage of the work approached. One day, without warning, he would begin to criticize his own ideas with the utmost severity, as though he had never felt the slightest enthusiasm for them, and all matters connected with them he would subject to the same severe scrutiny. The most complete distrust followed on the most complete enthusiasm. While before he had discussed his idea with everyone, he now worked it out jealously on his own, became secretive, lived on self-criticism, on raising and allaying his own doubts, grew difficult to deal with. . . . When in this stage he was never cheerful and pleasurably excited as in the first stages of his plans, but often dejected and always sceptical, reserved and without any enthusiasm. . . .'

This pessimistic mood had distressing consequences for his family and colleagues. 'Rathenau,' says Riedler, 'was a man of unusually simple tastes. His personal requirements were very modest, and he judged others by his own standard. Now when the pessimistic mood came over him, this showed itself in money matters also; in every point he demanded the greatest economy. His friend, the banker Carl Fürstenberg, once said: "Rathenau understands and approves everything up to the limit of three hundred marks, but beyond that there is a vast interval in which he is money-blind. Only when three million marks are reached does he begin to see again." This thumb-nail sketch must, however, be supplemented in one respect: small sums had to be kept separate; if they were added up or multiplied he would become adamant even against requests for less than three hundred marks. . . . The spending of money without any adequate return he would not tolerate. . . .' That explains what Walther Rathenau is alluding to in his *Apology* when he says: 'I grew up in an atmosphere, not of want, but of anxiety.' And also the deeper, and somewhat pathetic, meaning in the funny little birthday greeting he sent his mother when he was thirteen, words written in a graceful childish hand under the drawing of a money-bag:

> Die, thou monster!
> Of every care
> And every sorrow
> The burden vile.

His father's quick changes between boisterous affection and brooding reserve seem to have galled the boy deeply. For in complete contrast to his father, Walther Rathenau was, even as a child, remarkably good-tempered and patient, and, however trying the circumstances, always serenely cool and reserved. Even at that time nothing was more foreign to his nature than emotional outbreaks or excitement. In her charming book on him Etta Federn-Kohlhaas relates how his mother told her that when she inflicted little punishments on him for some trifling misdemeanour, he met these with a smiling indifference, which in itself nullified the punishment. 'His mother would put him in the corner, and there he would stay without a trace of bad temper, smiling gaily and completely unconcerned, till some urgent reason, such as his father's return, or bed-time, caused her to fetch him out of it. At which he would come to her cheerfully and lovingly, showing no sulkiness, but also no remorse, and she would see how ineffective the punishment had been.'

Along with this cheerful reserve there went a very pronounced feeling of his own dignity and responsibility, a strong childish self-esteem. Etta Federn-Kohlhaas relates concerning a French governess 'with what charm and sweetness, and in his

11

childish way with what sense of responsibility, the little boy promised to work for her and earn her a living, so that she might have beautiful clothes and good food and nothing to do.' His father's alternating fits of tenderness and indifference must have cruelly wounded the boy's self-esteem.

His and his father's characters were, indeed, very different. Walther's chief traits, his good nerves, his kind heart veiled behind a cool reserve, his strong self-esteem, he clearly inherited from his mother, who came from Frankfort, of a well-to-do Jewish banker's family, the Nachmanns. She was a lady of almost stolidly good nerves, and of an imperturbable calm and dignity; a Puritan, whose granite-like profile none can forget who saw her in the Reichstag at her murdered son's funeral. As a young woman she was very beautiful, of a southern type, with dark eyes and hair, which she attributed to Spanish ancestry. She came from a rich Frankfort town house, with numbers of retainers, splendid carriages and every luxury, to the shabby-genteel surroundings and circumstances of the Chausseestrasse, and it took her a long time to get over the change. She found some consolation, however, in her little sons and in music, went in for literature, was sentimental and romantic after the fashion of her day, but hard and austere in her dealings with men; and with her own husband and children passionately jealous. Being quick and clever, and a good diplomat, she understood how to win her son to her side, whereas between him and his father little conflicts and difficulties were continually occurring.

These were further nourished by the outward circumstances of Emil Rathenau's life during Walther's early boyhood. When Walther turned fourteen his father had been without regular occupation for nearly ten years—just when he felt his capacity for work at its height. Hence he was soured, inclined to fret and brood, and, with no interest in life but work, inwardly con-

12

sumed by a desire for something to do, without any prospect of his wish being fulfilled. When the war broke out in 1870 he had sold his factory in the Chausseestrasse, and soon after the financial crisis of 1873 he retired also from its management. 'Too young for the position of a rentier,' he threw himself into the study of applied science in all its branches. In the course of his studies he visited the rapid succession of great exhibitions, which in the last third of the nineteenth century went side by side with the development of world trade: Vienna in 1873, Philadelphia in 1876, Paris, where he came across the first arc-lamp, in 1878, and again in 1881, when Edison was showing his incandescent lamp for the first time. Rathenau, the mechanical engineer, had so far taken little interest in electricity. But the new incandescent lamp came upon him as a revelation: 'Rathenau recognized,' says Riedler, 'that to the incandescent lamp belonged the future, that it was destined to be not only the lamp of the wealthy, but also of the poor, the lamp of the garret and the stable, whereas the arc-lamp could serve neither luxury nor poverty.' In one of those moments of visionary optimism which were peculiar to him, he bought Edison's European patents at the exhibition itself. And as his own means were inadequate, he borrowed money from some German firms with whom he was on friendly terms, and with it proceeded to found an experimental company immediately on his return to Berlin. The year after, in 1882, at the Munich electrical exhibition, he was already able to exhibit a galaxy of incandescent lamps which created a sensation. While the exhibition was in progress, the director of the Court Theatres, Baron Perfall, entrusted him with the lighting of the Royal Residenztheater; on the comfortable understanding, however, recorded by Riedler, that 'you do the job at your own risk; if it is a success, I will pay you; if not, so much the worse for you.' Finally, in April, 1883, the 'Deutsche Edison-Gesellschaft für angewandte Elektrizität'

13

(German Edison Company for applied electricity), the original of the subsequent A.E.G. (General Electric Company), was founded in Berlin under Emil Rathenau's management with a capital of five million marks ($1,250,000).

When his father secured the Edison patents and entered on his new profession as an electrical engineer, Walther was fourteen. The ultimate effect on his relations with his father was profound and had a decisive influence on his future and the philosophical ideas he subsequently developed; the immediate result, however, so far as the boy was concerned, was that his father, absorbed by his new profession, vanished, as it were, from the family circle. 'Throughout a period of more than ten years,' says Riedler, 'the working day of Rathenau and his colleagues lasted from early morning till late at night, with half an hour at midday for luncheon. At table, business was discussed at length; in the evening, factories were inspected; over night, Rathenau took work home with him, which he attended to even on Sundays, for on Sundays one is not disturbed. . . . For ten years Rathenau hardly allowed himself a free afternoon. His leisure really consisted only in some change of work; leisure and amusement in the usual sense of the words were alien to his nature. Necessity alone could make him interrupt his work. Like Napoleon, he could say of himself: "I am born and built for work, I have never known the limits of my activity." '

The effect of this tremendous activity on the entire industrial system of Germany was nothing short of revolutionary. As managing director of the new firm, Emil Rathenau soon became one of the leading captains of industry, an inventor of new forms of business, and a pioneer of large-scale capitalism. Riedler has given an illuminating account of the gift which secured him his supremacy. 'Rathenau could only understand what was *simple*. Therefore he applied himself only to those things and those situations which were clear and simple, or

14

which he could make so. He was able to extract the essential, the convincingly simple, out of the complex, where others could not see it. . . . He never approached matters which he could not simplify. . . . That is a great and fruitful gift. For no matter in itself is ever simple; every problem always presents innumerable aspects full of inner contradictions; the essential thing is the mind that gets to the heart of a problem.'

Emil Rathenau's influence was, indeed, decisive on German and even world industry. He made mass production possible in one of the most important branches of modern industry—*i.e.* electricity—by fundamentally rationalizing the conditions both of its manufacture and its distribution. He invented new forms of co-operation between banks and industrial concerns, being the first to secure the help not of one big bank only, but the joint participation of several in his own firm, the A.E.G., thereby teaching the world how huge sums of money could be made available for the benefit of rapidly expanding branches of industry. And over and above this, he paved the way for the 'horizontal trust,' by combining his own with other electrical firms, by incorporating many undertakings in one great economic unit under his supreme control, and by sharing interests with foreign companies such as the General Electric Company of America. All the fundamentals of modern big-scale industry: the cheap and economic incandescent bulb as a mass product, the municipal power station as the new heart of the city, the distribution of electric current in the shape of light and power in rural districts, the economic exploitation of water power for the production and distribution of electricity, the introduction of electric instead of steam power into industry and locomotion—all these which we take for granted today are due to him more than to any one else—that is to say, to that unique combination of the highest technical and commercial skill which was his. Walther Rathenau has summed up what was revolutionary in his father's activity in these words: 'What happened

15

when applied electricity came into being [through Emil Rathenau's activities] was the mapping out of a new province of industry and the transformation of a great part of the prime conditions of modern life; a transformation, however, which did not proceed from the consumer, but had to be organized, and, as it were, forced on the consumer by the producer. Countries which left this development to the consumer could only produce this result incompletely and indirectly. Electricity in its present centralized form really originated in Germany, a country without any special qualifications for this so far as capital or geography is concerned. It is true that in America electricity made stupendous progress as a result of enormous consumption, but nevertheless it retained right into modern times the form of the older industries, though certainly on the largest scale.' (Letter 20.)

Among the men of comparable stature who played a leading part in the shaping of present-day big business, Werner Siemens may be considered greater as a scientist, Edison more revolutionary and prolific as an inventor, and Ford more thorough as an organizer of labour and machinery. But Emil Rathenau remains the most typically representative figure of Germany and continental industry, because he embodied with the greatest intensity and singleness of purpose the two basic tendencies which distinguish modern big business from all earlier forms of industry: the immediate utilization of every technical innovation for mass consumption, and the immediate absorption of every new source of capital for the increase of production.

Indeed, the thoroughness with which Rathenau directed both tendencies to one goal, the inexorable logic with which he tested every step towards this goal, are the very elements of his industrial tactics and the chief reason why, in his long and adventurous career, he never met with a serious reverse. For many years he passed, even with some of his colleagues, for a mere

16

speculator to whom fortune had been kind. The very president
of one of his own boards of directors once exclaimed in be-
wilderment: 'But you do not mean to say he really understands applied electricity?' Now, in point of fact, his triumphs
were the result of the almost fanatical concentration with which
he applied his immense knowledge of technical matters to commercial ends. Not that he cared personally for money; his love
of gain so far as his own pocket was concerned was of the
faintest. But, as Riedler records, he pressed on every one of his
colleagues as his fundamental principle that 'it is our duty to
make money for the shareholders; that is our sole business, it
is for that we are appointed; only when our establishment is
yielding large profits have we fulfilled our trust.' That gave
him his standing with the banks and made it possible for him
to raise almost unlimited sums; big and steady profits gave him
the confidence of the investor. Thus he made sure of the one
factor indispensable for the world-wide expansion of his business: the influx of almost unlimited capital. The other pro-
pelling force of modern big business, the rush of technical invention, he harnessed with equal thoroughness by diverting and
concentrating it, like Ford thirty years later, on mass production and cutting of prices. Thus, while in his inner life as an
inventor and creator he remained a dreamer and idealist, in his
industrial activities he became a complete, indeed a stupendous,
example of the 'purpose-ridden man,' as Walther Rathenau
afterwards called this type, the man who completely subordi-
nates himself and his soul to some purpose which lies outside
himself. 'He never touched,' says Riedler, 'anything which did
not fit in organically with what he was planning and scheming,
however important it might seem or be in itself; activities in
which mastery was out of his reach, he disdained. He avoided
frittering away his energies. And in accordance with this self-
restraint, his personal range of interests, compared with modern
standards, was very narrow. His only real interest was his pro-

fession. Yet his outlook was wide. Rathenau had an excellent general education; but everything that did not move him personally was soon forgotten. From his school days he had retained little more than a knowledge of geography and natural science. . . . His only permanent interest was the world of facts, the many-sided developments of applied science and industry. Art in the ordinary sense of the word attracted him but little. Everything in the way of literature left him cold; the theatre he considered merely as an amusement unworthy of serious attention; he only half heard what they were saying on the stage, and saw the same play several times without becoming aware of the fact.' Stendhal has an anecdote of Napoleon during an opera adding up the number of his battalions and cannons, Cimarosa's music only serving as a stimulant to strategical considerations. That was Emil Rathenau's attitude towards art.

It might be unjust or misleading to state that Walther Rathenau was thinking of his father when he drew up his indictment of the 'purpose-ridden man,' the man who sells his soul for material success. There were elements of greatness in Emil Rathenau which are lacking in the vulgar type of the 'purpose-ridden man,' the business man with nothing but facts and hard cash in his mind, such as Dickens's Bounderby or Mr Sinclair Lewis's Babbitt. Deeply imbedded in all Emil Rathenau's activities, as their source and impulse there lived creative imagination, vision, intuition, a sort of second sight independent of any plans for making money or ousting competitors. But outwardly, as a great financier and captain of industry, he cannot but have shown many of the traits and limitations from which Walther Rathenau recoiled. And over and above this, Walther realized that his father was not the master but the servant of the industrial Frankenstein's monster he had himself created. The huger the machine grew, the more did it feed on his freedom. Now, nothing was more abhorrent to Walther Rathenau

18

WALTHER AND ERICH RATHENAU

than any kind of personal servitude. Every limitation of his independence caused him acute pain, and he always rather despised those who did not share this feeling. And yet, here was
his father agreeing, without any outward necessity, to an unparalleled restriction of freedom. The jealous care with which
Walther Rathenau, as a sixth-form boy, shunned every suggestion of control is shown by a story which his mother told
Etta Federn-Kohlhaas. She was attending one of the public ex-
aminations in the Wilhelm Gymnasium, and had taken her seat
in the front row. 'When her son came up with his class he took
no notice of her, but purposely answered none of the questions
put to him, remaining completely dumb. His mother felt intensely distressed in her front seat and returned home angry
and mortified, with the intention of scolding her son. He, however, came in as if nothing had happened and in the best of
spirits, merely asking her whether she would soon attend another examination.' And some years later, as a young clerk, he
writes to his mother from Neuhausen: 'It fills me with despair
that I should be dependent and that so far as I can see there is
no escape from it and no end to it. To be under someone's control day by day, to have work set you day by day, to have to
submit to questions, to have to humiliate yourself by making requests and sometimes even apologies, when you believe yourself
to be in the right; to have inferior people as colleagues . . .
years of this are enough to drive you mad, if you value your
freedom above everything.'

These were the views and feelings with which he witnessed
his father's growing enslavement. Emil Rathenau's defects, his
fitful moods, his hardness in money matters, had always caused
friction; but now his acquiescence as a great leader of industry
in a state of practical slavery produced a worse and more profound estrangement.

Thus it came about that in his boyhood and early youth
Walther was deeply and completely devoted to his mother

19

alone. In her he thought he saw the embodiment of the ideal world of Goethe and of the great German Romantics; whereas his father personified to him another world, breathless in its pursuit of gain and technical innovation, undignified in its sacrifice of personal freedom. And yet, so insistent was the impact of this new world rising about him, so impressive his father's genius, that both forced their way into the very depths of the boy's soul; and the clash between the equally powerful influences of his father and mother produced or fostered in him a sort of dual personality, a conflict which from then on never ceased raging in him between an unquenchable desire for the pure life of the spirit and a mysterious, irresistible urge towards commercial and technical activity, and outward material success. It was this conflict which finally made of his life a tragedy, and, when it became an open secret through his writings, a sort of public scandal for millions of his countrymen, till a violent death appeared even to himself, as it did to many of his friends, his foredoomed and inevitable fate. But it was this same conflict that made of Walther Rathenau a tragic symbol of our civilization, which, rent in twain as it is between the ever-increasing need for soul-destroying labour and the no less insistent calls of the spirit, also has to choose, unless it find a compromise, between sudden catastrophe and, still worse, slow extinction.

CHAPTER II

THE WAY OF THE INTELLECT

Walther rathenau's dual personality, the peculiar character of his spiritual life, which seemed to revolve round two disconnected axes, developed in him early under the conflicting influences of his home. Many a boy is divided equally between some form of romantic idealism and competing mirages of worldly success. But, as a rule, youthful idealism is finally disposed of by 'sound common sense' when he goes into business or one of the professions. Or if his mind and spirit happen to be of a finer and rarer stuff, idealism gains the day, and unity is restored by the boy's definitely turning prophet or poet. Now the case of Walther Rathenau differs from the norm by the persistence of both tendencies in him through life, each getting the upper hand in turn, each proving itself in turn a master passion, each triumphing, only to be immediately challenged and defeated by its rival. The result, apart from far-reaching effects on his reputation and career, was a peculiar iridescence of Rathenau's intellect which seemed to clothe every idea it evolved in a brilliant and multicoloured halo. He had a vast, indeed a unique, store of knowledge, economic, scientific, literary, historical, political, and a no less unique store of business experience. Now all this was kept perpetually moving to and fro between two systems, introspective asceticism and shrewd worldliness, each complete in itself, each hardening rather than compromising with its rival as life proceeded, and each illuminating every idea, as it rose over the horizon of Rathenau's mind and passed on its way, with brilliant and ever-changing hues. His intellect thus came to resemble an astonishing coat of many colours, which he displayed for the delight or the discomfiture of those who approached him, and behind which he concealed, from himself and others, the painful hesitations of a nature torn between two mutually destructive passions.

Outwardly he ran a very ordinary course as a boy and youth. He never shone particularly at school. It was only in German literature that he excelled, and the drill inherent in German education went against the grain of his nature. Unsatisfactory reports led to repeated friction with his father. Once, we are told, he was near committing suicide. However, he was only seventeen when he left school for the university. He studied in Berlin and Strassburg: mathematics and physical science with the great Helmholtz, chemistry with Hofmann, and philosophy with Dilthey. In 1889, when he was only twenty-two, he graduated with a dissertation on 'Light Absorption by Metals.' He then went in for electro-chemistry, the new branch of industry which was just in its beginnings, giving the significant reason that his father had no say in it, his father's firm not yet having turned its attention that way. In order to fit himself for the profession of an electro-chemist he took a postgraduate course in Munich, where he remained a year; and then accepted the post of a subordinate technical official in the 'Aluminium Industry' Company in Neuhausen, Switzerland, where he perfected a process for producing chlorine and alkalies by means of electrolysis. In 1893 he took over the management of the 'Elektro-chemische Werke G.m.b.H.' in Bitterfeld in the Prussian province of Saxony, remaining there for seven years in a prolonged struggle with all sorts of difficulties and ill-luck. He did not give in, however, and stayed till he had achieved success. When he left Bitterfeld, in 1900, his apprenticeship was at an end. He was thirty-three, with a reputation for technical skill and business ability already established and a mind richly stocked with knowledge acquired by extensive reading in the

22

dreary isolation of a small provincial town. Life seemed to open out for him a vista of easy triumphs. And yet, if one considers more closely the lines on which he was developing, one can observe the implicit tragedy drawing relentlessly nearer. The qualities which tied the knot of his destiny move on to the stage one by one and hand in hand like the Virtues and Vices in an old play, and gather unto themselves strength for the battle which was to end for him in catastrophe.

He was devoted to his mother. Yet even in his dealings with her, he was of a curiously secretive disposition. His mother's reminiscences, as quoted by Etta Federn-Kohlhaas, show how he drew a veil between himself and her, a very definite line of defence against that complete intimacy which for a child always implies a surrender of its independence. His mother, who was jealous by nature, was deeply mortified by this aloofness, and used to reproach him for it. One of his earliest published letters was evidently written in reply to some such reproaches. 'You must not imagine that I am an enemy to emotion or affection. But living amongst passionate people—and we are all passionate—has made me shy of excess. I think it a fine thing to live in intimate communion with others without enthusiasm or self-annihilation, but with a steadfast and immutable sameness of affection strengthened and heightened by calm but indefatigable activity. But it is the expression of this, its outward proof, that I do not like. . . It may be that I go to the other extreme and that I should show more consideration for you, who are not made like that. But I cannot help it. It goes too much against the grain, and I find it difficult even to write you this, especially as one can never express adequately what one feels on this subject.' He was positively haunted by the fear of anybody's drawing him out and establishing an ascendancy over him. He reacted with a sensitiveness which seemed almost morbid to the faintest attempt at influencing him. In his *Aphorisms*, jotted down probably in Bitterfeld, he says: 'Beware,

23

man, lest they love you as they love a beautiful animal, not out of affection, but out of covetousness.' Professor Saenger, who knew him for half a lifetime, records: 'Even when he appeared most frank, even in the middle of an intimate conversation, Walther Rathenau always seemed hidden behind a sort of veil. . . . He kept watch over the inner workings of his soul as though it had been the Holy Grail.' And he himself once wrote: 'Years ago I was inclined to make a present of my heart to any one. A kind word unlocked my soul. Although a Jew, I am not by nature suspicious, but, on the contrary, eager to trust people. But when I found out that I was being used as a means to an end, I felt crushed, dishonoured, disgraced, betrayed. I was ready to be helpful of my own free will, but to be taken for a fool and treated like a common, despicable tool, like a sort of swindler outswindled! Wounded vanity is slow to heal; it was some time before I found myself.'

He found himself by assuming the leadership in every relation with others, by making himself their superior, their prop and help, by always setting the tone. Thus he preserved his independence. There is a photograph of him with his younger brother Erich, when they were in their early teens, showing how soon this patronizing tendency expressed itself even in his gestures: Walther's arm is laid on his younger brother's shoulder, as though he were protecting him, a habit he came to adopt almost as a matter of course when in prolonged conversation with a friend. Up to the very end of his life he delighted in playing the 'big brother' even to casual acquaintances, who often failed to appreciate his condescension.

The weapon with which he imposed his leadership on others was his intelligence. His Jewish blood and remarkably gifted family had endowed him with an intelligence far above the average; and this he had still further widened and trained, made supple and brilliant, by his own indefatigable industry.

24

To intelligence was added an extraordinarily active imagination; and both together seemed to stretch out like an Indian idol with a thousand arms to seize and hold all who came within their reach, friends and enemies alike. Yet he himself thought little of the origins of the intellect, reviling it as the product of fear. 'Fear and courage, as seen in the movements of the will, the tendency to oppression and assault, and the tendency to defence and flight, form,' so he says, 'the great antinomy which runs through all Creation . . . these are the antagonistic primal elements of all human impulses, uninfluenced by experience, independent of thought and will, of faith and knowledge. These impulses (one or other of them) govern from first to last the life of men, of peoples, and of races. . . . Courage is the outcome of strength, fear of weakness. The weapon of the strong is confidence and strength, the weapon of the weak is fear and flight. . . . With his eyes anxiously fixed on the future the man who is fear-ridden becomes conscious of the power of his intellect, which dispels the surrounding darkness. He thinks and plans, strives and covets, seeks and broods. Thus he forges as his defence against fear the new weapon of intellect. . . .' (*Weakness, Fear and Purpose*, p. 13 ff.)

The principal fear-ridden race and hence the race with the highest intellectual powers is the Jews. 'When has a man of the blond type of the Nordic Gods ever achieved greatness in the world of art and thought?' (*Aphorisms*.) From the very beginnings of their history the Jews have been a race governed by fear, driven by their experiences, by their 'God,' to a one-sided, stupendously exaggerated cultivation of this one organ, the intellect. In one of his brilliant table-talks (it must have been about 1906), sitting after supper with the poet Hofmannsthal and myself, he expounded to us his view of the history and origins of the Jewish people: 'This is what happened. When God created the world he acted after the manner of a good French cook, who gets ready in the morning an ingredient he

25

WALTHER RATHENAU

will be wanting for dinner in the evening. He allowed himself
the luxury of setting aside a portion of pure mind,[1] a certain
quantity of brain matter; this he sealed up in a jar and sent it,
so to speak, to the bottom of the sea for two thousand years. In
this watertight jar he enclosed one book, one single book, and
apart from this he left it, hermetically sealed against the rest
of the world, to ferment by itself. And what has been the result? For two thousand years this mass of mind has gone on
thinking over the same thoughts, till it has brought them to the
last pitch of refinement and complexity. Having written commentaries on every sentence in the Bible, the Jewish mind then
wrote commentaries on its own commentaries, and then commentaries on the commentaries of its commentaries. On this one
book was heaped a mass of knowledge so stupendous that only
a few men could master it. But, from time to time, such a man
arose, and then from Cordova to Cracow, from Posen to Lis-
bon, people would make pilgrimages to see him. The power and
prestige of the intellect, of this quite unpractical but most
highly refined and complex Talmudic intellect, grew and grew.
And thus was created an intellectual *form*, which now, in the
twilight of civilization, has become indispensable for our modern world, for the international economic life of today. Without
it world trade in the modern sense is unthinkable. And yet I
consider this mere intellect to be in itself unfruitful. Simmel [2]
is the most perfect example of it among scientists. And what do
we find? In reality he merely runs a sort of broker's shop in
which to barter ideas. And the same is true even of trade when
we look closer into the activities of Jews in this branch of
human affairs. The Jews are the salt of the earth; but you
know what happens when one takes too much salt. I have always found that people who are clever and nothing more come

[1] In a letter to Frau Minka Grönvold, Rathenau defines 'Mind' as 'consciously
differentiated thinking. Lower form: intellect. Higher form: reason.' (Letter 69.)
[2] The German philosopher Georg Simmel (see Index).

26

to grief even in business. And they richly deserve it; for in themselves they are unproductive.'

The legacy which his forefathers had bequeathed him, Rathenau felt, was fear, and, as the product both of fear and of a peculiar history, a stupendous intellect, overcultivated to the point of sterility. Whatever one may think of the myth of dark intellectual races governed by fear and a blond unintellectual race impelled by daring and born to rule, the fact that Rathenau believed in this myth and made it the starting-point of his philosophy of history is in itself a confession. Although Rathenau was, as he proved later, physically fearless, he yet felt himself to be one of a dark, timid, servile race. Somewhere within him he felt fear lurking as his basic instinct, haunting him like a ghost, possessing him in a thin, highly intellectualized Jewish form, torturing him whenever he was faced by the brutal violence of things, or by any intellectual, moral or social superiority. In those very years which were decisive for his future career this lack of self-confidence was deepened by an experience which made him at the same time painfully conscious both of the fact that he was a Jew and of the harshness of the world.[3] In his essay *The State and the Jews (Staat und Judentum)* he says: 'In the youth of every German Jew there comes a moment which he remembers with pain as long as he lives: when he becomes for the first time fully conscious of the fact that he has entered the world as a citizen of the second

[3] It is, perhaps, necessary to explain for the benefit of English and American readers that there have been no *legal* disabilities imposed on the Jews in Germany for over a century. In Prussia they were emancipated by an edict of Frederick William III. in 1812. But their real status differed almost as widely from their legal status as the real status of negroes from their legal status in the Southern States of America. Jews were practically debarred from the Army and the Civil Service, and only very gingerly received into Society till the days of the last Kaiser, who himself, by the way, received them at his Court and thus contributed a good deal to the removal of the prejudice against them. But in Rathenau's youth, when a Jew of genius was ruling the British Empire in the interests of British aristocracy, the Jews in Germany were still looked down upon almost as dangerous aliens and segregated in a moral Jim Crow car.

27

class, and that no amount of ability or merit can rid him of this status.')During his year's service in the Horse Guards, though he proved himself an efficient soldier, he was not promoted. His romantic admiration for the fair-haired Prussian Junker caste must have made this humiliation particularly painful to him. And so he let himself be guided, though he despised himself for it, by the wisdom of his fathers, and not seeing any other way of mastering his sense of uneasiness, trusted for his defence to his intellect. In his violent philippic against the purpose-ridden man, Rathenau has himself described, though with much exaggeration, the mood in which he let himself be driven along the path of worldly shrewdness: 'Feeling that he cannot out of his own strength wield power, he attempts to substitute authority for strength. A slave by nature, he seeks to dominate over slaves; tortured by fear, he seeks to awaken fear in others.'

The first step on the path of worldly cleverness was the renunciation, in spite of a talent and inclination for painting, of an artistic career, and the choice of a technical and commercial, *i.e.* lucrative one. In the short introduction to the Swedish edition of his book, *In Days to Come,* he notes: 'Choice of vocation; hesitation between painting, literature and natural science. Decide on physics, mathematics and chemistry, as the foundations of modern technology and science.' He took this decision because he feared that he might have to remain dependent on his father, if he chose a career which gave no sure prospect of financial success. He notes with satisfaction in his *Apology:* 'By the age of seventeen I had finished my schooldays, at twenty-three I entered on my profession. And from then on, as was customary in my family, I neither asked nor accepted any further assistance from my father.' And at the age of twenty-four he writes to his father: 'You know me well enough to judge how I suffer from my subaltern position. I would never of my own free will be a subordinate official in any works.

I find it unspeakably hateful to have my work assigned me every day by a superior, who comes from time to time to see if I am doing what I ought, to whom I owe an account of everything I do, and who is in a position to give me orders, etc. . . .' (Letter 7, 14.11.92.) Against such a state of material dependence the only protection is money; money, which is obtainable by industry, brains and strict economy, and which protects like golden armour the all-too-thin and tender covering of the soul.

Perhaps it really was the soul of the Jewish race, downtrodden, humiliated, persecuted, and hunted from ghetto to ghetto for two thousand years, which kept Walther Rathenau for seven years of his youth earning a competence in the dreary manufacturing village of Bitterfeld. There he stayed, the son of rich parents, without any other motive; without a wife or family, against his artistic leanings, solely in order to achieve his material independence. Once every month or two he paid a short visit to his mother in Berlin; in between, it was only work, work, work, at experiments which yielded but scanty profit. The work was often exhausting, and sometimes even physically disgusting. His assistant at Bitterfeld, Hugo Geitner, relates that on one occasion, in the so-called 'disintegrating chamber' at the works, in which the electric current was sent through hydrochloric acid in order to produce alkali-lye, the fumes became so suffocating that, in spite of the sponges steeped in vinegar which they had strapped to their mouths, the workmen ran away, leaving their apparatus; at which Rathenau stepped into the breach and himself attended to the apparatus throughout the night.

On one occasion, when he himself had doubts as to the ultimate success of his technical experiments, he wrote to his mother: 'But if no practical use can be made of my results—and I begin to have doubts on the matter—what then? Yes, indeed, what then? I don't know. I ponder and ponder, and still

29

I don't know. Another career? . . . A new course of study at the University? No; so long as I have not got enough money to live independently, no, emphatically no. . . ' These words sound like the passionate disclaimer of an emancipated slave who, having won his freedom, is terrified at the prospect of falling back into slavery.

But money alone is not a sufficient protection against humiliations. The intellect provides yet another weapon against social injustice, namely, social diplomacy, the art of appreciating at their true value and turning to account the conventions of society and the secret impulses, weaknesses and prejudices of influential people. What is needed for this is sympathy and insight; when these go hand in hand with imagination they crystallize into intuition, that is, the ability to build up before the inner eye the workings of another soul, the conflicting tendencies of an entire society, to study its laws, so to speak, in the model, and to calculate its rhythm and output like that of a machine. Rathenau possessed this gift from a very early date, as is shown by a play which he wrote in Strassburg in 1887, at the age of nineteen. He had it printed anonymously, offered it to a theatre, and when it was refused, destroyed all except one copy of it, secreting it even from his mother. This was the hitherto unpublished play, *Blanche Trocard*. In judging it one should remember that it was written at a time when the German theatre seemed dead and buried: a year before Sudermann's *Ehre*, two years before Gerhart Hauptmann's first play, *Vor Sonnenaufgang*, at a period when Ibsen had hardly been heard of in Germany, and Oscar Wilde had only just begun to experiment on the stage for the benefit of a highly exclusive set of English aesthetes. This work by a student still in his teens is something quite different from the usual type of schoolboy drama. It is neither conventional nor revolutionary, but based throughout on the observation and expression of the most delicate, scarce-perceptible

30

half-tones in thought and feeling, of the most subtle shades in social relationships. In his complete avoidance of all theatrical convention, of clichés and of rhetoric, and in his supple imaginative sympathy for the lightest stirrings of affection or distaste between people, for the most transient fluctuations of the social barometer, he stands much nearer to the modern French dramatists, Charles Vildrac or Porto-Riche, or at least the little poetical *Proverbes* of Musset, than to the models which the theatre of that day offered him: the Parisian successes of the younger Dumas or of the author of *Le monde où l'on s'ennuie.*

Blanche Trocard is worth studying more closely for the light it throws on Rathenau's precocious insight into people and their relationships. It is a short drama of marriage, in which the tragedy is only just suggested between the lines, in which passions and conflicts, which threaten to destroy two human lives, glimmer but faintly, with a light dimmed by social convention, behind the simple, everyday words. There are two married women. One of them, Madame Rozan, a former musical-comedy star, has bought herself a husband; the other, Blanche Trocard, a respectable girl without money, has been bought by her husband. The two men are partners, and they and their wives live together in the same country house. Between the two women there exists a not unnatural aversion. The former musical-comedy star obtrudes herself on Blanche, from whom she has secretly, as she thinks, stolen her husband. Blanche, however, is aware of the situation, and without complaining repels all Madame Rozan's advances. The play opens with the arrival of a young man named Berthier, who had formerly loved Blanche, but, believing his love unrequited, had made way for her present husband. Here, as a specimen, is the first conversation between Blanche and her former lover:

MME TROCARD. Don't your memories of France and the friends you have left there have any influence over you?

BERTHIER. It is just my memories of France which drive me away from it, for they are part and parcel of what makes life so particularly hateful to me and turns all my other worries into indifferent trifles. Nor do my memories of my friends hold me back, although they are for the most part rather amusing, indeed very amusing. If it comes to that, I cannot think of anything that could be more amusing than my friends and my memories of them.

MME TROCARD. I should never have expected a man like you to think unkindly of his home, you, who hardly seemed to know what it meant to have a wish unrealized—spoilt by fortune, spoilt by your surroundings, loved by all, and envied by so many. . . .

BERTHIER. You would never have expected it—that I can well believe; but you understand it. Even as you understand, alas, that a woman may be young, beautiful and wealthy, and nevertheless unhappy. And that is much more strange!

MME TROCARD. I don't know what you mean.

BERTHIER. Yes, dear lady, our fates are similar; and I must confess that I find some comfort in the fact. To have found you unhappy is indeed sad; but I don't know what I should have done if I had found you happy.

MME TROCARD. You are wrong, M Berthier, I am not unhappy. What makes you think I am? Really and truly you are wrong.

BERTHIER. I grant that to all appearances you are happy. Your words are those of a happy woman. So is your laugh and the tone of your voice—perhaps indeed a little over-cheerful —but I know you too well. I can tell the difference.

MME TROCARD. Please don't think that I am acting. I have no need to.—Why should I feel unhappy?

BERTHIER. How often have you put yourself this question, and how often have you answered it! But *I* have no right to do so.

(Short pause)

32

MME TROCARD. I know what you mean, M Berthier, and I dare to put it into words: you think that my husband neglects me. But you are wrong. My husband is more considerate than he wishes to appear. Don't you believe me? But suppose he were not—should I then have a right to complain or be unhappy? Certainly not. I cannot forget that I was nothing at all before my husband made me his wife, and that it was through him that I first learnt what consideration was.

BERTHIER. Is that his view too?

MME TROCARD. I don't know.

BERTHIER. If you wish it, I will gladly believe—what I have never noticed, but also have never denied—that Trocard is conscious that in you he possesses one of the best of women. All the deeper and more hidden, then, must be the grief which feeds on your happiness, and which has torn from your heart that gladness which was so beautiful and so unconscious of itself.

MME TROCARD. In heaven's name—what do you mean by that?

BERTHIER. Have you still the same trust in me that you used to have in Paris? You have, haven't you? And I thank you for it from my heart.

Why shouldn't we speak openly with each other? We meet again after a long separation. Through unfortunate circumstances, which I cannot explain without wounding you deeply, my happiness has been destroyed. Through circumstances of another kind, for which, however, you are not responsible, so has yours. We both know these circumstances and feel them equally deeply—so why deny that they exist? If it is your wish, not another word shall be spoken on the subject of your grief. But at least you will not forbid me to share it.

MME TROCARD. Tell me, M Berthier, what you know. I beg of you. . . . Let me hear everything.

BERTHIER. I know no more and no less than you.

Mme Trocard (*with growing uneasiness and agitation*). And even if I did know it! . . . Tell it me to reassure me. I implore you. I cannot bear this uncertainty.—Does it concern my husband?

Berthier. Forgive me, dear lady, but you can hardly expect it from my lips.

Mme Trocard. Don't drive me to despair with this uncertainty. Tell me whether apart from him . . . Tell me whether a woman . . . Oh, I implore you, please. . . . Mention a letter of her name. . . .

Berthier. Why this word-game? Well, then, so be it. I was thinking of Madame Rozan.

Mme Trocard (*bursting into tears*). O my God! that it should be so obvious!

The way in which in this dialogue, as in the further conversations between Berthier and the former musical-comedy star, between her and Blanche, and between Blanche and her husband, the tragic situation shines through the simple indifferent words, like a lower layer of paint which cannot be completely hidden by the picture itself; the way in which this situation becomes gradually clearer, then reaches its crisis, and remains finally without a solution—as in life—all this proves not only Walther Rathenau's dramatic gift, but even more his natural talent for the intimate refashioning of everything which brings about coolness or warmth, compliance or firmness, weakness or power, ascendancy or subjection, between people in their relations with one another.

In fact, Rathenau belongs to that group of writers—in Germany a very small group—who in France are described as 'moralistes': men of the world, philosophers and statesmen, like La Rochefoucauld, La Bruyère, Vauvenargues, Chamfort and Rivarol; men who have pierced with intelligence, sympathy and creative imagination into the secrets of the human heart and social relations, illuminating them with their brilliantly polished aphorisms; men, for the most part, of a timid, over-sensitive nature, or who have become so through external circumstances, like Oscar Wilde or the German Lichtenberg, who seek in their image of the world an inner support against the real world. But whatever in a particular instance may be the source of this gift for revealing the essence of social life, what ultimately matters is whether the insight so gained can be put to practical use. And Rathenau rightly estimated this gift of his more highly than all his others.

One could make from his works a selection of concise and vivid images, which would provide a general view, a consistent and convincing model, of the entire modern world, starting with the smallest and obscurest wheel hidden away within the individual soul, and leading by a series of intermediate stages to the great fly-wheels, pulleys and shaftings of social, commercial, political, economic, religious, national and international life. Doubtless in Rathenau's own mind there existed some such model as this which at any moment he could set going. In his long years in Bitterfeld he had built it up piece by piece for his own private use. Buried away in the comfortless little manufacturing village, where he fought for material independence, he sought, not diversion, but composure and inner stability, by making the great and mysterious world beyond his factory chimneys visible to his inner eye and accessible to his imagination. His studies were voyages of discovery to their various spheres; efforts to conceive of everything in the form of images, and to comprehend all activity in terms of its function. Sociology, political economy, history, philosophy, and literature, just as much as balance-sheets, business journeys, and negotiations with financiers or competitors, were subordinate to the aim of building up and formulating an—in this case rightly so-called—*outlook* on life ('Weltanschauung').

In the first place it was his concern to gain a clear conception

of his most immediate environment: the Jewish question and
the world of business. Two essays, which he gave Maximilian
Harden for the *Zukunft*, namely, *Hear O Israel!* (*Höre Israel!*) and *The Physiology of Business* (*Physiologie der Ge-
schäfte*), formulated his ideas on both subjects so definitely
and, for him at least, so finally, that his insight into the rest of
the world followed naturally from this firm foundation.

'I will confess from the outset that I am a Jew.' So runs the
first sentence of *Hear O Israel!* published in Maximilian
Harden's *Zukunft* for March 6th, 1897, in which he appeared
in print for the first time.[4] It is a bitter and fateful sentence, like
the opening theme of a tragic symphony. For Rathenau's Judaism was his ruin.—Then, in a style still trembling with self-
laceration, he struggles to give a clear picture of the Jewish
problem. Whoever wishes to see it 'should wander through the
Tiergartenstrasse at 12 o'clock on a Berlin Sunday morning, or
else look into the foyer of a theatre in the evening. Strange
sight! There in the midst of German life is an alien and isolated race of men. Loud and self-conscious in their dress, hot-
blooded and restless in their manner. An Asiatic horde on the
sandy plains of Prussia. . . . Forming among themselves a
close corporation, rigorously shut off from the rest of the world.
Thus they live half-willingly in their invisible ghetto, not a living limb of the people, but an alien organism in its body. . . .'

'Yet I know,' he goes on to say, 'that there are some among
you who are pained and shamed by being strangers and half-
citizens in the land, and who long to escape from the stifling
ghetto into the pure air of the German woods and hills. It is to
you alone that I speak.' This was no cry of hollow pathos, but,
as Rathenau proved by his life, a cry for help out of the depths
of his distress; for he, the Jew, was in his heart on the side of

---

[4] Two small essays on 'Electro-chemical Works' and 'Industrial Securities,'
which he published in the *Zukunft* in 1895, may be left out of account, as they
were concerned with purely technical matters.

36

his opponents from the beginning. He says in one of his aphorisms: 'The epitome of the history of the world, of the history of mankind, is the tragedy of the Aryan race. A blond and marvellous people arises in the north. In overflowing fertility it sends wave upon wave into the southern world. Each migration becomes a conquest, each conquest a source of character and civilization. But with the increasing population of the world the waves of the dark peoples flow ever nearer, the circle of mankind grows narrower. At last a triumph for the south: an oriental religion takes possession of the northern lands. They defend themselves by preserving the ancient ethic of courage. And finally the worst danger of all: industrial civilization gains control of the world, and with it arises the power of fear, of brains and of cunning, embodied in democracy and capital . . .' *The tragedy of the Aryan race,* not of the Jewish! That was his feeling, and that is the peculiarity of Rathenau's attitude to the Jewish problem. And for this reason none of the current solutions satisfied him; for example, the removal of all restrictions, or conversion to Christianity, or Zionism. Suppose the social boycott and the 'citizenship of the second class' removed; that would be an act of justice and an advantage to the subordinate race, but not enough to loose the tragic knot. 'So what is to be done?' he asks in *Hear O Israel!* 'An event without historical precedent: the conscious effort of a race to adapt itself to alien conditions. Adaptation, not in the sense of Darwin's theory of mimicry, according to which certain insects have the power of adapting themselves to the colour of their environment, but an assimilation, in the sense that racial qualities, whether good or bad, which have proved repugnant to their fellow-countrymen, should be discarded and replaced by others more suitable. . . . The goal of the process should be, not imitation Germans, but Jews bred and educated as Germans.'

He developed this solution further at a later date when he

had ceased to assign a deeper meaning to differences of race, and had come to recognize only differences of temperament, the difference between people who are governed by fear and those who are governed by courage. During the war he wrote to a nationalist friend: 'I am convinced that religion, language, history and culture are of far greater importance than physiological questions of blood mixture and that they cancel them out.' (Letter 191.) And a few months later to the same friend: 'You say incidentally "my people" and "your people." I know that you do this merely for the sake of brevity, but I should like to say a word or two on the point. "My people" are the Germans and no other. For me the Jews are a German race, like the Saxons, the Bavarians, or the Wends. . . . The only qualifications I recognize for membership of a people or nation are those of heart, mind, character and soul. From this point of view I put the Jews somewhere between the Saxons and the Swabians. They are less near to me than Brandenburgers or Holsteiners, and perhaps somewhat nearer to me than Silesians or Lorrainers. I am speaking, of course, only of German Jews.' (Letter 208.)

Thus the conscious adaptation of the Jews to German life came to appear merely as a matter of will and perseverance. This conviction of Rathenau's hardened from year to year. It offered him the surest support against the spectre of fear, which he felt within him. And from this starting-point he laboured at moulding his own personality. His appreciation of Junker ideals, his preference for old Prussian forms of art, as exemplified by his purchase and restoration of the little castle of Freienwalde, the peculiar bareness in the style of 1813 which he loved to have around him, in short his Prussianism, proceeded, at least in part, from this conscious adaptation to the race of which with such passionate pathos he longed to be a member. Hence to some they seemed affected, to others superficially romantic, because few, and those only gradually, became

38

aware of the deep necessity from which they sprang. Above all, his enemies questioned his sincerity, and took advantage of the alleged dubious nature of his German sentiments as the most effective means of agitation against him, until the nationalistic circles, whose ideals he really shared, ended by bringing him to bay and murdering him. In the sentences quoted from the essay *Hear O Israel!* this tragic development is already implicit.

The second and already completely mature product of Rathenau's persistent endeavour to attain to a clear conception of the world is *The Physiology of Business*, which appeared in 1901 in Harden's *Zukunft*. In spirit and in form this work bears a close affinity to that of the French 'moralistes'; it is witty and pointed, opening out perspective after perspective with such insight and at times with such clarity that some of his sayings have already become classical:

'To recognize and create a demand is the secret of all sound business.'

'An organization should cover its territory like a spider's web: from every point a direct and practicable route should lead to the centre.'

'Business concerns should be run monarchically. Committees at their worst are very bad, but at their best they are only indifferent.'

'To have colleagues is to have enemies.'

'Put yourself constantly in the other person's place. Propose what you yourself would accept if you were in his position; and when anything is said to you, consider what interests lie behind it. Do the thinking for others, as well as for yourself.'

'With intelligent people who know each other and are experienced in negotiation, few words suffice to make important decisions. An inexperienced listener would hardly realize that they were dealing with the point in question, and would often not know whether the outcome was refusal or consent.'

'When one considers how often the origin and fate of great

39

undertakings is decided by a walk or a lunch, a yawn or a nod of the head, one may well doubt whether man's strength or his weakness is the more to be wondered at.'

'I don't care a straw for what are called "great ideas." They can be had for the asking. They come by the dozen, this rabble, when we are dreaming, or digesting our food, or seeking recreation. And that is their proper time and their proper place. . . . I can imagine a king of industry reading his own biography, and seeing how the "great thought" of life is set out and interpreted and extolled. How the good man must laugh over the chroniclers' credulity! For when he took it up the great idea had already become a well-worn platitude, an heirloom, the common property of all sensible people; what had been lacking was the man, the will, the industry and the perseverance. And if genius was needed, it was the genius for dealing with a thousand different methods and complications, the genius of obstinacy and persuasive force.'

'I hate clever thoughts and distrust brilliant and paradoxical sayings.'

'People who fit successfully into an organization are always Germans or Anglo-Saxons. Of all form of racial superiority this seems to me the most important. Jews are never officials. Even if it is on the most insignificant scale they are employers and business people on their own responsibility.'

'A young man of good family was once commending his abilities to me, and asked me what he could earn by a commercial career, provided that he only worked five hours a day. To which I replied that in business only work of seven hours and upward is remunerated, and induced him to enter the Civil Service.'

The views which are formulated in the last aphorisms of the little collection are of decisive importance for the further development of Rathenau's ideas:

'*Plutocracy*. There is nothing more depressing than the

knowledge that we are irretrievably committed to plutocracy. Three or four Teutonic states still hold out against it; but for how long?'

'*The Future*. I see the rulers of the future and their children. Horrible people with huge skulls and burning eyes, men who sit perpetually, sit and count, calculate and advise. Every word an act, every look a judgment, every thought directed to that "which is." Perhaps they will be somewhat more cultured than their brothers of today, probably less healthy.

'And their descendants!—They are their heirs in everything except intellect and strength. A feeble, nerveless rabble, morbid, pampered, ill-tempered and irresolute. The dragon's brood, they exist on the treasure that has been left them, too lazy to increase it and too weak to keep it. The best of them and those who will earn the gratitude of sensible people will be those who by gambling, extravagance or passion restore to the world that which belongs to it.—The golden spectre approaches inexorably.'

'*Euplutism*. If the accumulation of riches must be taken for granted, then I confess that the sceptre of wealth in the hands of men like the elder Krupp, Pullman or Montefiore seems to me less dangerous than the insignia of political power in the hands of legitimate and constitutional princes such as Louis Philippe or Frederick William the Fourth.

'The most tolerable kind of plutocracy, and therefore the one most worth striving for, seems to me to have been reached, when the most clever, efficient and conscientious people are at the same time the richest. For the sake of brevity I should like to use the word *euplutism* for this state of things. Darkly and confusedly the popular will and legislation of all countries is striving towards euplutism. In the long run, why should not this aim be frankly recognized, and pursued by the appropriate means?

'The condition of euplutism will only be approximately at-

41

tainable; with the same degree of approximation perhaps as in our present-day efforts to make the wisest men into representatives of the people, the bravest into the leaders of our armies, the justest into judges, and the noblest into rulers. But if the goal is in itself worth striving for, then the ways of attaining it follow naturally.

'Such ways are: graduated income-tax; heavy duties on inherited wealth, dowries and settlements; taxation of capital unproductively employed, especially of foreign loans; diminution of arbitrary monopolies by the right to nationalize mines, transport and urban land; abolition of monopolies where government contracts are concerned; state control of combines, cartels and trusts.'

These passages written in 1901 when he was thirty-four and had just emerged from obscurity already contain Rathenau's future programme. But there is still more behind them: the clear image of a world whose problems are no longer national, but international; the new world of the twentieth century which has already superseded that of the nineteenth. His systematic exploration of reality made Rathenau—who in his tastes and ideals remained throughout his life a thorough Prussian, in so far as he was not a Jew of the Old Testament type—much against his inclinations into a representative of European, indeed cosmopolitan, thought. And from this point he progressed inevitably to those views which are embodied in his great theoretical works, and from which proceeded his two historic achievements: the organization of the supply of German raw materials at the beginning of the war; and, after the collapse, the foundation of a new German foreign policy, the so-called 'policy of fulfilment,' to which Germany owes the beginning of its recovery, and Europe the beginning of its rehabilitation and pacification.

CHAPTER III

SOCIAL INTERLUDE

'IN 1899,' says Rathenau, 'after I had spent seven years in the little manufacturing town of Bitterfeld, the undertakings began to prosper. I decided to retire from industry in order to devote myself to literature. The A.E.G., however, invited me to join their board of directors and take over the department for constructing power stations. I undertook the work for three years, and built a number of stations—*e.g.* in Manchester, Amsterdam, Buenos Aires and Baku. I retained the directorship of the electro-chemical works, and became at the same time delegate of a great foreign electricity trust. . . . In 1902 I left the A.E.G. in order to enter finance. I joined the management of one of our big banks, the Berliner Handelsgesellschäft, and reorganized a great part of its industrial undertakings. I gained an insight into German and foreign industry, and belonged at that time to nearly a hundred different concerns.'

With his return to Berlin Walther Rathenau started on a career in society—a further advance along the 'path of the intellect' in the form of social diplomacy and of insight into the mind of modern Germany in its focal point, Berlin, and in its typical representatives, the Berlin bankers, Berlin Court Society, and the Kaiser. Any one who met him then will remember a slim and very tall young man, who startled one by the abnormal shape of his head, which looked more negroid than European. Deep-set eyes, cold, fawn-coloured and slow; measured movements; a deep voice; and a bland address—these formed

43

the somewhat unexpected, and, as it were, artificial, setting for a dazzling display of intellect.

In Court Society, where everybody knew everybody, his intrusion seemed strange at first. But once one had noticed him, it was impossible to forget his appearance and the peculiar impression he made: an impression of massive strength and at the same time of a certain weakness, perhaps, for all one knew, of a too tender skin. He was fascinating and somewhat mysterious. He reminded one of Stendhal's Julien Sorel, with his dark frock-coat and piercing eyes, or even more perhaps of another young Jew, who had forced his way into society seventy years before in another country, with an equally brilliant intellect, but adorned with ear-rings and an embroidered Turkish waistcoat—Benjamin Disraeli. With Rathenau it was only the intellect that glittered, the intellect and the rush of images crowding each other in his conversation. His bearing and gestures, and his neat and unobtrusive, but always fashionable dress, revealed a well-considered intention to oppose to the simple military style of Prussian Court Society another, still more simple, of his own. Never for a moment did he forget, or allow others to forget, that he was a Jew; he seemed to want people to feel that he was proud of his race, that it made of him a distinguished foreigner who had a right to special courtesies and to pass through doors closed to others. He contemplated the great ladies, and the young nobles of the Horse Guards, as though they belonged to another planet. Herbert von Hindenburg's novel *Crinett*, which had just appeared, and which gave an unfriendly but authentic picture of this world, Rathenau studied like a Baedeker. 'Important material for getting at the ideas of the Prussian nobility,' he sets down in his diary.

His delight in being received into this strange Berlin Court Society, whose rays had shone as from some distant star upon his childhood—and no less his pride in his old middle-class

Berlin ancestry—are both reflected in the following (unpublished) early letter to a woman friend:

'Today I am not pressed for time. I have the night before me, my coffee machine is on the boil, and I have just come from my old friend, the Countess Kalckreuth, *née* Babette Meyer.

'Mme Abeken spent the whole evening telling me of the 1840's. Her mother was Schubert's "Fair Maid of the Mill," which you sang to me; she was a Staegemann by birth and in her house the Miller songs originated. Mme Abeken (a sister of Marie Olfers, who was also there) is almost beautiful by her excess of ugliness. She was wearing a little jacket of light grey velvet with three large strings of pearls, and her teeth, which are grey pearls too, were all set in gold. But she told me how Tieck read, how Sonntag sang and Elsler danced. Elsler wore long clothes and danced the ballet *Sylphide*, in which she used to die with the utmost grace. Mme Abeken cannot understand how Elsler could put up with that old fool, Friedrich von Gentz, who was a friend of Rahel's. "One" [viz. members of the Court Circle] was friends with Varnhagen till '48; after that he became too radical.

'I know you care nothing about all this; *but to me it is something rare and strange that I, the little electrical engineer, should actually touch with my fingers the magic ring of the Romantics.*[1]

'Who else was there? Voss [the novelist] and his wife, and the two von Wildenbruchs; in all eight women and four men. At the end Exzellenz Wildenbruch [an official of the Foreign Office] made himself agreeable to me. . . . "Have you been long in Berlin?" "For just four generations." "And may I ask what profession you are going to take up? The Foreign Office?" "No, I am a banker." "And very nice too!"

'The fourth man, on the other hand, a Count Baudissin,

[1] The italics are mine.

45

was better informed. He took me for the art critic of the *Zukunft*. . . .

'Mme Abeken also knew Bettina. On the site on which the Roland Fountain now stands [near the Tiergarten and not a hundred yards from the Rathenaus' house in the Victoria-strasse] there was a certain very tall poplar tree; beside this, in the Kempergarten, they used to eat cold beer soup—which tasted quite different in those days—and cherry tarts. Tieck had the most beautiful blue eyes, and read the female parts in a kind of falsetto. His friend, the Countess X, wore a green eye-shade. Sonntag, by becoming Countess Rossi, advanced to the position of an ambassador's wife. Nevertheless she sang the *Iphigenia* in society, and had some young girls to make a chorus. In '48 she lost all her money, returned to the stage, earned half a million, and died in Mexico.

' "Historians," said Mme Abeken, "are no use. They have no knowledge of the people they are dealing with, and try to classify everything rigidly, however complex it may be." '

Rathenau's two booklets, *The Kaiser* and *To the Youth of Germany (An Deutschlands Jugend)*, give a terse account of the other impressions the new German Empire made on him after his return to Berlin:

'We had become both rich and powerful, and we wanted to show it to the world. . . . The feverish life of a great city, hungry for realities, intent on technical success and so-called achievement, clamorous for festivals, prodigies, pageants and such-like futilities, for which the Berliner has invented the nicknames Klimbim and Klamauk, all this produced a sort of combination of Rome and Byzantium, Versailles and Pots-dam. . . .

'The monarch was surrounded by the Court, which untiringly and self-sacrificingly idolized him, regarded the State as the All Highest's family affair, and shielded him from any kind of unpleasantness. "He must have sun," they said.

'The Court consisted of the aristocracy, landed, military, or bureaucratic. Prussia was its private domain, which it had helped to make; and it was bound to the Crown by mutual interests. . . .

'Round Society the plutocratic bourgeoisie lay encamped, demanding admission at any price, and prepared to defend anything and countenance anything. . . .

'Beyond lay the people. The people of the countryside, conservative, uninformed, resigned to the authority of the nobility, the church, the drill-sergeant, and the sheriff; the people of the towns, restless, disrespectful, yet easily impressed, spending themselves in a feverish rush for money and enjoyment. And in the background the working-class, resentful, despised and despising, systematically denying the present and living on the future.

'The promising young man making for a "career" was generally a coxcomb; bloated, insolent and cynical in his bearing, with hair pasted down on his scalp and duelling scars on his face, in tight breeches and spurs, with strident voice, aping the officer's tone of command. He looked down on his professors and passed the paltry examination standard with the help of crammers; his manners were aggressive and defiant, except where influential connections were concerned, and he spent his time in duelling, getting drunk, and telling dirty stories. Boys of this stamp were tolerated, in fact welcomed; they were destined to become the rulers and judges, the pastors and masters and doctors of the people.'

This type, which, as Domela [2] attests, is not even yet completely extinct, at that time controlled all the avenues to power in the State. The attack direct against it and its representatives in the Civil Service and the Army was difficult and perilous

[2] Harry Domela, a young adventurer who impersonated the eldest son of the former Crown Prince, and who has recorded his adventures in post-war Germany in a very entertaining book, *A Sham Prince*, published in an English translation by Hutchinson and Co., London.

47

even from above, from the highest positions; Bismarck himself
confessed that it had defeated him. From below, it had to be
circumvented by strategy. Rathenau, to whom a superiority
based solely on brutality and arrogance must have seemed particularly objectionable, managed to evade it by finding his way
into that section of Court Society which appreciated intellect
and individuality. This small, but very exalted set, which
breathed a little fresh air and culture into the upper regions of
the Prussian Army and Civil Service, combined elements from
the circles of the late Empress Augusta and Empress Frederick
with those younger or more advanced members of the Aristocracy who had a European rather than a bureaucratic outlook.
This tradition of culture had been passed on from great lady
to great lady, as the salt of Berlin Court Society, from the days
when the wife of the Prussian Minister of the Royal House-
hold, Frau von Schleinitz, afterwards Countess Wolkenstein,
intrigued against Bismarck and patronized Richard Wagner,
and when, a little later, the Empress Augusta scandalized old
Prussian country gentlemen by employing a French poet, who
happened to be Jules Laforgue, as her reader, to the little
Court of the Empress Frederick, the friend of artists and
musicians, and thence to the small company of fashionable and
high-born women who about 1900 were the leaders of Berlin
Society: the beautiful Mistress of the Robes, Countess Harrach,
née Pourtalès; the daughter of Prince Münster, Frau von
Hindenburg; the daughter of Meyerbeer, Frau Cornelia
Richter; the dark and rather mysterious Russian beauty, Princess Guido Henckel-Donnersmarck; the formidable niece of
the great Talleyrand, Princess Marie Radziwill; and, above all,
the wife of the Chancellor, the stepdaughter of Minghetti, the
self-willed, lively and witty Italian Princess, Marie Bülow. All
these were Europeans, had great European family connections,
were independent by reason of their wealth, could snap their
fingers even at the Kaiser, and by their prestige, their tact and

intelligence exerted an influence which actually counterbalanced that of official circles when it came to making important appointments, especially under the chancellorships of Prince Bülow and Bethmann-Hollweg, both of whom were intimately connected with this set. Soon after 1900 Rathenau, as the only representative of his class, became a welcome guest in this inner circle, from which the New Rich were still ruthlessly excluded, and to which even Ministers, if they were not either very well born or very clever, were only admitted on probation. One of the great ladies of this group not long ago wrote to me in answer to my question about her acquaintance with Walther Rathenau: 'It is more than twenty years since I first met Walther Rathenau at a small dinner party given by Frau Cornelia Richter. When her son, Gustav Richter, told me that Rathenau was to take me in to dinner I was rather annoyed, as I was accustomed at the Richters' to being taken in by some old friend of mine. Gustav was very much amused, for Rathenau was also annoyed. Cornelia, however, smiled; it had been her intention to bring us together! And we understood each other at once. With Rathenau, I never had the feeling that I was under critical observation, which with others I am apt to feel acutely. When he was free, he often came to see me; the very day after this first meeting he told me how delighted he was about it.'

Between these lines one can read the secret of Rathenau's social success. In society, just as at a later period in diplomacy, he could adjust himself to those he met with lightning intuition; he took their measure so rapidly that they never noticed he was observing them; and he so captivated them by the play of his astonishingly versatile mind that most people left him with the desire to meet him again as soon as possible.

This was the key to his relations with the Kaiser. Fundamentally the two had many traits in common, for the Kaiser also was timid at heart and governed principally by the impulse to mask his weakness by brilliant talk and assumed leadership; the difference was that he was more of an actor than Rathenau and entirely lacked his gift of intuition. Starting from this dissimilarity in similarity, one can follow in Rathenau's essay on *The Kaiser*, written immediately after the Revolution, the manner in which he felt his way into the monarch's mind and veiled whatever criticism he had to offer in the semblance of heartfelt sympathy. From 1901 onwards Rathenau saw the Kaiser, as he says, 'on an average once or twice a year, often for several hours at a time.' 'On the first occasion, I had to repeat before him a scientific lecture which I had already delivered before a larger audience, and which I thus had at my fingers' ends. The Kaiser sat right in front of me so that I was able to observe him closely.

'How different he was from what I had expected! I was familiar with pictures of a dashing young man with heavy cheekbones, bristling moustachios, and menacing eyes; and also with the dangerous telegrams and the sabre-rattling speeches and mottoes.

'And now there sat before me a youngish man in a bright uniform covered with exotic-looking medals. His hands were very white and decked with many coloured rings, and on his wrists he wore bracelets. His skin was delicate, his hair soft, his teeth small and white; a veritable prince; intent on the impression he was making; for ever struggling with himself, and tyrannizing his nature in an attempt to win from it mastery, dignity and strength. He had scarcely an unconscious moment; he was unconscious only—and this was the pathetic thing—of the struggle within himself. His was a nature unwittingly directed against itself.

'Since then many have confessed to me how they were struck by a certain feeble longing for support and friendship, a violently suppressed childishness, which one felt at the bottom of his displays of physical strength and feverish and boisterous activity. Here was a man who needed some strong arm to

protect him from dangers which he darkly felt, yet did not
realize, and which all the time were dragging him towards a
precipice.

'A friend asked me my impression of his bearing and conversation. I said: He is an enchanter and a man marked by fate.
A nature rent, yet not feeling the rent. He is on the road to
disaster.' (*The Kaiser*, p. 26 *f.*) [3]

At this stage of his career Rathenau could probably have
obtained some high state appointment. For as a result of his
social diplomacy, which had opened to him the inner circle of
Court Society and put him in close touch with the Emperor,
he was looked upon as a 'coming man,' as a possible Ambassador,
or even Minister. The only visible difficulty in his way was the
fact that he was a Jew. The reason why he did not remove
this difficulty by becoming a Christian is, in spite of his own
explanations, not quite clear. He could have had no conscientious objections on the score of religion; for he was a Christian by conviction, and acknowledged himself as such. Thus, in
his pamphlet *Polemic on Belief* (*Streitschrift vom Glauben*),
he writes: 'Perhaps you have read some of my writings. Then
you will know that I take my stand on the gospels.' The reason
which he gave himself was that it would have been a con-
temptible thing to purchase a personal advantage at the cost
of conversion, and thereby countenance the wrong done to the
Jews. Thus in a letter to Frau von Hindenburg, who wanted
him to become Foreign Minister, he wrote: 'My industrial
activities give me satisfaction, my literary activities are a necessity of life to me, but to add to these a third form of activity,
the political, would exceed not only my strength, but also my
inclination. And even if I were inclined to take to politics, you
know, dear lady, that external circumstances would prevent it.
Even though my ancestors and I myself have served our coun-

[3] As early as 1906 Rathenau spoke to me of the Kaiser almost in the same
words.

51

try to the best of our abilities, yet, as you know, I am a Jew, and as such a citizen of the second class. I could not become a higher Civil Servant, nor even, in time of peace, a sub-lieutenant. By changing my faith I could have escaped these disabilities, but by acting thus I should feel I had countenanced the breach of justice committed by those in power.'

That is convincing, so far as it goes, but it is inadequate. Certainly there must have been still more weighty reasons: possibly some doubt whether he would be able to achieve any-thing worth while in face of the opposition which his appoint-ment as a Jew to an important political post would inevitably involve. Then, too, there was his opinion of the Kaiser's per-sonality and of the Prusso-German system of government, whose methods seemed to offer him scant hope of being able to attain any profitable goal. But the strongest motive, conscious or unconscious, was his reluctance to break finally, not only with the religion of his childhood, but also with those more recent tendencies of Judaism which are based on an undogmatic mysticism, and to which the unworldly, ascetic side of his nature was very specially drawn.

So he hesitated on the brink of power, half hoping, half desponding, because the preliminary run he had taken never seemed to lead to an actual take-off. So much the greater, then, became his longing for intellectual ascendancy. Soon after his return from Bitterfeld he found himself in the very centre of the artistic and intellectual life of Berlin. The painter Max Liebermann, the head of the new and revolutionary 'Secession' art movement, was his cousin. Those literary and artistic circles which came into prominence through their violent feud with the Kaiser and the boycott with which the imperial art critic honoured them were his daily environment: Maximilian Harden, who in the *Zukunft* led the opposition against the Kaiser and was then at the height of his success, Max Rein-hardt, still a beginner, but already boycotted officially, Frank

WALTHER RATHENAU, FROM THE PORTRAIT BY
EDVARD MUNCH

Wedekind, the dramatic author who was somehow climbing from failure to failure towards a niche in the German Pantheon, Hofmannsthal and Dehmel, the two most prominent poets of the day, Gerhart Hauptmann in the flush of his first triumphs, the literary circles centring around the two periodicals *Pan* and *Insel* which had introduced into Germany the impressionist art and symbolist poetry abhorred by the Kaiser, the architect Henry Van de Velde and the Norwegian painter Edvard Munch.

All these people used to foregather and discuss artistic, literary, economic and political questions in Rathenau's modest flat in the Victoriastrasse, not far from the house of his parents, or else as his guests at the Automobile Club. His conversation on these occasions sounded like a tale from the *Arabian Nights*, even when it was only a matter of electric power stations or bank balances. He clearly felt most at home with Maximilian Harden, with whose cynical and brilliant mind his had much in common. But he always kept up the part of the distinguished foreigner, as it were a Prince from some distant Oriental land, gently discouraging too great an intimacy. He hated to be contradicted; arguments irritated him; and a downright attack would sometimes completely disconcert him. What he liked best was to do the speaking himself. Just as he had drawn a veil of smiling reserve between his mother and himself, so now as the years wore on, he spread a web of magic formulas around him, woven word by word, and more or less consciously designed to conceal his inner self and give him power over men and things. He was deeply pained if any one lifted his hand against this magic veil, and could get positively angry if the attack was violent or clever enough to risk tearing it.

For he either could not or would not give reasons in defence of his views. Perhaps he had lived by himself too long; perhaps he was afraid of the Jewish tendency to endless argument slumbering within him; perhaps he really disbelieved in the efficacy of argument. In the *Physiology of Business* he had said: 'It is not possible to convince a man, and certainly not by arguing with him. Quote new facts and new points of view, but never insist. The best policy lies in thinking out fresh proposals as soon as strong objections are raised.' More important was it that behind the deceptive mask of intellectualism which he still flaunted before the world a revolution was taking place. The second axis about which his soul moved, the longing for a deeper spirituality, was rapidly gaining strength, attracting to itself the forces of his inner life, and preparing the way for a repudiation of the mere intellect and a revolt against its ascendancy.

CHAPTER IV

THE REPUDIATION OF THE INTELLECT

THIS is the turning-point of Rathenau's drama; at this point it becomes tragedy. The impulses which his intellect had forcibly repressed rise up in open rebellion. Too weak for final victory, yet too strong for final defeat, they poison his inner life with fruitless longing for their ascendancy, and compromise him before the world by their ever-undecided strife. As in *The Pilgrim's Progress*, the opposing tendencies of the soul take on material shapes and battle with each other: courage with fear, trustfulness with wary cunning, free imaginative creation with designing business capacity, visionary intuition with the critical intellect, the wish for full humanity with a placid acquiescence in the narrowing of the soul in the interests of material gain. Homeric antagonists, Homeric, too, in their insults. No one, except Harden at a later date, has so pitilessly dissected Rathenau piece by piece or so ruthlessly laid bare his worst tendencies as did Rathenau himself in his essay *Weakness, Fear and Purpose*, which appeared in Harden's *Zukunft* in 1904. In this pamphlet, in which the rebellious forces of the soul openly pillory those others against whose lordship they are revolting, the 'purpose-ridden man,' or 'fear-ridden man,' or 'cunning man,' may in almost every case be taken to mean that worser self which haunted Walther Rathenau's imagination. And the picture he draws does indeed give, in a rough way, an idea of the darker depths of his personality.

Here, in abstract, is his description of the spectre he sees before him: 'Laughter, to the vital man a natural expression of joy, is to the cunning man a reaction to wit: half *Schadenfreude*, a malicious pleasure in other people's misfortunes. To admire is hateful to him, for instead of exalting, it abases him. He is curious, eager to learn, greedy for knowledge. A mechanical lucidity and a straightforward theory seem to him desirable. He does not realize that existence in itself is a source of happiness. He does not know the joy in one's own strength and in the beauty of the world. So he hankers after that which is to him a substitute for joy, after pleasure. Laying the blame for his own deficiencies on the outer world he hopes, by striving for what is difficult, to gain that pleasure which is denied him by his own nature. The weak man envies the strong man his strength. The opinion of other people is important to him. He is himself only what he appears to others. He craves, asks and begs for recognition. Hence, that which men are used to call vanity and arrogance is in him the deepest modesty, for it is in truth servility. And thus he becomes an object of loathing. For he demands of others two things they never give together: admiration and bond service. And therefore as master he is impossible. With some people, so great is their human covetousness that they can hardly set eyes on their neighbour without desiring to possess themselves of all about him. They must know who he is and what he does; they must make an impression of some kind on him, please him, impress him or strike him, and, if all else fails, at least master and possess him in their own way by criticizing him. Even when the mind of such a person is left, without restraint, to choose its own path, it concerns itself with highly personal and practical matters: "Granted that such and such a thing happens, how shall I reply? How shall I behave? What will be the effect of my action?" And thus he becomes an actor playing the part of his own life.'

Rathenau turned in horror from this picture, which in the course of long years of intimate contact with hard-headed 'purpose-ridden men' had gradually grown to completion. By relentless self-discipline he had succeeded in suppressing in himself a number of the tendencies he loathed, even transmuting them into their opposites. Thus he was practically free from base envy, pleasure-seeking, *Schadenfreude* and the itch to criticize everything. On the strength of this he believed that any one can, by the persistent exercise of the will, bend and twist his own nature into new shapes. 'That which makes the superficial person shrink from there being no free-will,' he writes about this time, 'is the fear that he will be condemned, by reason of his weakness, to lead an inner life which is contrary to his will: "So must thou be, thyself thou canst not flee!" Goethe's statement is true; not so the inference from it. What, then, is the truth of the matter? If your fear of yourself is strong enough to set in motion a strong will, then you will be able to penetrate to the innermost cells of your body and soul.' He felt himself to be an experiment, one who was chosen out to test on himself how far a 'man of fear' can change himself into a 'man of courage,' 'a man fettered by his purpose' into 'one whose soul is free.' In an unpublished letter to his closest friend he writes: 'Both in my good points and my bad you will not look upon my like again. For with me God has set going an experiment which even if it proves a failure—and that seems to me more likely than the opposite—will at least have been an interesting one. And the best of it is that I am honestly and earnestly awake to the position, and follow the threads in all their windings, whithersoever they lead.'

But yet at the same time he had a secret affection for the 'man of fear' whom he was seeking to slay within himself. He wrote to Frank Wedekind in 1904 with reference to the pamphlet *Weakness, Fear and Purpose*: 'The man of fear. Only an ideal reader, with the gift of divination, could feel that I love him—if only to justify God's ways to man. For is he not the only truly unhappy man? And is not suffering the only true nobility? Lucifer and Prometheus, are they not the most sublime of man's dreams? And are not the Olympian gods—

57

and men—cold, heartless idols? Let me for once confide what I believe, but do not actually assert: genius consists in the closest mixture of the two elements. Whence otherwise has pain its receptivity, its insight and sympathy? And all profiles prove it. The Greeks were fear-men, and I dare to say so.' (Letter 22.)

Thus the struggle proceeded between the opposing forces of his soul. And as the conflict which raged under the smooth, or artificially smoothed, surface of his nature was the same as that which rages under the glittering surface of our western civilization, the revolt of his repressed spiritual forces against the crippling of his full humanity was transmuted into a revolt against the crippling of mankind through its bondage to material ends.

But where find a gift more powerful than the intellect, capable of overthrowing the forces opposed to the unshackled development of man? Rathenau believed that he saw this gift at work in his father. Till his return from Bitterfeld his relations with his father had been cool, to say the least. Now they were both working together in the A.E.G., Walther as manager, Emil Rathenau as chairman of the board of directors. In his *Apology* Walther says: 'These three years [from 1900 to 1903] were the only ones of my working life which I spent in my father's own particular province.' In 1903 a family bereavement brought them into the closest personal touch. This was the death of Walther's younger brother, Erich, who, unlike Walther, was his father's idol. Even as a child he had suffered from severe articular rheumatism, and his parents, warned by the doctors, foresaw that he had not long to live. He died suddenly on January 18th, 1903, at Assouan, while on a trip to Egypt with his father. Emil Rathenau's despair knew no bounds; indeed, he was so distracted that people feared for his reason. He could no longer conduct the most simple business negotiations, he forgot the relevant figures, broke down at general meetings, and began to weep because Erich's coffin

58

suddenly came back to his mind; he was completely helpless. It was at this point that Walther Rathenau leapt into his place, accompanied him, conducted the necessary negotiations for him, addressing meetings in his name, and became in fact his second self. It was the conclusion of a long and painful family drama, resembling that between Frederick William I. and his son Frederick, which had a decisive influence on Walther Rathenau's philosophy of life. He realized, when working in close association with him, what it was that gave his father his superiority: not the intellect narrowly set on its goal, but visionary intuition eliminating the goal from its consciousness.

The Physiology of Business contains an anonymous portrait of Emil Rathenau: 'My chief was anything but a diplomat. When an important question of principle busied him, he enlisted the advice of all who came his way. He discussed it with his employees, with his wife, with his competitors, and where possible with his servants, much as it is commanded to the Jews to discuss the Law "when thou sittest in thine house, and when thou walkest by the way, when thou liest down and when thou risest up." He not only allowed objections, but conscientiously reported to each new person what his predecessor had said. At last, often weeks later, when every one else had ceased thinking about the matter, he produced his proposal. Badly propounded, with long digressions this way and that, his solution gave the impression of something quite trivial, uninteresting and obvious; it resembled much that had already been discussed high and low—and yet it was not quite the same. His directions were quietly followed, and only much later for the most part did it become evident what prospects were opened out by the new way, the peculiar quality of which had not at first been visible. . . . As with the artist, so with the industrialist and the trader, the highest gift is "the eye for the essential." . . . If you are seeking for genius in this sphere of human activity it is to be found—following on from the just-mentioned gift for

59

the essential—in what I should like to call a divinatory survey
of the needs of today and tomorrow, and in the perception of
possible ways of fulfilling them. This power of divination was
possessed by the industrialist of whom I have just been speaking. . . . He had no love for theoretical considerations, and
would not look at anything but the matter immediately in front
of him. Some chance remark would suddenly reveal in part the
idea he bore within him, somewhat as a section of the brightly
lighted stage is partly shown through a chink in the theatre
curtain.' (*Collected Works*, Vol. IV, p. 324.)

This description reveals what it was that Walther Rathenau
rated more highly than the analytical intellect, what seemed to
him a more effective means of imposing one's authority on men
and things: that was, an eye for the essential, a visionary and
imaginative quality of thought and perception; in short, a grasp
of the world such as the artist possesses. The painter does not
set out to *prove* that his picture is correct; he convinces by the
picture itself, or not at all. Nor does the dramatist offer a
scientific psycho-analysis of his hero's character; he sets him on
the stage and convinces the spectator by the logic of his words
and actions. Art does not work by proofs, as does the intellect,
but rather by visions, which are often truer than the so-called
truths of contemporary science. Rathenau believed his father's
superiority to be based on his visionary penetration of reality.
And it pleased him to deduce from this the inferiority of the
intellect. 'The intellect,' he says in his *Unwritten Works*, 'must
lose itself sooner or later in the unessentially real; only the
imagination can find the way which leads up to the essentially
true. The materially enterprising world of today can carry
on only if it turns from its crass admiration for the analytical
intellect and bows to the ideal. Only by sacrificing itself can
the intellect maintain its existence.' (*Collected Works*, Vol. IV,
p. 210.)

About this time Nietzsche's posthumous works were pub-

EMIL RATHENAU

lished. Rathenau, who read everything, almost certainly read these. They contain a fragment *On Truth and Falsehood in their Ultramoral Sense*, which gives to intuition and intellect much the same values as Rathenau. 'There are ages when the rational and the intuitive man stand side by side, the one in dread of visionary intuition, the other full of scorn for the abstract; the latter just as irrational as the former is inartistic. Both desire to impose their will on life; the one by knowing how to meet the most important needs with foresight, prudence, regularity; the other as an "over-joyous" hero by ignoring these needs and taking life as real only where it is all make-believe and beauty. Wherever perchance intuitive man, as for instance in the earlier history of Greece, wields his weapons more powerfully and victoriously than his opponent, there, under favourable conditions, a culture can develop and art can establish its rule over life. There, make-believe, a determination not to give in to every-day needs, a splendour of meta-physical ideas and especially a directness of belief in the unreal, accompany all manifestations of life. Neither the house of man, nor his way of walking, nor his clothing, nor his earthen jug suggest that necessity invented them; rather, it seems as though all these were intended merely as expressions of a sub-lime happiness, an Olympic cloudlessness, and, as it were, a gay game with the serious sides of life. Whereas the man guided by concepts and abstractions uses these only to ward off misfortune, without even gaining happiness for himself out of these abstractions, and whereas he strives only after the greatest pos-sible freedom from pain, the intuitive man, on the other hand, safely encamped in a culture of his own, garners from his visionary intuitions not only the warding off of evil, but also a continuous enlightenment, exhilaration and redemption.' (Nietzsche's *Works*, Vol. X, p. 190.)

As a matter of fact the repudiation of the intellect and the exaltation of visionary intuition as a profounder and more fruit-

ful form of perceiving were rather the fashion about 1900. Just
then the eloquence of Bergson was investing intuition with so
seductive a magic that for some years, in the Paris of Madame
Verdurin and the Duchesse de Guermantes, his works were to
be found on the tables of the most advanced and fashionable
Parisian ladies hobnobbing with the latest thing in curios, old
Persian bowls, Maillol statuettes and Han terra-cottas. Indeed,
the idea that visionary intuition unfettered by any ulterior
purpose can pierce deeper into the reality of things than
analytical intellect enslaved by its goal is as old as the world.
The first saying of the most ancient of all philosophers, Lao-
tse, runs:

> 'He who stands at a distance, sees clearly;
> he who takes a part, but dimly,'

and his second:

> 'The perfect man lives without goal,
> rules without word,
> acts without motive,
> creates without object,
> thinks without aim,
> does without doing.'

And yet for Walther Rathenau the superiority of visionary
intuition over the intellect was undoubtedly a personal experience, gained from observing his father, whose example illustrated for him daily and almost hourly the difference between
administrative and creative activity, and the part played in
creative work by intuition. Hence, he evolved on his own, on
the strength of experience which to him was convincing, a new
set of values, which he catalogues as follows in his *Unwritten
Works*, published in 1907 (*Collected Works*, Vol. IV, p.
21 *ff*.):

> 'Eye for the essential,
> admiration,
> trustfulness,

goodwill,
imagination,
self-consciousness,
simplicity,
joy in the senses,
transcendence.'

These values he sets up against the 'tendencies of the servile soul,' the tendencies against which he is struggling in his own self:

'Delight in novelty,
pleasure in criticizing and in argument,
scepticism,
Schadenfreude,
desire to outshine others,
love of small-talk,
affectation,
aestheticism.'

Thus did he justify to himself the repudiation of the intellect and make the way clear theoretically for his later ideas.

But to imagine that the struggle within him was thus at an end would be to misunderstand his personality. The intellect with its brilliance and its barrenness, with its bondage to purpose, remained for him, as for our civilization, the most powerful of all impulses, against which the qualities that, as he expresses it, 'compose the aristocracy of the soul,' can at best continually rebel.

CHAPTER V

FRIENDSHIPS

R ATHENAU was passionate by nature, and, as his artistic temperament and love of beauty would lead us to infer, sensual. But in his immensely complex being sensuality, with all the impulses derived from it, was never more than one of the many notes that sounded in him simultaneously. Indeed, it was never strong enough to silence even for a moment his most powerful instincts—his self-esteem, his tendency to reserve, his hatred of any sort of dependence, and, above all, his intelligence, which impelled him with the momentum of an unbridled force of nature. Hence, one often finds in his letters and other writings a craving for friendship, for self-sacrifice, for the complete surrender of his own self in love, and, over and above this, much delicate insight into the workings of the heart as in his play *Blanche Trocard*. But nowhere is there any evidence of one single moment in which he succeeded in hushing the many voices of his nature by the one clear tone of love. Whenever the sweet flute solo of the love motif tries to make itself heard, it is drowned by the furious fiddling of the intellect; and one feels how desperately, but ineffectually, the conductor raps his baton to secure silence for it. In those letters whose words come nearest to passion the script is always business-like, regular, somewhat flamboyant, but never agitated, betraying a constraint which either will not or cannot allow the veil to lift completely from his soul. With Rathenau passion never ran its course; never did its insistence conquer his dread of being caught in a trap, nor the pleasure of the senses deceive him as to the possibility of the mystic union of two souls. 'I know this longing,' he writes to his friend Lore Karrenbrock, 'and feel with you about it. And yet I know how vain it is. Union only exists in the sphere of the senses, and even there it is a fleeting illusion. The souls of men whirl after one another like the stars in their courses, but they cannot leave their orbits and they cannot meet.' (Letter 645.)

He often honoured very insignificant people with his friendship. True, such friends usually belonged to the fair-haired Siegfried type, thus satisfying his romantic admiration for the Nordic race. In fact, their limitations only served in his eyes to increase their resemblance to his Nordic ideal. Such friendships often showed, almost to the point of caricature, how peculiarly his emotional life was influenced by abstract theory. Because of this theoretical element in his reactions to men and women his insight, and sometimes even his instinct, used to fail him when faced by some quite irrational passion or fanaticism, by what Goethe calls *'das Dämonische'* in man. One is struck here by curious points of resemblance between Rathenau and that other great Jewish agitator and Socialist, Lassalle. He, too, suffered from this inhibition, this all too loud accompaniment of the intellect. 'I am, as perhaps you have noticed,' he writes to his friend Lina Duncker, 'not as other men are. I am, if I may say so, a thoroughly theoretical being. I live in the intellect and can only love similar beings. Diminish or destroy my respect for your intellect or, even more, for your character, and my love is gone, hopelessly and beyond recall.' But Lassalle was more primitive, more romantic and crude than Walther Rathenau. For, as a matter of fact, passion did once conquer his intellect—and impel him to run away with the 'tragic comedian' Helene von Dönniges. But Rathenau never surmounted the inhibition, never got beyond a mere state of longing. *'I know this longing!'* he writes to Lore Karrenbrock; the longing for that complete self-surrender which his complex nature never allowed him. He understood, after the manner of a poet, the

65

emotion of self-surrender; he could feel himself into it, was capable of expressing it verbally, but yet, behind even his most passionate words, he could never really bring it into being. This halfway inhibition made the affairs of his heart mysterious and puzzling to others. He often bitterly disappointed those who had been led by his words to expect complete devotion, and he finally became more and more isolated, because the bridge he sought to build between himself and others always broke down before reaching the farther shore.

Hence, he never got beyond mere friendship, beyond a sort of emotional helpfulness, a readiness to sympathize with the most delicate movements of other people's souls. Even with women this seems to have been the strongest emotion his nature allowed him; an emotion indeed which he directed with almost equal warmth to men or women. In his letters to men like Wilhelm Schwaner, Ernst Norlind and Constantin Brunner, passages occur in which the sentimental colouring is no less pronounced than in those addressed to women which are almost love letters. Everything that opened out a prospect of friendship, of that attenuated and bridled form of sentiment which in him took the place of sensual and unbridled passion, he seized on greedily and almost naïvely; and then, usually very soon, disenchantment followed on both sides, and the friendship rapidly cooled down. Thus friendship followed on friendship, with men and women, significant or insignificant, renowned or unrenowned, unscrupulous or over-scrupulous, simple or subtle; they lasted usually only for a matter of months, weeks or even days, and left not a trace behind. And so it was not without justice that some one who followed all this, year after year, said of him, half regretfully, half in fun, that he was only 'a Don Juan of friendship.' In one case, his friendship with Harden, the disappointment of the other party grew into implacable hatred, lasting to his death and beyond; in many other cases it faded into a somewhat contemptuous indifference.

Some contented themselves with what he was able to give them and responded with a lasting affection to his sympathy and helpfulness. On the whole, however, this emotional life, so peculiarly inhibited and yet so active, made him more enemies than friends, and created a core of the disenchanted, whose hatred radiated outwards into other and wider circles.

This inhibition of his emotional life through the complexity of his nature also accounts for his attitude to art. He once formulated a 'fundamental law of aesthetics,' laying down that: 'Aesthetic enjoyment arises when one becomes aware of an underlying order.' (*Collected Works*, Vol. IV, p. 49.) This formula takes for granted the dethronement of the senses and emotions through abstract reasoning; for laws are apprehended by the intellect. If you consider the perception of an underlying order to be the ultimate effect of a work of art, and not at best the first step to enjoying it through your sensual and emotional faculties, you are like a man who imagines love to be merely a method of propagation, and not a sensual and emotional communion between two souls in which all their faculties are involved. For that also is the essence of great art, an emotional communion between the artist and him who is captured by his work, the art 'lover,' an emotional communion involving all their faculties and without any further purpose than its own intensity. Reason, the perception of an underlying order, may in certain cases contribute, but always merely in a secondary way, to this emotional communion. All this is self-evident to the point of being trite. But all the more significant was it for Rathenau's state of mind that he entirely ignored it, giving paramount importance in aesthetic enjoyment to some more or less conscious form of reasoning. It is not surprising therefore that like most natures debarred from the depths of sensual experience by some inhibition he did not really appreciate great art. He had a gift for painting and architecture, both of which he practised; his pencil sketches go beyond mere amateurishness; and his restoration of the little eighteenth-century pleasance of Freienwalde, and also his Grünewald house, which he designed himself, show a delicate, if rather frigid, taste. His preferences in art went to the charming, somewhat provincial Prussian classicism of the beginning of the nineteenth century; a classicism giving the impression of delicate frozen flowers, somewhat akin to that of Sheraton, the brothers Adam, and Wedgwood, or the late colonial style in America, in that it was a Roman shoot grafted on a Puritan stock, and thus entirely different in spirit from the florid and pompous French Empire style. He took pleasure in works of art which were graceful and simple, designed in accordance with easily comprehensible rules and in a style which had stood the test of time. But beyond this his taste did not go. In a letter to his most intimate friend he says: 'Much as I admire the powerful in art, or rather the powerful subdued by art, the bold, intense, abrupt kind of art is not to my taste.' A Van Gogh was to him an eyesore. Among the works that he purchased for his collection there is not a single really great work of art.

After all this, it is not surprising that the only one of his relationships which was really tinged with passion failed like the others to reach fulfilment, for it was like them enmeshed in the net of his inhibitions. Some letters which have been entrusted to me and which I am enabled to publish here and later in the book throw a dim but curious light on this one great semi-passion of his life. They sound as though they were addressed to an ideal being, a sort of lay figure away somewhere in the Empyrean, but retaining enough of the flesh and blood of a woman to set his senses on fire, to give him joy and pain and to lure and bewitch him, as Helen of Troy lured and bewitched Faust, and even to unseal his lips to the brink of self-revelation. Indeed, as one reads these letters, the feeling grows upon one that perhaps unconsciously he was all the time using this one great love of his life as a looking-glass in which he saw himself—often in romantic poses, sometimes with uncanny realism, and always with a sincere uneasiness and a deadening sense of impending doom.

The sequence of the letters is no longer ascertainable. Most of them are undated; but those which follow in this chapter range over the period from 1906 to 1911.

Your beautiful, earnest letter touches me deeply. I have had it with me since yesterday.

In Schreiberhau, on the way to Agnetendorf, I told you with complete candour what it is that men find puzzling in me, and what compels even those who love me most to fear and hate me. In the first place I cannot belong completely to any one. I am in the grip of forces which—whether good or bad, whether they control me in jest or in earnest—determine my life. It seems to me as though I could do nothing of my own free will, as though I were led—gently if I comply, roughly if I resist.

If I follow out my past life, I find no external landmarks except in my ideas; these always seem to me different— whether stronger or weaker I don't know—from those of other people (which to my mind are usually very much like each other), and in real life they have brought me many strange successes, and in my spiritual life much fresh enlightenment. But I am in no wise master even of my thoughts; you are yourself acquainted with my hopeless periods of mental extinction.

Secondly: it is true that my nature is polyphonic. The melody rises like a treble above the other parts, but it is very seldom unaccompanied. And in the bass and tenor other sounds are heard, sometimes harmonizing, sometimes in utter discord with the song. I know incomparably greater men, in fact great men, in whose every word and thought I detect the same phenomenon; in this I find I do not stand alone. Indeed, it sometimes

69

seems as if it were this very strength or weakness which like a shell re-echoes, though faintly, the rush and roar of the whole world. Meanwhile the pure flute notes of more simple natures seem to me monotonous, charming and rather dull.

Now, this is why people are mistaken in me, because in this medley of voices they fail to recognize a melody. But I recognize one, and know that it is there, and that it controls all the rest.

And the proof of it is this: Life itself does not deceive, even if all else does. Now, consider my life. Do you know of another more earnest, more self-denying? And this is not due to lack of sensibility or dulness. Nor is it due to any wish of mine. For I wish nothing. Ruthlessly though I have questioned my inner self, I have never found anything of this world that I wish. I wish what I must, otherwise nothing. And what I must, I see, as a wanderer by night sees by the light of his lantern only a few steps in front of him. That this my life is an oblation, offered gladly and willingly to the powers above, not for reward, nor in hope, this I may say, and you yourself know it; that I forfeit the love of my fellow-men in the process I know, and feel it cruelly.

Now, when I say that your life is a game, this does not mean that it is frivolous, but rather that it is not an oblation. You have been created for the sake of your beauty and your Greek nature, and this and this alone can be my light.

Remain what you are, and remain to me what you are to me. Adieu, I am leaving today for Cologne. Farewell!

Your W.

Now, what do you really want of me? You know that with Nature, with my God and with myself I stand on good terms. Even you are sometimes quite well disposed towards me, and spoil me off and on. What more would you have me do? What concern have I with the rest of mankind? Do you really want

me to set a window in my heart in order that you may thank
me afterwards for 'the interesting sight'? Or would you like
me to set aside a few years of my life for acquiring a label, so
that I shall not be taken straight away for a silly ass?

On two points you do me an injustice. Over-estimation of
self, indeed! I realize my limitations very precisely and have
always respected them. But you do not realize them, for one
does not exhaust a man's possibilities in conversation. And despite everything, you are bound by the established opinion:
'witty, subtle and cold.' No matter.

But that you of all people should reproach me with being
cold and unfeeling, that I do resent. That is your egoism,
which defeats your better judgment.

God be thanked. You may squabble as much as you like.
For in the long run I would rather be scolded by you than
praised by any one else.

Affectionately yours,

29.vii.06 W.

This is the third we have had of these belated summer days,
cloudless and mild; a summer has slipped by unheeded. Your
letter has made me very sad; I read it early in the morning, and
since then these empty days have become still more unreal.

And the four songs you transcribed for me are oppressively
sad too. But they are beautiful, tender and delicate, like everything good in the art of sensitive Jews; they remind me of your
brothers, especially of Robert. Beside such warm and gentle
work I seem to myself like a primitive savage who shatters
and mangles, not one who shapes and builds. It is only in tangible things that I succeed, perhaps, in being more delicate; I
have spent these evenings in building with pencil and paper,
and have made six plans for the house, which please me. I
will make three or four more and then show you the lot. But

all this work seems to me unsatisfactory; it is too easy and irresponsible, almost woman's work.

I know that you suffer, and it tortures me; and I want to say something loving and comforting to you, and yet I cannot. Now you will think I am cold and heartless, but I am neither of these. We both suffer under this eternal constraint, from which we can only dream to be free. And when I once again examine possible hypotheses and motive forces, I see that it could not have been otherwise. Constraint and misunderstanding are responsible for this, and if we shrink from each other now and then, it is because we merely flash across at each other like planets whose orbits and revolutions are never in harmony. That other lesser reason lies in our own natures which do not *want* to live in harmony with one another.

So it seems to me at present; but I don't wish to write any more on the subject, however obscure it may sound, either now or later.

Farewell. Tell me that things are going better with you. If you find that what I have written to you is cold analysis, then I have no hope of ever making myself understood. Read it over quietly; you *must* understand me.

From my heart,

Your W.

I have been trying to do another hour's work, and was just about to go to bed. But on my way through the dining-room I passed the large black sideboard and stopped to take one more look at the lovely branch of fir with its seven cones which you gave me. Just think: a veritable miracle! The branch has blossomed! Everywhere the bright spiky flowers are breaking through the pine needles. Good-night! I had to tell you of this.

W.

What do you mean by belittling yourself and talking as though I could give you something, when you are so much more rich and enlightened than I? My one merit is that I love you and that you are sure of my love. I feel as though I had never suffered through you and could never suffer through you, but only through my heart and its narrowness. But your dear words have stirred and troubled me, and your beautiful image haunts me, and I am able to feel again warmth, light and peace. But early tomorrow I will tear up your letter, and go into the country. I hope for snow.

Ever and only,
Your W.

CHAPTER VI

THE REALM OF THE SOUL

IN MAY, 1906, Walther Rathenau made a journey to Greece. In his sketch-book, between views of Delphi, Corinth, Taÿgetos, etc., there is a brief entry under the title of *Breviarium Mysticum*, which records a decisive moment in the development of his philosophy:

'1. The picture which each man has of the world is the measure of his soul.
2. Many are born with a soul; all can attain to one.
3. Every one who is *bonae voluntatis* is vouchsafed a soul.
4. The soul is the image of God.
5. The powers of the soul are threefold: Imagination, Love, Awe.
6. With the Imagination the soul comprehends the world, with Imagination and Love God's creatures, with all three powers God.
7. The soul is disinterested, the intellect is the slave of purpose.
8. In its conflict with the intellect the soul attains to victory, because the intellect defeats its own ends.
9. Art and unconscious creation are the expression of the soul, science and conscious creation the expression of the intellect.
10. The soul derives its nourishment from the urge to life, the intellect from fear of death.'

In this entry there is a word which strikes one as weighted with a new meaning, or rather with a new significance, a new pathos: the word '*Soul*.' Why did this word suddenly acquire such a high value for Rathenau? What was its meaning to him?

In his principal work, *The Mechanism of the Mind* (p. 30 *seq.*), he describes the '*birth of the soul*'; and behind his words we seem to see, only thinly disguised, three experiences connected with his visit to Greece: Greek scenery in its sublime grandeur, a new delight in artistic creation, and the urge of a passionate, unfulfilled craving for love. Every one familiar with Greek landscape will recognize it in this vision of the world as it appears to the eyes of youth. 'A nature not touched by age surrounds him; not stones, plants, air and water, but a mysterious Cosmos teeming with life, mind, blood, light and love. Things no longer speak the language of everyday life; they whisper of the Unspoken and Unspeakable. A second Nature lies veiled behind the visible, ready to burst forth; speak but a word and all reality will be dissolved. The Spirit of the World breathes majesty and love, and the soul when it is still young demands nothing but to give itself up to the forces of the world and be absorbed in their workings.'

The second experience that moved Rathenau deeply while he was sketching in Greece was the joy of creation for its own sake as vouchsafed to the artist. In the passage just quoted relating to the 'birth of the soul' he continues: 'There remains the faculty of creating; but no longer for the sake of the material values it produces; there remains solicitude, but not for the sake of the object to be attained. Creation now means the transmutation of the soul into visible form, giving shape to what the imagination has conceived; a process of nature comparable to the behaviour of the mussel and the spider, which with joy and pain weave their clothing and their armour out of the sap of their being in accordance with an inner necessity.'

Most decisive of all, however, is love; and the words in which he describes the part love has in the birth of the soul— words which are in very close relation to the *Breviarium Mysticum*—are so loaded with real feeling under the artificial warmth of their palpably affected style, they reflect so clearly his vain struggle for sincere and unfettered emotion, that they are more eloquent of the strife which preceded what he calls 'the birth of the soul' in himself than an explicit confession could be. 'The love of man is not devotional as is the love of a

75

woman, for it is a love which demands; and yet in a certain sense it goes further than the devotion of woman: it is prepared to sacrifice itself. Woman desires to accept and to yield, whereas man desires to possess, but at the same time to sacrifice and bestow himself: thus at the very moment when it is most intense the will to live is stultified and purpose is destroyed.' And a little later in the same paragraph: 'There remains love; the more pure and glowing the fire of the senses, the more brightly is it surrounded with the aura of supersensual clarity. The love of humanity stirs within us, and the love of God, and there is awakened the love of St Francis, which embraces all creatures, including the stars, and which reaching up to heaven compels God to descend. For this love is transcendent. It is divination and comprehension of the seen and the unseen, it is surrender and sacrifice, but it is also fulfilment and transfiguration. It grasps the world, but not with the talons of the intellect; rather it dissolves itself, is submerged, unites itself, becomes one and, in that it becomes one, comprehends. Thus out of nature and creation, love and transcendence, the soul of man is born; in truth it is born only out of love, for love embraces in itself the other three powers.' (*Mechanism of the Mind*, p. 32.)

Thus Rathenau gives the name of 'Soul' to inner experience when it is devoid of purpose, that is to say, when it follows only its own inner impulses, not the lure of material or other outer ends. (*Breviarium Mysticum* VII.) 'Soul' is the collective name he bestows on all those inner experiences which are alien and hostile to the schemer, the man enslaved by purpose; it is the rallying-cry of all those faculties which Rathenau summons up within his own self to fight the dreaded and detested intellect: a cry to which they immediately respond in serried ranks.

But 'soul' is more than a mere word: the elements of experience which it summarizes have in common something real, something which distinguishes them from all other moments of

76

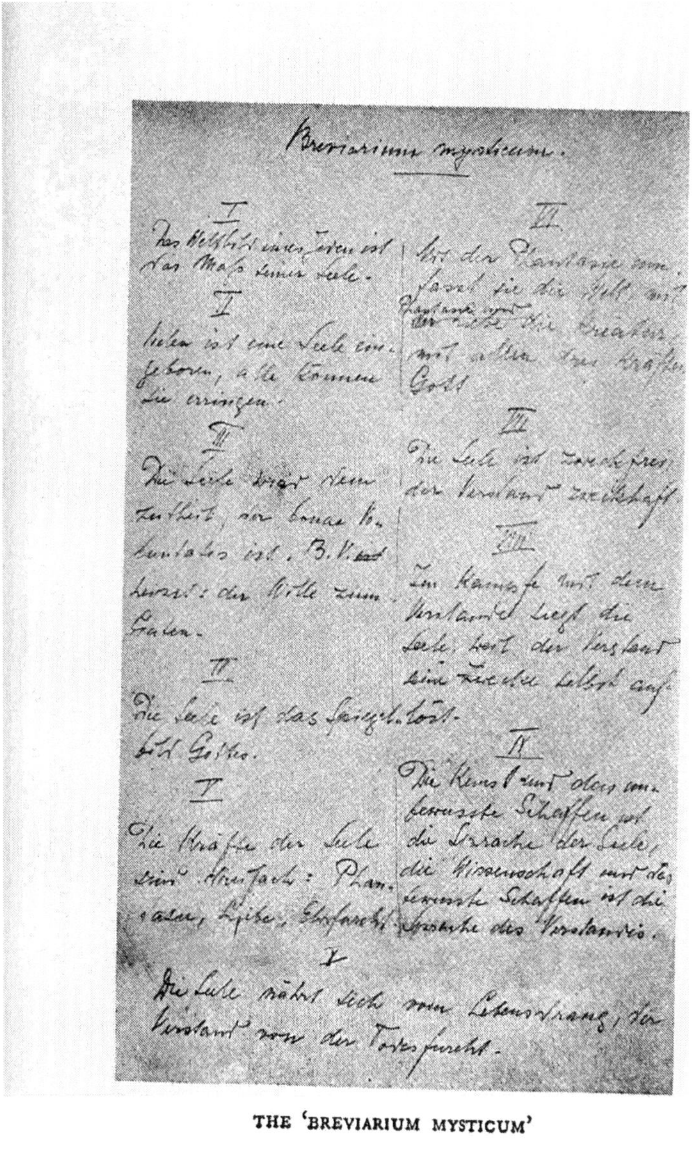
Breviarium mysticum.

I
Das Weltbild eines Jeden ist das Maß seiner Seele.

II
Jedem ist eine Seele eingeboren, alle können sie erringen.

III
Die Seele wird dem zuteil, der bonae voluntatis ist. B. V. heisst: der Wille zum Guten.

IV
Die Seele ist das Spiegelbild Gottes.

V
Die Kräfte der Seele sind dreifach: Phantasie, Liebe, Ehrfurcht.

VI
Mit der Phantasie umfasst sie die Welt, mit Phantasie und Liebe die Kreatur, mit allen drei Kräften Gott.

VII
Die Seele ist zweckfrei, der Verstand zweckhaft.

VIII
Im Kampfe mit dem Verstande siegt die Seele, weil der Verstand sein Zwecke selbst auflöst.

IX
Die Kunst und das unbewusste Schaffen ist die Sprache der Seele, die Wissenschaft und das bewusste Schaffen ist die Sprache des Verstandes.

X
Die Seele nährt sich vom Lebensdrang, der Verstand von der Todesfurcht.

THE 'BREVIARIUM MYSTICUM'

inner experience, and which sets them above them—namely, the fact that only in them is man completely himself, that is to say, truly free. That such moments of inner freedom can be attained, that they, and they only, are fraught with happiness, that they are, in truth, the only moments in life which are really valuable—this was what Rathenau brought back with him from Greece as a matter of experience, as an unshakable fact of his inner life.

The typical example of such experience, and one with a significance apart, he chose to see in disinterested, transcendent love. The reason why to him this transcendent love was so fundamentally important is apparent from the previous chapter: he realized with anguish that the fullness of earthly and human love was removed beyond his reach by insuperable inhibitions. Nevertheless, it was the one earthly passion of his life which opened to him the conception, and enriched him with the experience, of the 'Soul.' He himself hinted as much in a letter which, many years later, he wrote to the woman whom he had loved, on sending her a copy of his book *The Mechanism of the Mind*. 'You think that nothing in this book belongs to you? But when you have fully mastered it—and you will master it—you will feel that it is not only a confession, but also the transmutation of personal experience.'

When he left for Greece he was quite aware of the fact that his passion, both for outward and for psychological reasons, was hopeless. Possibly the journey itself was a gesture, a conscious or unconscious gesture of renunciation. Yet we find him writing from Athens to the woman he loved, with a last faint hope:

'More calm and a better frame of mind. Yesterday I spent at the ancient seat of the mysteries: Eleusis. Tomorrow I shall greet the Delphic Oracle. I have much to ask it (including your whereabouts).'

From Delphi, he informed her that he had consulted the

77

Oracle about her. By way of answer, in the sublime solitude of Parnassus an eagle had suddenly started up before him and risen to the sky.

Some days later he writes again from Athens (May 23rd, 1906): 'Many thanks for your letter. It was waiting for me at the gates of Athens and thus fulfilled a part of the Delphic Oracle that I hinted to you. This Oracle itself was phantastic and almost magnificent, so that I shall probably have to keep it secret. The drive up to Delphi, the deep, cool ravine and the distant greeting of the sea, quite thrilled me, and I was content to linger a little longer than the ordinary tourist. Today I must take leave of Athens. I have sketched out a wonderful journey through the Peloponnesus which involves eleven hours of riding. Its end and consummation is to be Sparta and the Taÿgetos with its ravines. Even here in Greece I have my heretic moments: I avoid the desecrated fields of ruins sweltering under a pitiless sun, and keep to the perennially youthful realm of water, air and earth. . . . The snow-capped Parnassus was impressive, facing the sea on two sides, bleak, unflinching. Its unseen presence hovers over the Delphic landscape, and its deep shadow falls upon the animated valley. The Campagna is only a dull image of this purity and greatness; here the fundamental elements are at work in eternal calm; vegetation and humanity are merely a faint breath which scarcely colours the picture. . . .'

The question which he put to the Oracle is not recorded; but we can easily imagine it, and also how Rathenau interpreted the eagle's flight: 'Rise up above things earthly, and you will find redemption in transcendent, heavenly love.' But what kind of redemption? The answer had been revealed to him when he set down the *Breviarium Mysticum* in his sketch-book: *Redemption through the birth of the soul*. As Dehmel, the great German lyric poet, who, in his philosophy, was nearer to

Rathenau than any of his other contemporaries, said in the Induction to his epic *Two Human Beings:*

> 'Arise, arise with thy passions,
> Abjure lukewarm complaining,
>
> .   .   .
>
> Round the hub of life revolve,
> Equally blessed, joy and pain;
> See, with irresistible yearning
> Man leads man onwards to God!'

For Rathenau this revelation of the 'Soul' was the most important thing that ever happened to him, his greatest adventure, coming on him suddenly somewhere on Parnassus or in the mountain passes beyond Sparta, a profoundly disturbing, uprooting, revolutionary inner experience, because it suddenly blazed forth a sort of glory on the shortcomings, the inhibitions, the negative part of his being, and gave them a positive significance, making of them marks of superior humanity.

Indeed, over and above this, the 'Soul' seemed to give a new significance to life in general. And this revaluation of life in general was no less revolutionary and important to him than the revaluation of his own being.

For he was hopelessly puzzled—as is sooner or later every human being not completely primitive, and every civilization as soon as it outgrows the myth from which it originally sprang— by the fundamental question: Why do I exist? What is the purpose of my life? What is the purpose of life in general? What is the purpose of the world? Is there any purpose anywhere? Or is everything without any sort of significance, just a meaningless play of atoms? When civilization gets to the point of not being able to answer these questions convincingly, it must needs discover for itself a new myth, or else take the

79

irretrievable plunge into the formless abyss which Nietzsche
describes as 'Nihilism.' ('Nihilism,' explains Nietzsche: 'no aim,
no answer to the question: Why?' *Will to Power*, p. 11.)
Classical civilization, when it reached this point, invented Christianity and planted in it the seeds of the medieval and modern
world. Our civilization is now at the same crossroads and, like
Classical Antiquity two thousand years ago, needs a 'transmutation of all values' in terms of a new myth in which it can
grow new roots and find new impulses. Nietzsche propounded
'the eternal recurrence of all things' and the 'superman' as such
myths. Rathenau found an answer to the great 'Why?', and,
bound up with it, a myth, in his experience of the 'Soul.' Why
is man here? Nature or God, answers Rathenau, evolved him
in order that he might feel ever afresh the pure joy of freedom
and the 'Soul.'

The personal significance of this answer to Rathenau is obvious. Up to this moment his writings and letters bear witness
to a perpetual war between his two dispositions. 'I am a German of the Jewish race,' he says in his *Appeal to German
Youth*, which he published soon after the Revolution, 'my people is the German people, my home is Germany, my faith is
the German faith which stands above all creeds. Yet Nature in
mocking perversity and arbitrary liberality has brought the two
springs of my ancient blood into tempestuous opposition: the
urge to actuality, and the yearning for the spiritual. My youth
was passed in doubt and strife, for I was conscious of the con-
tradictory character of my gifts. My action was fruitless and my
thinking false, and I often wished, when the horses bolted with
the bit between their teeth, that the cart might dash itself to
pieces.' He had now had a revelation that would, he hoped, put
an end to the struggle. Indeed, he felt so certain about this that
before he got home he had made up his mind to retire from
business. He told me so when I first saw him after his return,
explaining that he had asked himself why he did all he did—

and had been unable to find a satisfactory answer. Actually the answer that was in his mind ran: 'All my business activity is much ado about nothing; yet something exists or could be made to exist, which would make life worth living: my soul. I must adapt my way of living to this revelation; for that alone can give my life significance.'

The reserve which had been characteristic of him since childhood now took on a new quality; behind the veil which he drew around himself he seemed henceforth to shelter from the crudeness of the world not only his timorous soul, but some kind of mysterious knowledge about which he maintained an awed silence. But when for a moment he contemplated abandoning his business activity, he misunderstood his destiny, the incurable nature of the rent within him; the impossibility of integrating his divided life. He could not by mere resolution thrust aside his most powerful driving force, his practical intelligence, or subordinate it to weaker impulses.

Instead, something else took place, which made him a creature unique and strange: he branched off a part of his business capacity, of his immense experience of men and affairs, of his restless energy and practical intelligence and set it to the task of reconstructing economic, social and political life in the interests of the Soul.

That Rathenau's philosophy had its ultimate roots in personal experience cannot be doubted; that, like every other philosophy, it also derived nourishment from alien sources, is no less certain. In his case, however, such sources are not easy to discover, because he purposely never, or hardly ever, disclosed them himself, and because he had no use for other men's ideas until they had been transmuted for him by the light of his own personal experience. His explicit references hardly go beyond the words of St Paul on love in the First Epistle to the Corinthians, and the words of the Gospel: 'For what shall it profit

a man, if he shall gain the whole world, and lose his own soul?'
(Mark viii, 36.) Plato himself he hardly mentions. But there
can be no doubt that he was deeply influenced by the most recent and most impressive manifestation of Jewish mysticism,
Hassidism, a philosophy inaugurated in the first half of the
eighteenth century by the 'master of the good name,' Baal-
shem-tov. He studied Hassidism and accepted it in so far as it
confirmed his own experience and gave a significance to life. It
happened that just at the critical time he met the historian of
Hassidism, Dr Martin Buber. He read Buber's first book on
the subject, *The Tales of Rabbi Nachman*, when it came out in
the late autumn of 1906 (indeed after he had written down
the *Breviarium Mysticum*), and found there the very answer
he himself had given to the question regarding life's 'Wherefore?': that life was intended as a means of experiencing joy
in God; that its aim and end must be the soul's spontaneous
entry into God, and that this end was attained most completely
in ecstasy. 'But ecstasy,' explains Martin Buber, 'is not [in the
view of Hassidism] as in German mysticism, a dissolution of
the soul, but its unfolding; it is not the soul which contracts and
renounces itself that merges into the unconditioned, but the
soul attaining to its own perfection. In ascetic renunciation the
spiritual being, the Neshama, shrivels up, becomes limp, empty
and dulled; only in joy can it grow and perfect itself until, free
of all limitations, it ripens into the Divine. Never has a teaching
based the "finding of God" so firmly and clearly on "being
one's self."' (Martin Buber, *The Hassidistic Books*, 1928,
p. 14.) [1]

[1] Dr Martin Buber writes to me:
'Heppenheim, 16.1.28. I knew Rathenau well. It is true that we rarely met
during the time in which I was living in Berlin, *i.e* up to the end of 1915 (and
after that time we had no further personal contact, although our inner relationship was not weakened), but when we did we always had a long talk. As I
gleaned from all sorts of remarks and hints, he was an attentive reader of my
books on Hassidism. We discussed Hassidism with one another repeatedly; I had

Certainly also Rathenau was influenced by Spinoza, as is evident from the Latin title of the *Breviarium Mysticum*, its series of numbered propositions mimicking Spinoza's style, and the essence of its philosophy. When Rathenau states, in the *Breviarium Mysticum*, that 'the soul is the image of God' he is not only recording a personal experience, but resting it on Spinoza's conception of God as the one infinite substance of which space and time, mind and matter, and we ourselves, are mere transitory manifestations. For Rathenau's proposition follows logically from this conception: the soul, being a manifestation of God, must needs be His image. Rathenau's personal experience—the divine quality of the soul when unfettered by purpose—confirmed for him the truth of Spinoza's conception. In the same way, when Rathenau speaks of the transcendence of love as of something experienced by himself, this experience becomes fused with Spinoza's conception of love as an emotion of God, an expression of God's love of Himself, wherefore human love, our love of ourselves, and of other finite beings is ultimately nothing more than man's incomplete and partially expressed love of God, or, more precisely, nothing more than a particle of God's own love of Himself. Whence it may be said that love always is transcendent and, beyond and through the beloved, always seeks God. Thus Rathenau takes Spinoza's metaphysic, illuminates it from within and uses it as a basis for further development.

It became in the first place a basis for a new interpretation of Fichte.[2] Rathenau was influenced more by Fichte than by any

the impression that it signified for him an extension of his self-knowledge, and that what he derived from it and from my *Addresses on Judaism* was not without influence upon a change in his attitude towards the nature and destiny of the Jewish people. He was desirous of working back to the original sources himself and, as you are well aware, he studied Hebrew zealously for some time; his teacher, whom I met again in Palestine many years later, told me on that occasion how seriously and thoroughly Rathenau pursued this study. Why he subsequently abandoned it I do not know.'

[2] The philosopher Johann Gottlieb Fichte, born in 1762, died in Berlin in

other philosopher except Spinoza; he was fascinated by the ascetic, Spartan-Prussian spirit of which Fichte's philosophy was an ideal, highly intellectualized embodiment, and by his disdain for utility and purpose. Fichte evolved his ethical postulates directly out of Spinoza's concept of the relation between God and man. As every man is a unique manifestation of God, it follows logically that his highest duty is *always to be himself* without allowing any outward purpose to deflect him from his path: for every contradiction with himself involves him in contradiction with God. 'As certainly as man possesses reason,' says Fichte, 'so certainly is he his own purpose; *i.e.* he does not exist because something else is, but he exists quite simply because *he* is: his mere being is the ultimate aim of his being. . . . Man is an end to himself; he must condition himself, and never permit himself to be conditioned by anything outside himself. . . . I will therefore express the fundamental precept of moral philosophy in the following formula: Act in such a way that you can conceive the maxim of your will as an eternal law *for yourself*. The final vocation of all finite, rational beings is therefore absolute unison, continuous identity, complete accordance with their own selves.' (Johann Gottlieb Fichte, *Über die Bestimmung des Gelehrten*, Jena and Leipzig, 1794, p. 8-12.) It is hardly necessary to point out how convincing these passages must have sounded to Rathenau; for they merely gave expression to what he had himself experienced and henceforth valued as his most precious possession.

Thus by a natural process of growth Rathenau's personal experience of the 'Soul' broadened out into a philosophy to which the New Testament, Hassidism, Spinoza and Fichte each contributed something, without however obscuring that personal revelation which remained the live core and motive of all

1814, the great exponent of an ascetic Prussian view of life, who by his teaching instilled into the youth of Germany the spirit which made it rise against Napoleon.

Rathenau's thoughts. This live experience even brought about a fundamental difference between Rathenau's philosophy and that of Fichte and Spinoza. For they did not distinguish between different states of the soul; Spinoza conceived all workings of the soul as equally complete manifestations of God— and Fichte's man was man without any qualification. But Rathenau bestows the name of 'soul' on inner experience only when it is impelled by its own tendencies alone without any outward purpose—only in those moments when it is not twisted and crippled by bondage to outward, material ends, is it the pure image of God. From this premise he was led inevitably to two startling propositions: First, that there are men who possess no soul—a view incompatible with Spinoza's conception, but acceptable to the Jewish Cabbala, which on the other hand also conceives of men who have two souls or even several. Men who are without a soul have failed to evolve one, either because external bondage or sheer misery has left them no leisure to acquire one, or because business and pleasure so engross them that they never have a single disinterested moment, never a breathing space when they are not the slaves of some scheme or purpose. And from the same premise follows just as inevitably that in most men the soul has yet to be 'born.' 'Many are born with a soul,' says the *Breviarium Mysticum*, 'all can attain to one.'

Hence the *'Birth of the Soul'* advances to the rank of a mystery, of a kind of miracle of the Holy Grail around which centres Rathenau's philosophy, as Christianity centres around the mystery of the admission to the fellowship of Christ through Baptism and Holy Communion. Men are different from one another not according to whether they are 'good' or 'bad'—for Rathenau's moral philosophy, like that of Nietzsche, is 'beyond good and evil'—but according to whether or not the birth of the soul has taken place in them, whether they are 'soul-less' or men who have a soul. This mystery, this initiation, which a man

85

must go through before he emerges on the side of Redemption, is obviously nothing but the first experience of his own individuality and uniqueness, of his being a child of God. It is therefore identical with the religious experience on which so many great mystics have founded their teaching: not only the Jewish Hassidim, but also Lao-tse, Buddha, Plato, Christ, Plotinus, and later the great German mystics Meister Eckhart, Jacob Boehme and Angelus Silesius. And to English readers it will suggest Wordsworth's lines in *The Prelude* which describe a mystical experience in a wild Alpine pass, curiously like Rathenau's revelation on Parnassus:

> Our destiny, our being's heart and home
> Is with infinitude, and only there.
>   .   .   .   .   .
> Under such banners militant, the soul
> Seeks for no trophies, struggles for no spoils
> That may attest her prowess, blest in thoughts
> That are their own perfection and reward,
> Strong in herself and in beatitude. . . .

The idea that not everybody has a soul and that in every man the soul must first be 'born,' though limiting and narrowing Spinoza's and Fichte's concepts, actually supplements the latter's fundamental proposition—that the paramount duty of every human being is to prevent the pure light of God as revealed in his soul from being obscured—by pointing out that man has first to throw off the bondage of material purpose in order to acquire a soul. With Fichte's proposition thus supplemented and reinforced, Rathenau finds himself justified in demanding with insistent vigour what is as revolutionary today as it was two thousand years ago—that nobody shall be hindered in his efforts to acquire a soul; and hence to proclaim that every limitation of man's freedom on the path to his soul is intolerable, and constitutes an injustice which upsets the divine order of things and a tyranny which it is man's duty to destroy.

And yet another consequence can be deduced from the concept that man is not necessarily born with a soul, but nevertheless can evolve one subsequently: the hope that the painful disharmony between man and the world which Christianity describes as sin, can be resolved even on earth—provided that, faced by the world, man first breaks through to his soul, and henceforth secures to it the upper hand. To this hope however there is a sinister corollary. For if a man later on, after he has discovered his soul, fails to establish and uphold its supremacy, then the strife and pain in him become worse than before. That is the meaning of the parable of the rich young man in the New Testament, and also of the belief prevalent in the ancient world that the man initiated into the mysteries who did not in life remain true to the divine revelation was punished by an avenging God. In Rathenau's case it is a fact that the dangers latent in his dual nature did not become threatening until, at those cross-roads in Greece, perhaps not far from the cross-roads where Oedipus met his fate, he stood face to face with his soul, but, turning back and hindered by a thousand inhibitions, was only able to give it half a hearing.

And yet the divinity of every human soul, its uniqueness and its paramount importance, which Spinoza conceived as a semi-mathematical formula expressing the relation between man and infinity, and Fichte used as an abstract hypothesis on which to found a new system of ethics, stood before Rathenau's imagination as a magic ring of indisputable facts vouched for by his own personal experience and liberating him from the depths of misery. 'He who has experienced the first stirring of the life of the soul,' he says, 'needs no proof. His inner certainty, which is more living than any other experience, assures him of a new activity of the spirit which, entirely separate from the intellect,

87

opens the way to new powers, new joys, new sorrows, and to a life above life.' (*Mechanism of the Mind*, p. 36.)

But it is not only in the individual that this miracle, the birth of a soul, this infinitely delicate, mysterious process, can take place; a community also can give birth to a soul, a communal soul, strange as this idea would presumably have seemed to the old Mystics. Just as according to the Cabbala several souls can have their home in one body, so modern philosophy and folklore recognize that thousands, even millions, of men can participate in one soul; and not only millions who are contemporaries, but also generations past and to come, all of whom through the fact that they have a share in this one soul constitute, as it were, only one body. Thus families, races, peoples, nations, religions, and civilizations arise round this central miracle of the birth of a soul which is what truly forms the community, just as the birth of a soul in man is what makes him truly human. As a man only experiences himself in the soul which comes into being within him, so does a community only experience itself when a communal soul works within it, which reveals itself in its customs, its speech, mythology, poetry, art, life and culture.[3] By means of this concept German classical philosophy made a decisive advance beyond pure individualism. Formulated by Herder, developed and carried to its logical conclusion by Fichte, this concept became the living core of revolutionary nationalism, the most powerful lever of the political upheavals of the nineteenth century. For, as Herder recognized, it implies that the soul of a community is no less a manifestation of God in Spinoza's sense than the soul of an individual; and that, according to Fichte's fundamental proposition, a community therefore has, no less than individual man, the right and the duty to demand of mankind that it shall in no

[3] See Professor William McDougall's *Psychology*, Home University Library, pp. 228 ff. and the writings of Professor Durkheim. It need hardly be pointed out what use the French nationalist writer Maurice Barrès and his friends made of this concept in their agitation for the reconquest of Alsace-Lorraine by France.

way be interfered with, or shackled, or hindered from realizing its individuality. 'The peoples' right of self-determination': here is its transcendental root.

But how is the birth of a communal soul possible? How can numbers of men participate in one soul and even pass this soul on from generation to generation? Rathenau explains this by two psychological principles, which he calls 'addition' and 'radiation.'

Just as in a family between husband and wife, parents and children, a communal soul arises through the medium of love, so in a larger community a soul arises through processes similar to love: through the feeling of solidarity and the willingness of individuals to sacrifice themselves to the community. Every community, whether it be a family, a race, a nation, or a confederation of several nations (as, for example, Switzerland), within which solidarity and the sense of sacrifice hold sway, possesses the soil from which a communal soul can be born. The birth of a soul in such a community Rathenau explains through the process of 'addition,' since through solidarity and sacrifice the part-souls of the individuals 'add themselves up' into a communal soul (*Mechanism of the Mind*, p. 55 *ff.*); its survival, through a process which he calls 'radiation.'

'Radiation' (*Mechanism of the Mind*, p. 131 *ff.*) is the process which in a community takes the place of memory, enabling it to organize its spiritual life into a continuous experience. This radiation can best be explained by means of an example. The shape of the waterspout which rises out of the round pond in the grounds of Sans-Souci in Potsdam is exactly the same as in the days when Frederick the Great watched it. Now, since Frederick's death the water has never been the same for an instant, yet for a hundred and fifty years the form of its jet has never altered—in a thousand, in two thousand, years, provided the water comes out of the same pipe, it will always be the same. This principle of radiation, as Rathenau rightly

89

recognized, is the law of all life, its fundamental law. Everything is in flux, yet at every moment matter in its onward rush is caught up in a millionfold net of forms, which give the world the appearance of permanency because, from the form of the Universe to that of the atom, they are, according to human standards, immutable. This 'radiation'—in a paper published in Harden's *Zukunft* in 1906 I first called attention to its bearing on the phenomena of *Nationality*, naming it *the principle of permanent form-tendencies*—is paramount also in the realm of the mind, giving individual experience the chance of surviving the individual in the shape of a form-tendency ingrafted into the community. It is the rise and survival of permanent form-tendencies that explain how the same experience, the same tastes and urges can recur mysteriously in generation after generation of men. It is not blood, but a body of permanent form-tendencies, forcing matter and mind ever again into the same forms, that gives a community its individuality and, in Rathenau's sense of the word, its soul,—in the forms of its speech, its art, its morals, its religion. The birth of a soul in man and the birth of a soul in the community are twin manifestations, twin mysteries which cannot be separated, and as such dominate Rathenau's moral philosophy and his schemes for industrial, social and political reform.

Great thoughts, as Rathenau himself says somewhere, are to be had for the asking: it is easy to conceive them, but difficult to put them into practice; and when a complicated nature, hemmed in by more inhibitions than Hamlet, undertakes the task the result is likely to be tragic. With the object of preparing the way for the 'realm of the soul'—which was a concept similar to Fichte's 'perfect society'—a realm in which both the individual and the community should be given scope for the unfolding of their souls through freeing them from the bondage of material purpose, Rathenau outlined in three revolutionary books the fundamental features of a new human, social, industrial and political world-order. These three works are: *Criticism of the Age*, published in 1912, *The Mechanism of the Mind*, published in 1913, and *In Days to Come* written during the war.

With a ruthless determination to get down to realities he asks of the world of today: *What of the soul?* In seeking for an answer he comes upon a fact which appears to him the fundamental cause of the present soulless state of the world: *mechanization*. 'Mechanization,' says Rathenau, 'is the amalgamation of the whole world into one compulsory association, into one continuous net of production and world trade.' (*In Days to Come*, p. 28.) [4] In this oppressive organization, in this stranglehold, the soul droops and withers. A problem is therefore set before humanity: How to save the soul out of the grip of mechanization, how to give it back its freedom in a world thoroughly enslaved by purpose? Now the problem Rathenau thus exalts to the position of a world problem is in fact the problem of his own personality. 'With the gigantic search-light of his egocentric spirit he projected the image of his inner fate upon his century,' says Emil Ludwig in his essay on Rathenau. But Rathenau was entitled to do so, because his fate and the fate of the world were curiously alike, and he was thus led to realize more vividly than most people what must happen unless the conflict between the two tendencies which rend the modern world ends in the victory of the spirit.

Fate governs this struggle because mechanization, as Rathenau shows, is the ineluctable consequence of the unprecedented increase of the world's population in the course of the last century, and indeed is the sole effective means of preserving it. If freedom of the soul proves finally incompatible with a mechanized world, mankind will one day have to choose between its

[4] The page references throughout are to the English translation of *Von Kommenden Dingen*, published by Messrs George Allen and Unwin, Ltd (London, 1921).

overgrown body and its soul. Rathenau experienced to the full the tragedy of this dilemma. Hence the pathos of his writings: the pathos of a tragic personal fate raised to the unthinkably terrible fate of mankind.

But is it true that an unprecedented increase of the population is responsible for this? According to Sombart (*Hochkapitalismus*, Vol. III, p. 355), between 1800 and 1914 the population of Europe increased from 180 millions to 452 millions and the white population of the whole world from 185 millions to 559 millions. The chief cause of this increase is certainly, as Sombart shows, the decrease in the death-rate, not the increase in the birth-rate; but that is not to the point at present. For whatever may have been the causes of this unprecedented increase, in order to meet the needs of such a huge population, 'there remained,' says Rathenau, 'only one thing for the peoples to do, and that was to acquire completely new customs and laws of life and work, with the object of increasing material production to the utmost and adapting it to the teeming millions of mankind. This was only possible in one way: by a ruthless adaptation of means to end, which greatly increased the effectiveness of human labour and at the same time utilized the product of this labour to the fullest extent. The formula which lies at the basis of the mechanizing of the world is increase of production secured by economy of labour and material.'

This end is brought about by the aid of organization and technology, 'organization, in that it directs production and consumption into the desired channels by means of division, unification and ramification; technology, in that it controls natural forces and places them at the disposal of new organizations for production and transport either by power, by chemistry, by electricity, or by skilful mechanical devices. . . . If in this manner mechanization had its original roots in the creation of commodities it did not long remain confined to this province. Admittedly even today this is still the centre from which it rami-

fies and casts its shadow; for the creation of wealth remains the
central province of material life; that which all others touch
at one point at least.

'But we encounter mechanization over whatever department
of human activity we cast our eyes, although its forms are so
complex and varied that it seems presumptuous to attempt to
grasp the whole sweep of the ever-changing picture. To the
economist it appears as mass production and distribution of
goods; to the industrialist as division of labour, accumulation
of labour, and manufacture; to the geographer as development
of transport and communication, and colonization; to the tech-
nician as control of natural forces; to the scientist as the application of the results of research; to the sociologist as the organization of labour; to the business man as capitalistic enterprise;
to the politician as realistic economico-political statecraft. But
all these have in common something which separates them in a
definite and peculiar fashion from the modes of life of earlier
centuries: a spirit, namely, of specialization and abstraction,
standardized thinking devoid of surprise and humour, complicated uniformity; a spirit which seems to justify the name
"mechanization" even when applied to the sphere of emotion.'
(*Criticism of the Age*, pp. 42-56.)

Thus mechanization signifies a complete revolution of the
whole mental, social, economic and political outlook. First of
all, with regard to economic life:

'From all parts of the surface of the earth raw products of
mineral and organic origin are streaming along railroads and
water routes into the reservoirs of towns and harbours. There
they are sent to the various factories in which they are to be
treated and in which they are combined in prearranged proportions in order that, having been chemically or mechanically
modified, they may begin another cycle as semi-products. Again
separated and recombined and worked up, they appear as final
products, which in their third form are brought into the ware-

house of the wholesale dealer before they find their way along highly differentiated paths to the retail dealer and finally to the consumer, who converts them into waste material and sends them back into the process of production. Like the blood stream, the stream of commodities flows through the network of its arteries and veins. Every moment of the day and night, metal thunders, propellers churn, fly-wheels whir, retorts steam, to renew and to maintain this circulation. . . . If we consider this vision in its entirety, the earth cannot but appear to us a single and indivisible economic unit.'

Capital is the driving power behind this prodigious new world machine. 'If this economic bee-hive, which had attained to a visible unity, was to secure its life and existence, there had to be a system of tacit agreements, links and relationships to hold together the human elements in the organization, distribute labour, and at the same time chain the dead material to these living elements. . . . The core of this invisible organization of the economic world is the institution of property, and this particularly in the form of property which is most closely associated with the individual: inheritable property. For this highly personal institution to adapt itself to the manifold forms and movements of mechanized types of production, it had to become equally flexible and impersonal. Property had to be infinitely divisible, yet susceptible of infinite accumulation; it had to be mobile, exchangeable, active; its fruits had to be separable from their source and realizable in themselves. In fine, property had to learn to correspond to the pattern of mechanized actuality, of division of labour, accumulation of labour, organization and combination; it had to be mechanized. Mechanized property is what we call capital. That procedure which, regarded physiologically and from without, presents itself as mechanized production, appears, regarded from within from the human and organizational point of view, as capitalism. Hence capitalism will persist as long as the mechanized system

94

of production is in existence. . . . One can therefore speak of the cessation of private capitalistic society, but not for the present of the cessation of the capitalistic type of production.' (*Criticism of the Age*, pp. 61-62.)

From the revolution in industry there follows an equally fundamental revolution and crisis in political thought: 'Alongside of the anonymous, autonomous and rational organization of property there stands a second, supporting it and supported by it, which is built on the basis of custom, prestige, power and sanction—the organization of the state. In it, for an incalculable period, the mystical principle has fought with the mechanical, the first invoked to reinforce custom and purpose, the second called into being by the increasing tasks and difficulties of the moment. The mystical power of the state lay in its age-long association with religion. From the time when the changes in industry, the growth of population, the policy of expansion, compelled the state to exercise tolerance and no longer to regard heresy as a crime, but rather to recognize the rights of the religious beliefs of its neighbours, the basis was transferred from the unconditioned and the transcendental to the conditioned and the utilitarian; the religious state was a sacrament, the modern state a contrivance.' There remain indeed, as indispensable functions, foreign policy and defence, law and police. 'But actually and normally nine-tenths of the political activity is devoted to the industrial demands of the moment, and the remainder to the industrial demands of the future. It would perhaps be premature to depict the state of today as an armed confederacy for production on a national basis; but it is certainly out of date to regard it as a mystical institution on a higher level than mechanized industry and business.' (*Criticism of the Age*, p. 68.) Thus the inevitable consequence of mechanization is a weakening—an irrevocable weakening—of the conception of the state, its subordination to economic considerations.

Thus we have a world turned upside down, in which economic interests are on top, political interests subservient, and the soul crushed and suffocated beneath both. But in what way, we ask, does this new condition of things effect the crushing of the soul? Rathenau describes this in detail. To begin with, the world today strangles the soul in a network of organizations which hinder it in every one of its natural activities. 'A German citizen returning home from America without a penny in his pocket has only the right, if he is not going to solicit charity, to proceed along the public thoroughfares at a normal pace and to record his vote at parliamentary elections.' (*Criticism of the Age*, p. 70.)

Organizations throw their manifold, invisible meshes over every foot of the earth. 'If once upon a time a German was able to boast of being a Christian, a subject, a citizen, the father of a family and a member of a guild, today he is the subject and object of countless associations. He is a citizen of the Empire, of his particular state and his town, a resident in a district and a province, and a member of a parish; he is a soldier, voter, taxpayer, the holder of honorary posts; he is a member of a profession, employer or employee, tenant or landlord, customer or purveyor; he is an insured person, a member of a trade union, of a scientific society or a club; he is the client of a bank, a shareholder, a creditor of the state, the owner of savings certificates, mortgagee or mortgagor; he is a member of a political party, a subscriber to a newspaper, the telephone, the postal cheque system, an inquiry office, he has a season ticket on the tramways; he makes oral and written contracts and agreements; he is sportsman, collector, connoisseur, dilettante, traveller, reader, pupil, student; the possessor of testimonials, a passport, diplomas and titles; he is agent, member of a firm, a 'reference,' a competitor; he is an expert, confidant, arbiter, witness, magistrate, juror; he is heir, testator, husband, relative, friend. These are the ramifications of the nervous system of mechanized industry laid bare in all their complexity.' They imply that the behaviour of the individual reflects to an increasing degree not himself but a system. And no less than the individual have the professions and occupations lost their outer peculiarities through the effects of mechanization. Formerly, but two or three generations ago, one could at least recognize every man's occupation by his outward appearance: one could distinguish from afar a doctor, an artist, an artisan, a farmer. But today all are 'middle-class': the mason looks exactly like the journalist, and the boxer like the priest. Every one tries to be as like as possible to every one else, since 'living machinery (like mechanized society) must, in order to maintain the productivity of the earth, consist of uniform, normal and solid material' and 'its parts must be producible and exchangeable on a mass scale.' (*Criticism of the Age*, p. 71.)

Thus, out of these two elements, mechanized organization and mechanized occupation, there develops 'the decisive characteristic of mechanized society: its homogeneity. . . . A lawyer of today resembles his medical colleagues very much more than a linen-weaver used formerly to resemble a cloth-maker. And there is still more resemblance between their domestic arrangements, their way of living, their clothing, their mode of thought and their desires.' (*Criticism of the Age*, pp. 70-72.)

That men become more and more similar to one another in their outward aspect—first within each particular country, and then all the world over—is probably the most obvious result of mechanization; but of course it affects them in ways still more fundamental and revolutionary.

Thus, it creates a completely new spiritual atmosphere by increasing to an unprecedented extent the personal experience and the knowledge of each single individual; not, be it well understood, his 'culture,' as one used to say, his breeding and assimilated knowledge, but rather the mass of sheer facts which are forced down his throat. The average German 'leaves school

97

with some general knowledge of the past and the present, and a superficial acquaintance with several languages and with mathematics; he has some idea of the multiplicity of human institutions and of the classification of natural phenomena. Countless reproductions of works of art of all periods, styles of architecture, countries and their peoples, are put before him. A walk in any town shows him more goods and contrivances of every kind than Babylon, Bagdad, Rome and Constantinople together had even heard of. He is trained to understand the working of machines, communications, and manufacture; he can look without surprise at men of every occupation and every country, at the animals and plants of every region of the earth. . . . But the flood of insistent information does not cease with his schooldays and his entering on a career. At least once a day the curtain of the world-theatre rises and the newspaper reader is presented with murder and violence, war and diplomatic intrigue, horse races, discoveries and inventions, expeditions, love affairs, public works, accidents, theatrical productions, stock exchange business, the weather report: in one morning over his early coffee more remarkable events than his forefathers were vouchsafed in the course of a lifetime.' (*Criticism of the Age*, pp. 81-83.)

In these days of wireless and cinema Rathenau's indictment seems almost old-fashioned; the stupendous flood of new ideas has increased enormously since then, penetrated into the remotest villages, into furthest Asia and Australia. But does the inundation bring nourishment to the soul? All this information, these visions, these ideas, rush past as though carried away by a roaring torrent. Very few ever succeed in taking hold; most of them whirl past, merely serving to provide man with moments of self-forgetfulness, to make him from day to day less intimate with himself, to draw him away more and more from the depths to the mere outer trappings of his soul.

But still worse than this devastating mass of cheap informa-

THE REALM OF THE SOUL

tion are the effects of the mechanized methods of work, of our latter-day division of labour carried to such a point that the work of most men has become a purely mechanical operation having nothing in common with the craftsmanship of former times. 'With the exception of a few creative occupations, such as the artist's and the scientist's, the mechanized occupations are as it were mere "jobs." The workman sees no beginning and no end, the finished article is no concern of his; for the products he makes and the stages he deals with are intermediate. . . . Thus is man strangely modelled in the school of his calling. If labour is a joy to him, it is no longer the joy of creation, but rather that of getting through his work. A task is done, a danger obviated, a stage reached: all that matters is what comes next, what follows.' (*Criticism of the Age*, pp. 84-87.)

The man who, in a factory with a thousand other men, makes the same movement of the hand twenty times a minute is not an image of God, nor even truly a man, but just a machine, a soulless piece of clockwork of which the artificial men of Karel Capek, the 'robots,' are not even caricatures. His work takes no account of his individuality; and when he walks out of the factory gate he might as well have been dead for eight hours. Who has still the effrontery to preach to him about the 'joy of labour'? The *Vossische Zeitung* of March 8th, 1928, printed this letter from a machine-worker, Franz Flächsenhaar of Mannheim: 'Put yourself in the place of a worker who formerly gave himself heart and soul to his work, who breathed his spirit into it, grew with its progress and found his own self in the completed work. And now he stands beside the band and makes the same movement of the hand day after day, hundreds and even thousands of times, and always at the prescribed speed. He has been forced to bury his pride as a craftsman, for what he is making can be made equally well by anybody else. He has been forced to sacrifice his soul to rationalization.'

99

Hence in order to tap man's creative energies other impulses than the joy of labour must be aroused: fear of hunger, delight in superfluous possessions, ambition, the pursuit of pleasure. And actually the typical mechanized man is a compound of greed, lust and vanity. It is this last remnant of his soul, his 'iron ration' of spirituality, which suffices to keep him and the world going.

But have we not forgotten the other side of the question, the spiritual forces fostered by mechanization? Has not the age of mechanization witnessed the growth of an ideal which has overshadowed all others, namely nationalism? Not patriotism, but nationalism. Patriotism implies a willingness to sacrifice oneself for one's own people without any ulterior motive, a pure sacrifice for their defence and welfare. A striking and graphic illustration of patriotic sacrifice pure and simple without thought of any advantage is offered by the poet Theodor Däubler's description of the saving of the Greeks of Asia Minor after the catastrophe of 1921 by the poor Greek sailors and fishermen of Santorin, Paros, Naxos, Syra, etc.; it exhibits the element of patriotism, one of the most precious in the human soul, so well that it deserves to be quoted in full as he wrote it down for me:

'Coming from Santorin, I left the Greek steamer at Paros in order to pay a visit to the marble quarries on the island and its wonderful Byzantine church. The people seemed to me profoundly unhappy. A great disaster seemed to be in the air, but no one mentioned it. After having spent two days there, I wished to leave Paros; but the old fishermen in the harbour shook their heads as they gazed out to sea and said: "There is no ship in sight." "When will one come?" I asked. "Perhaps in a month," answered the pilot, "perhaps earlier." I had with me a government paper which invited all Greek officials to give me their assistance. I was able to make good use of it, for that very afternoon the port officials succeeded in getting me

THE REALM OF THE SOUL

aboard a sailing ship which was conveying fish, packed in ice, to the Piraeus. It was the last which set its course for the capital. All the Greek steamers had received instructions to proceed to the coast of Asia Minor in order to collect refugees. The Greek army had been routed; Ionia, the native land of Homer and of the great philosophers of the ancient world, had been surrendered. The victorious and exasperated Turk had fallen upon the towns and villages of his rebellious subjects. This time the Greeks and Armenians were to be exterminated. The islanders were aghast. Through a violent nor'wester every ship, even small sailing boats which were scarcely of a size to battle with the threatening waves, could be seen taking an eastward course. Every Greek who possessed a boat of any sort was moved by the soul-stirring cry: "Hellas in Asia is lost!" Everywhere along the coast of Asia Minor that faces Europe the cry rang out: "If there are Christians here, or Greeks, come! Your brothers are waiting to take you away." A miracle took place: nearly half a million men and women, old people and children, had been brutally butchered, yet three times as many were saved and transported to Europe. I saw this with my own eyes. I am not romancing, but reporting.'

Opposed to this readiness for unselfish sacrifice is nationalism, the policy of armed expansion, claiming special rights as the perquisite of a chosen people. Since mechanization has overrun the world, nationalism thus understood has blossomed to a remarkable degree; but it is in no sense a new departure, as Rathenau seems to hold. Wherever there have been greedy business men and ambitious states, there have also been nationalists. Alcibiades, Socrates' fair pupil, the déclassé aristocrat and boon companion of the rich Athenian corn-merchants, who drove Athens to her doom in Sicily, was a nationalist who conducted a policy of armed expansion in the name not, of course, of the Athenian corn-trade, but of the 'higher mission' of Athens. Nor has a nationalistic policy by any means always led to disaster; the British Empire from Cromwell to the younger Pitt is a masterpiece of ruthless nationalism, with Providence on its lips and plenty of powder and shot in the holds of its men of war. Nor would it be fair to deny to nationalism an ideology. The assurance of belonging to a chosen people and having on that account a right to a privileged commercial position does foster idealistic tendencies, however uncertainly they may flutter around the solid core of good business.

So much we can grant. But can we therefore hope to see nationalism free man from the strangle-hold of mechanization? Millions certainly believe it. Even after the fruitless orgy of nationalism in the Great War and subsequent Peace it still remains the peculiar faith, the sole religion, of masses of people everywhere. Yet obviously nationalism can never by any chance free the soul from the meshes of mechanization. For it is itself scheming, purposive, profiteering—a growth of the same materialistic, pettifogging spirit as mechanization, and thus essentially related to it, its elder brother so to speak—but if an elder brother, a hostile one, stranded halfway between the old world, which was cut up into economic units, and the new, which has willy-nilly become welded into one economic community. Nationalism, therefore, though apparently dominating the age as its only substitute for religion, is really involved in a life-and-death struggle with the spirit of the age and fated to go under in this contest. For both these reasons, because it is itself materialistic, and because its day is on the wane, it cannot fulfil the hopes of the Italian Fascist or German 'Völkische' and become the seedling of a new type of soul raised above mechanization. That is why Rathenau, although to a certain extent sympathizing with it, finally rejected it, and took up the line he did, before, during and after the war. 'If it looks as though nationalism, because it is a question of bread, must remain with us for all time, one can only reply: It is not so; for

THE REALM OF THE SOUL

that which is contrary to reason cannot persist.' (*Criticism of the Age*, p. 116.)

Mechanization thus leads to outer bondage and inner starvation of the soul without providing it with any redeeming ideal. And yet, however severe this indictment may seem, it is not complete; for we have not yet considered the worst crime of mechanization, its fostering of an immense 'Proletariat,' a class of human beings which has no share in the means of production and is therefore entirely dependent on those who have. The question of how man shall free his soul from the strangle-hold of mechanization becomes an even more urgent and terrible problem for the proletarian than it is for the bourgeois, a special problem which keeps him in a state of permanent unrest and which he must solve if he is not ultimately to go under both physically and spiritually. Seen in this light, the so-called 'Social Question' is a special case of the much more general problem set humanity by mechanization.

By conceiving the struggle for the emancipation of the proletariat as part of the much more extended and complex struggle for the emancipation of man, Rathenau broadened the basis of the proletarian claim and envisaged a task far beyond the mere economic improvement of the proletarian's lot. Marx justified the 'class war' by a sort of legal title: the employer class, the 'bourgeoisie,' do not refund to the proletarian the full value of his labour in the form of wages, but only a fraction of that value: the rest (Marx calls it *'surplus value'*) they pocket, giving nothing in return; to this sharp practice they owe their income, their capital and their very existence. The proletarian demands that the 'surplus value,' the fraction of the value of his labour out of which he is habitually swindled, be refunded to him; but in mechanistic (or 'capitalistic') society his claim is turned down, not because it is not just, but because the employer class have laid hands not only on the means of production, but also on the state, and can therefore deflect justice by

103

bringing political power to bear on it. Hence the proletarian must conquer both the means of production and the state, viz., political power. And in this 'class war' justice is on his side; on the assumption, of course, that Marx is right and that the employer really does deprive the working man of a portion of the value of his labour. Such is the ethical basis of Marxism. To the agitator it has proved invaluable, and for the purposes of attack on the bourgeois position most effective tactically; but it is narrow and obviously weak, since it rests entirely on an assumption which to say the least is disputable.

Now Rathenau also starts from the assumption of an injury inflicted on the proletariat by the bourgeoisie, but this injury is clear and undeniable. Whether the employer appropriates a part of the value due to labour, says Rathenau, may be doubtful. But what is not doubtful is that the institution for which he is responsible crushes and destroys his workman's soul. 'Not any inherent necessity of the principle of mechanization,' says Rathenau in *In Days to Come*, p. 34 *ff.*, 'but mere expediency, has turned the inevitable distinction between hand and brain work into a permanent and hereditary separation; and brought into being in every civilized country *two peoples*, of one blood and race, yet eternally separate, and related one to the other as were racially distinct upper and lower layers of population in former times. They are divided and governed *compulsorily*. . . . This compulsion is intolerably hard on the second people. . . . The proletarian's (forced) labour enjoys, it is true, a sort of deceptive anonymity, called subordination; he receives not orders, but instructions; he obeys not a master, but a superior; he does not serve, but of his own free will enters into a contract; his rights in law are the same as those of the man he contracts with; he is free to change his habitat and situation; the authority by which he is governed is not personal; even though it take the shape of an individual employer or firm it is in reality Bourgeois Society. But the proletarian's life, however he may ar-

WALTHER RATHENAU BEFORE THE WAR

range it within the bounds of his sham liberty, will run its course from generation to generation in the same dreary uniformity. . . . Whoever realizes that this life never ceases, that the dying workman sees the long sequence of his children and grandchildren doomed to undergo the same fate, will feel the conscience-pricks of a great crime. Our age calls out for state intervention when a cab horse is ill-treated, but finds it natural and right that one people should have to go on slaving for centuries for the benefit of another which is its kith and kin, and is indignant when that people refuses to vote for the maintenance of the present state of affairs.' (*In Days to Come*, p. 34 *ff.*) Later on in the same book he returns to the insurmountable barrier which separates the proletarian from the bourgeois. However strenuously the workman attempts to rise to the social class above him, he cannot do so. 'The charmed circle is closed. Money is the shibboleth. To him that hath, shall be given; what he has increases, but first, he must possess. . . . Thus walls of glass rise on every side, transparent yet insurmountable, and beyond them lie liberty, self-determination, comfort and power. The keys to the forbidden land are knowledge and property, and both are hereditary. Under the mask of liberty and self-determination, we find anonymous slavery, not of man to man, but of people to people. It is incompatible with the claim to the liberty of the soul and its development that one half of mankind should condemn the other half, which is endowed by God with the same features and gifts, to be its drudge for all eternity.' (*In Days to Come*, p. 69 *ff.*)

Rathenau has epitomized his moral judgment on this state of affairs in the words: 'A moral vindication of the proletarian relationship is impossible.' And further: 'The will to become a free people is incompatible with the will to class division. You must choose between having German citizens, and German proletarians.' (*In Days to Come*, p. 201 *ff.*) One hears the voice of Fichte: 'The choice of a status in life should be a free one; no man should be forced into or excluded from any status. Every individual action as well as every institution which is based on such compulsion is contrary to justice.' (*Über die Bestimmung des Gelehrten*, 1794 edition, p. 64.) And somewhat earlier in the same work: 'Every one who regards himself as the master of another is himself a slave. Even if he be not really a slave, he certainly has the soul of one and will cringe basely to the first man strong enough to subdue him. He alone is free who wishes to make all around him free' (*l.c.*, p. 39). Rathenau concludes: 'Thus the demand for redemption no longer appears as the demand for the liberation of one class, but as an aspiration towards the raising of industry and society in general to a higher moral plane, to the level of personal responsibility.' (*In Days to Come*, p. 85.)

But what is to be done? 'A proletariat stirred to its depths, terrifyingly silent,' Rathenau writes in the latter part of the war, 'lurks down below, a nation apart, a lake of darkness, out of which now and then a glance and a cry strike the upper air: the embodiment of the guilt and sins of mechanized society.' (*In Days to Come*, p. 201.) How is this nation apart to be redeemed from the lowest circle of the hell of mechanization and assisted to a soul? The task appears beyond human strength, and doubly so, because it is only a part of a much greater and bolder undertaking: the endeavour to raise both the proletarian and the bourgeois once more to the full status of man. And at this point it is only just to emphasize again the fact that the form in which Rathenau raises the so-called 'Social Question' —whether we agree with his answer or not—signifies an advance beyond Marx, not only because it proves the need for a fundamental reconstruction of Society by arguments much more general and less controversial, but also because obviously the solution of the greater task, the awakening of man out of the death-sleep of mechanization, is necessary if the proletarian is to become not a mere *petit bourgeois*, but a man. Rathenau never failed to recognize the enormous, the almost insuperable, difficulties of the task which he had set himself; in fact, they were only too familiar to him from his own inner backslidings and personal failures. For even though the mechanized world have no ideal, it is at least not based on mere material power, but on a general tendency of the age, which it is even more difficult to overcome: the pursuit of the purely rational. 'We must recognize,' says Rathenau in his *Criticism of the Age*, 'that never in the history of man has any system of ideas so uniformly dominated such a stupendous number of people as has the mechanistic. Its power seems inexhaustible, since it embraces both the sources and the methods of production and the forces and aims of life; and this power is based on Reason.'

'Nevertheless,' he says, 'nevertheless, mechanization has already received its death-blow. For in its heart of hearts this world of ours is terrified of its own self; its inmost impulses accuse it and strive to be free from the eternal domination of purpose. The world says that it knows what it wants. But it does not know, for it desires happiness and concerns itself with material things. It feels that material things bring it no happiness and that it is condemned to perpetual desire. It is like Midas, dying of thirst in a flood of gold. . . . But through all this confusion the voice of desire is doubly piercing because, repudiating the self-complacency of knowingness, it has to admit that it really does not know what it is yearning for.'

With these words, which sound like a personal confession, Rathenau introduces in the *Criticism of the Age* his search for counteracting forces which, if they cannot do away with, can at least lead us on beyond, mechanization. For there can be no going back on mechanization. 'After working for years at the fundamental problems of industry I have come to the conclusion that only mechanization itself can lead us on beyond mechanization.' (Letter 263.) But where are we to look for the forces strong enough to resorb mechanization and render it harmless? We have seen that nationalism is not equipped for this task. Can it be achieved by any of the traditional forms of withdrawal from the world?' 'Who can teach the man of this Age, anguished by doubt, what he should prize, love, desire and strive for? He addresses himself to philosophy. It replies: Some people believe this, some that; the choice of a creed is determined by character and circumstances; everything is true, everything is false. He turns to religion . . . he is presented with a history of God; God becomes a subject for natural history. . . . He inquires of Science; she advises him to specialize. Art opens before him a picture gallery which enshrines the beauties of all ages and peoples from Memphis to Paris, from Mexico to Pekin; extolling one epoch and abusing the other, with more than a hint that tomorrow it will do the exact opposite. . . . It is as if the world had become fluid and was trickling through one's hands. Everything is possible, everything is good. But man thirsts for faith and values.' (*Criticism of the Age*, p. 127.)

This is not to say that philosophy, religion, science and art are of no avail, but rather that they are not sufficient, that their driving power is no longer, or not yet, strong enough to force open the iron vise of mechanization without any outside aid. 'It is implicit in the consequences of mechanization, which faithfully reflects the present intellectual state of the world and vies with it with ever-increasing intensity, that these counteracting forces cannot be political, social or economic: in a word, they cannot be mechanical. Even the emergence of a theoretically perfect collectivistic state, the nationalization of the means of production and the pooling of commodities, would not destroy mechanization, but, at the most, effect a redistribution of property and power inconsiderable from the point of view of culture, and with no guarantee for its continuance.' (*Mechanism of the Mind*, p. 303.)

The world really presented itself to Rathenau as a macrocosm, as a stupendous image of his inner self. Just as his own intuition, imagination and emotions waged war on his intellect and purposiveness, the moment he had secured a competency, and suddenly in the experience of the soul revealed to him a meaning in life and an escape from the toils of mechanization, so, Rathenau believed, would these forces and others allied to them show man that there was a meaning in his history and raise him above the plane of mechanization, as soon as the material obstacles of poverty and intellectual inhibition were removed by a reorganization of Society and a new spiritual outlook. Rathenau thought he already saw the power of these anti-intellectual tendencies increasing 'without external or internal assistance, without any new creed, without any conscious reshaping of the aims of world politics or history, any deepening of spiritual experience.' Instead of the spiritual forces born of fear, 'qualities closely allied to courage, such as imagination, vision and inwardness, together with the less exalted qualities of energy, patience and tenacity, will come to occupy a central position among those forces which mechanization will need in its zenith and decline, and which in days to come will show the way to the complete development of the soul.' (*Mechanism of the Mind*, p. 332.)

At the same time the intellectualist impulses which had hitherto been the main driving forces behind mechanization—acquisitiveness, ambition and ostentation—would be ousted from their ascendancy. 'We are all aware that even today in this acquisitive age the most enlightened and spiritual people choose that mode of life in which property plays the smallest possible part. . . . We know that possessiveness, luxury and extravagance are the mark of this dissolute heir, of the mere grasping upstart; men of creative genius are independent of them. We know that nowadays men of great wealth are becoming more aware of their responsibilities, and are more and more inclined to rid themselves of this burden during their lifetime instead of leaving its disposition to the caprice of their heirs. It needs little foresight to recognize that the time is drawing near when, in so far as the institution of private property still persists, the right of inheritance will be stringently curtailed and the greater part of private incomes assigned to the community. . . . The worst conceivable work is that which is done from necessity, or purely for the sake of gain. If there is still anywhere a well-sewn pair of boots, then they have been made by a cobbler who has joy in his craftsmanship. Thus from a purely business point of view we see that the ground even of material life is being prepared for the future.' (*Mechanism of the Mind*, p. 298 *ff.*)

Indeed, the weakening of those impulses which have built up the mechanized world raises the question whether there is not a danger 'that the human motives which drive the social mechanism may be weakened, or even destroyed. . . . Is not this stupendous mechanism driven by greed and competition, by intellect and scheming? What will happen if the driving forces slacken, greed dies down, competition ends in love, the intellect is superseded by vision, and scheming ceases? Many will fear that, without driving forces, the world would not carry on for a single day, and they thereby testify to mankind that it does not deserve to live a day longer and that it would be better if it had never been created.' (*Mechanism of the Mind*, p. 290 *ff.*)

This question will have to be considered carefully further on, when we come to Rathenau's proposals for reconstruction. Here where we are only concerned with mapping out the two positions, the one defending and the other opposing the subjection of man and his soul to purpose, it must suffice to record Rathenau's answer: that although it be true that these forces have propelled the mechanism of the world, they have not been really creative. 'Ambition has never produced anything in this world but sharp practice, petty expedients and mere casual successes. . . . But if we consider the truly great, the creators in·

thought and deed, we find that they were men who served a cause. . . . Display, immediate results, and reward meant nothing to them; they were willing to give up property, power, and life itself for the sake of their cause. Such devotion is transcendental, for it is disinterested and intuitive; the spiritual forces which release it are the result of imagination and vision. Of such a kind were and are the men who have given to the things of the world their form. The passion that moves them is the same which inspires the artist, the scientist, the craftsman and the builder; it is the joy of creation. And they must have yet another emotion in an unusual measure, the consciousness of being called by the will of spiritual or divine forces to an activity which absorbs their whole being, demanding a ceaseless struggle against their own imperfections, incapable of delegation and endowed therefore with the dignity of a personal burden and necessity. This consciousness we call "responsibility," meaning thereby that the spirit must render its account to God and man.' (*Mechanism of the Mind*, p. 297.)

Behind these words is not only a personal confession to which the future was to give a tragic significance, but also the figure of Emil Rathenau. Walther turned to what seemed to him the driving forces of his father's personality, in the expectation that they would take the place of ambition and acquisitiveness, and become the mainspring of human activity long before these had died down.

This prospect, however, only applies to the leaders of industry, not—for the present at any rate—to the proletariat, the majority of whom have been robbed of every possibility of joy in creation by the division of labour. But in their case another impulse is gradually gaining ground which, he thinks, is destined to overwhelm like a rising flood the cold supremacy of the intellect and to reinstate the soul: the feeling of Solidarity, if by this we mean that within a community the individual becomes aware of the fact that one necessarily stands for all and all for one. The description and analysis of this impulse of solidarity is one of the central features of the *Mechanism of the Mind*. And rightly so; for the feeling of solidarity, which is in process of growth not only within each nation, but between different nations, and also within other types of community, corresponds to the increasingly close texture of human relationships and is therefore the most hopeful counter-movement against the mechanistic impulses of selfish acquisitiveness and personal ambition. But, says Rathenau, the sense of solidarity is not merely a harbinger of the soul; it is itself a part of the soul. And this enables the lowly and disinherited, whose souls are most in need of salvation, to play a quite special rôle in the overcoming of mechanization. Since suffering is their common lot, and their sense of solidarity is thus particularly strong, they bear within them, in the very midst of mechanization, an element of the future soul of man. They therefore are the truly elect, called upon to free the soul from the bondage of self-interest. 'Perhaps,' says Rathenau writing in 1912, 'no greater example of true fellowship is to be found today than among the oppressed Russian peasantry. We shall soon realize that it is not social and political formulas, not institutions and laws that make men free and happy; if only the superstitious belief in mechanistic contrivances could be shaken, there would arise from the depths of our own peoples the firstfruits of a spiritual life stronger than the faint stirrings of our neighbours. . . . Thus the last shall be first; the way of courage was too short, the way of intuition too narrow, but now the broad way of suffering and introspection is smooth and manifest for all. The sufferings of our soulless age have not yet reached their climax, but their end is in sight. Those very masses who today set the pace of mechanization, and are enslaved by and succumb to it, are hastening this end. It will come not by sacrificing the upper classes, nor by revolution, but through the rebirth of the

peoples themselves, redeemed by the sacredness of suffering.'
(*Mechanism of the Mind*, p. 334.)

That the forces opposed to mechanization would, if they
accomplished their task, completely reshape society, industry
and the state, that they must, in other words, be revolutionary,
is obvious. Rathenau himself drew up a programme for such a
reshaping. But as he has described it most clearly in the works
which he wrote during the war and after the collapse of Germany, the exposition of this aspect of his thought is better left
to a later chapter.[5]

But at this point we cannot but ask whether the abolition of
the proletariat and the elimination of self-interest would really
achieve Rathenau's ultimate aim: a solution of the problem of
the universe which will satisfy our age.

Nietzsche with the vision of genius realized what would have
to be the formal premises of a satisfactory answer: 'When the
nihilist asks "why," he is following the tradition according to
which life is given its aim *from without*—that is to say, by
some authority above man.' Such an authority is consciously
or unconsciously rejected by the great majority of men today.
Therefore an aim or meaning in life which is determined from
without can no longer afford a solution. 'But,' asks Nietzsche,
'could we not separate the setting-up of an aim from the process, and yet approve of the process? Such would be the case if an
end were achieved at every moment within that process, and that
end at every moment the same. Spinoza gained such a position
of acquiescence in life by assuming that every moment was *logically* necessary; and logic being his master passion he gloried in
such a texture of the world. But his case is only a special application of an attitude which can be stated in much more general
terms. Any trait so fundamental that it lies at the root of and
finds expression in every happening, would necessarily drive

[5] *In Days to Come*, chapter viii.

the individual, who feels it to be his, to glory in every moment of creation and to call it good. What is needed is that one should joyfully feel this trait to be good and valuable.' (*Will to Power*, p. 22.)

Now Rathenau did imagine he had discovered in man a fundamental trait—merely obscured by mechanization and modern man's exclusive preoccupation with material ends—in a yearning for the growth of his soul; man, he says, asks nothing better than to be his innermost self without interference from aims that come from without. If Rathenau was right he had thereby laid bare something that is indeed 'at the root of every happening, which finds expression in every happening, and which, when it is felt by an individual to be his fundamental characteristic, should lead him to approve of every moment of creation.'

Only the future can show whether modern man will recognize this to be his ruling trait and the final and satisfactory answer to his question: Wherefore do I exist? Nietzsche, we know, found the essential justification of life in something else: in the 'Will to Power.' But, one must ask, is Rathenau's yearning for the soul really, as it appears at first sight, merely quietistic, nothing but a turning of his back on the world, a flight into the beyond, a pure renunciation, or is it not also an embodiment of the 'Will to Power' in another dress? In his *Unwritten Works* there are two observations which seem to betray him: 'To the strong will all doors are open; non-willing lifts the world off its hinges'; and 'All power lies in the Soul; and all outer activity is vain' (p. 213). Non-resistance, the will not to will, may be the form assumed by the Will to Power in 'fear men,' in the weak and insecure, tempted to seek for power precisely in the pushing to extremes of their weakness, their lack of confidence, their instinctive recoil from the world. We now realize that the humility, the otherworldliness and the renunciation of many Christian priests, popes and saints, and of the great Jewish cabbalists, was but a highly spiritualized will to power. May we not therefore conceive of an epoch in which precisely this form of the will to power would prove to be the most effective and hence the most universal, so that its usual expression would be non-willing, non-resistance, contemplation and the yearning for the soul? And could not such an epoch succeed in overcoming mechanization? An epoch in which mechanization as a necessary evil was carried further in order to provide for the increase of population, but in which all real power was in the hands of those whose principal concern was with their souls—this seems to be the vision at the back of Rathenau's mind. For thousands of years of experience have driven deeply into the Jewish soul the consciousness of the power of powerlessness. Lion Feuchtwanger has given a striking expression to this particular bent of the Jewish mind in a passage of *Jew Süss:*

'To many it was not clear; only a very few could have expressed it; some shielded themselves from a definite recognition of it. But it pulsed in their blood, it was in their innermost soul; the deep, mysterious, certain awareness of the senselessness, the inconstancy, the worthlessness of power. They had sat so long, puny and straitened, among the peoples of the earth, like dwarfs, dissipated into absurd atoms. They knew that to exercise power and to endure power is not the real, the important thing. The colossi of force, did they not all go to rack and ruin one after the other? But they, the powerless, had set their seal on the world. And this lesson of the vanity and triviality of power was known by the great and the small alike among the Jews, the free and the burdened, the distant and the near, not in definite words, not with exact comprehension, but in their blood and their feelings. This mysterious knowledge it was that sometimes brought suddenly upon their lips that enigmatic, soft, supercilious smile which doubly provoked their enemies, because to them it signified an iconoclastic insolence, and because all their tortures and cruelties were powerless in front of it. This mysterious knowledge it was that united the Jews and smelted them together, nothing else. For this mysterious knowledge was the meaning of the Book.' [6]

Nevertheless Rathenau failed to allay the conflict within him. Although he despised the one way to power, the way of cleverness and industry, he yet pursued it; he could not continue to the end on that other more lofty way of the soul, the way of Tolstoi, Gandhi and the great mystics. Thus the sovereign power that comes from the soul remained beyond his reach. 'It sometimes happens,' says Rabbi Isaac Luria Aschkenasi in his 'secret doctrine,' which Lion Feuchtwanger quotes, 'that not one soul only, but two or even more, set out on their new earthly pilgrimage in one and the same human body. It may be the one is balm, the other poison, the one a beast's, the other a priest's or saint's; but now they are confined together, belonging to one body like the right and left hand. They permeate each other, grip each other, get each other with child, flow into one another like water.'

Rathenau realized this double nature in himself. 'Have I stilled the urge to power within me?' he writes to a friend. 'I fear not, but at least I know that I am fighting it. What you say is certainly just: that one is ruthless towards the passion by which one has been most dominated.' (Letter 366.) And to another friend he writes: 'The human race has never ceased to struggle, and each new affliction is more grievous than the last. Yet every affliction has only added to its stature. Even this intellect which we despise had to be fought for; today we are fighting for our soul. . . . But do not think that he who says this to you has a right to do so. I darkly realize these things, but I myself live unregenerate in the things of this world.' (Letter 374.) In these words he has inexorably depicted his own fate—perhaps also that of our age and culture.

[6] *Jew Süss*, English edition, translated by Edwin and Willa Muir, pp. 164-5.

CHAPTER VII

THE PATH TO THE ABYSS

THREE hundred men, all acquainted with each other,' wrote Rathenau in 1909 in an article in the Christmas number of the *Neue Freie Presse,* 'control the economic destiny of the Continent.' He himself was one of the three hundred. He was associated at that time with eighty-four large concerns, either as a member of the supervising Board or as a Managing Director. The centre of his activity was the A.E.G., which, as he wrote in 1907, was then 'undoubtedly the largest European combination of industrial units under a centralized control and with a centralized organization.' With its numerous undertakings and subsidiary companies, not only in Germany, but also in England, Spain, Italy, Russia, Switzerland and South America, it grew from year to year under Emil Rathenau's steady, yet enterprising guidance; and Walther Rathenau was his father's right-hand man. But apart from the A.E.G. there were many other undertakings in the founding and direction of which he played an important part: electrochemical works which made use of his own inventions and patents, transport concerns in the towns, motor works, cotton mills, and the mines and steel works of Prince Donnersmarck, who had requested him to join his board. From a statement which I owe to the courtesy of his private secretary, Herr Hugo Geitner, it appears that in the course of about ten years he played a leading part in the direction of eighty-six German and twenty-one foreign enterprises, viz., abroad: Italy 6, Switzerland 6, South America 2, Spain 2, Africa, Finland, France, Austria and Russia 1. And at home (joint stock companies and limited liability companies):

1. Electricity and allied industries 24
2. Metals 10
3. Mining, etc. 8
4. Railways and light railways 8
5. Chemicals 7
6. Telegraph and cables 6
7. Banks and trust companies 5
8. Spinning and weaving mills 4
9. Aviation 3
10. Glass 2
11. Rolling mills
12. Potash
13. Carriage-building
14. Motor-cars
15. Dockyards .... 1 each
16. Paper making
17. Pottery
18. Precious stones

Apart from the A.E.G. the Berliner Handelsgesellschaft and the Bank for Electrical Undertakings in Zürich, the most important of these concerns were the following:

1. (Electricity and allied industries)
Berliner Elektrizitäts-Werke,
Felten and Guilleaume, Köln,
Elektrizitäts, A.-G., vorm. Lahmeyer und Co., Frankfurt a.M.,
Osram G.m.b.H., Kommandit Ges., Berlin,
Schlesische Gas- und Elektrizitäts A.-G., Gleiwitz,
Deutsch-Uberseeische Elektrizitäts-Ges., Berlin;
2. (Metals)
Metallbank und Metallurgisch Ges., Frankfurt a.M.,
Gebr. Körting, Hannover,
Ludw. Loewe und Co., A.-G., Berlin,
Glockenstahlwerke vorm. Rich. Lindenberg A.-G., Remscheid,
Mannesmannröhrenwerke, Düsseldorf;
3. (Mining, etc.)
Schlesische Zinkhütten, Donnersmarck,
Internationale Kohlenbergwerks-Gesellschaft, Köln,

Braunkohlen- und Brikett-Industrie A.-G., Berlin,
Hohenlohewerke A.-G.;
4. (Railways and light railways)
Allgemeine Lokalbahn und Kraftwerke A.-G., Berlin;
5. (Chemicals)
Th. Goldschmidt A.-G., Essen,
Rütgerswerke, A.-G., Berlin,
Permutit A.-G., Berlin,
Elektrochemische Werke, G.m.b.H., Bitterfeld;
9. (Aviation)
Deutsche Luftreederei, Berlin;
10. (Glass)
Vereinigte Lausitzer Glaswerke A.-G., Weisswasser-Berlin;
12. (Potash)
Actiengesellschaft Thiederhall, Thiede;
13. (Carriage-building)
Linke-Hoffman-Lauchhammer A.-G., Berlin;
14. (Motor-cars)
N.A.G., Berlin;
15. (Dockyards)
Deutsche Werft, Hamburg.

Of the foreign companies with which he was associated these
were the chief:

Otavi Mines (Africa),
Officine Elettriche Genovesi, Genoa,
Unione Tramways Elettrici, Genoa,

and finally the two great electric railways in Valparaiso and
Santiago.

The initial period of concentration in big business involved
some momentous transactions, such as the fusion of the A.E.G.
with 'Union,' with Felton and Guilleaume, and with Lahmeyer,
all three of which Rathenau carried through. This necessitated
daily negotiations, interviews, committee meetings, inspections
of factories, and an enormous correspondence, the index of
which fills four volumes, as well as frequent journeys, chiefly

to the Rhine, Switzerland and Italy. In inspecting factories he used a particular method, which gave him a really intimate knowledge of the technical and commercial procedure employed; his visits were sudden and unexpected, and conducted with extreme thoroughness and precision. In his diary for the years 1911 to 1914 there recur as regularly as the days of the week the names of all the great German industrial magnates of that epoch: Carl Fürstenberg, Prince Henckel-Donnersmarck, Franz von Mendelssohn, Salomonsohn, Paul von Schwabach, F. von Guilleaume, Krupp-Bohlen, Eberhard von Bodenhausen, Klöckner, Ballin, Hagen, and Stinnes. Thus ever closer grew the network of his practical activity, of what he indicted in his philosophy as purposive scheming; while at the same time, his knowledge of the real nature of production and distribution on a world scale grew daily more intimate.

His *Physiology of Business*, written when he was still a small provincial managing director at Bitterfeld, had shown how acute was his faculty of observation even from there. But now he was in the very hub of German big business, able to add daily to his information and acquiring an insight into the mechanism of business—its wheels and gearing, the forces which drive it, the friction by which it is impeded—in a way only open to very few, while even fewer have the imagination and physical endurance necessary to take advantage of this insight. He got to know the whole European machinery of production and distribution, as a racing motorist knows the machine which he has dismantled and assembled piece by piece, tested on good and bad roads, and driven in every kind of weather. He knew every little wheel, every spring, every tube, the conditions under which it worked most safely and economically, the demands which one could and could not put upon it.

He knew its failings too: the points which could be improved, and those which were part and parcel of it and hence not susceptible of improvement. Above all he was aware of the weaknesses which result from the *political* construction of Europe and particularly of Germany. An unexampled industrial development had brought Germany in the course of a few years to the position of the third greatest industrial power of the world; an almost equally astonishing political decline during the same period had forced her from the first place among the great powers into a subordinate position. A frivolous policy which interpreted whims and fancies as necessities of state, which at one and the same time disquieted England over the Fleet, France over Morocco, and Russia through a blind championing of Austria, had led—by way of the Franco-Russian Alliance and the Anglo-French Entente—to a set-back at Algeciras in 1906, which, however camouflaged, was nevertheless the first unmistakable symptom of Germany's loss of prestige. The German Government replied to the danger-signal, not by altering its course, but by speeches and armaments; and when the Reichstag made difficulties, its dissolution gave an opportunity for more speeches and more armaments. The elections of February 5th, 1907, by crushing the Social Democrats and convincing the Centre Party of the wisdom of the Government's policy, opened the way which led from one false step to another, from naval estimate to naval estimate, straight to the World War.

On February 12th, 1907, a week after the elections, Rathenau made his political début in an article entitled *The New Era*, in the *Hannoverscher Courier*. This article is noteworthy, not only as Rathenau's first political statement, but also because it shows that he differed fundamentally even then with all the leading German politicians in his estimate of the relative importance of the forces making for success or failure on the political stage. His guiding principle was that the right method in politics is 'to look at the facts scientifically, and, after eliminating minor factors, to weigh up the chief forces involved and their interplay. For nature and stubborn fact are more powerful

121

than the wishes of men, whether single or combined.' The most important of all the factors which were at that time almost. universally thought to determine a country's international status was its effective armament, the number of men which it could put into the field, and the guns and warships which it could bring into action at short notice. Armaments were thus the principal concern of the Kaiser and his Government. The then Chancellor, Prince Bülow, formulated in his *German Policy* (p. 20) the lines along which he was thinking: 'The greatest and most urgent task of post-Bismarckian policy was the building of an adequate fleet.'

But in his article enumerating the forces that determine international status Rathenau made no reference at all to armaments, apart from a brief, sharp and ironical obeisance to the new armoured cruisers; and indirectly he denied them any real value, since 'in these days, even war fails to produce any decisive result. We realize that the wars of the future will be decided neither by single combat between heroes as in Homer's day (for "heroes" read "armoured cruisers"), nor by crack regiments. The War God of our days is industrial power. . . . But even war is seldom decisive. No longer are the peoples good enemies, they are bad competitors; and the game of foreign policy is directed towards manoeuvring oneself into a strong strategical position, rather than towards inflicting disaster on others. But in this game the protagonists have just so many counters as their economic power provides, and thus the principle which has at all times been active even if unperceived now becomes abundantly clear: a nation can win and retain just so much weight in foreign affairs as corresponds to its moral, intellectual and economic resources.' Thus it is not armaments, but moral, intellectual and economic strength, which has become the decisive element in international policy.

The German Government's policy, which, however desirous for peace, yet sought it chiefly through the reckless piling-up

of armaments, could not have been repudiated more fundamentally than it was in this article. Though cautiously framed,
it cut at the very root of the Kaiser's policy. In this Rathenau's
criticism of the imperial policy differed from that of the
Kaiser's chief adversary Harden, who, though much more
violent in tone, was not nearly so searching. Rathenau's methods and point of view were altogether those of the twentieth
century, Harden's, like those of the Government, were still of
the nineteenth. Still less had any bourgeois German politician
freed himself from those antiquated and misleading conceptions; their views were so remote from Rathenau's—which
were derived from his precise knowledge of the international
situation—that, in spite of enormous expenditure on the army
and navy, Germany entered the war completely unprepared
economically; and thus, by an irony of fate, Rathenau himself
had to intervene after the outbreak of hostilities to put Germany's economic house in order.

But Rathenau's first political announcement is noteworthy
in other respects also. For it was really directed against the
semi-absolutist imperial system and the privileges of the
aristocracy. It demanded the admission of the middle class to
influential government posts, the creation of a great middle-
class liberal party, and constitutionalism. The first Russian
Revolution had just ended with the capitulation of Tsarism,
while the Republic in France had been confirmed on the basis
of the Radical Left as a result of the clerical defeat in the
Dreyfus affair. 'The political climate of Europe,' wrote Rathenau, 'appears to be changing somewhat. In the East absolutism,
in the West clericalism, are running dry. How, we must ask,
can we justify the fact that Germany is ruled in a more abso-
lutist fashion than almost any other civilized country and on
more clerical lines than the majority of Catholic states. Germany is no longer the land of dreamers and professors. In the
economic battle the Germans hold third place for achievement

and first place intellectually. It will be difficult to show—
especially to foreigners, who are asked to respect us—why by
his Constitution the German is allowed so much less influence
in affairs of state than the Swiss, the Italian, or the Roumanian.
The Continental barometer stands today at "self-government,"
and we cannot very long continue to have a special climate of
our own. . . . Neither agriculture, nor feudalism, nor Catholic
clericalism can create the enormous increase of industrial
wealth which is required by our growing population; this is the
province of middle-class intelligence. But at present this intelligence is politically at sixes and sevens; it is of small significance
in legislation and as a factor in governing it is nil. . . . Sooner
or later the new elements must combine: the liberalization of
Europe, the resuscitated interest in constitutional questions, the
tension in foreign politics, the disappearance of phantoms which
belong to the past. And it is quite conceivable that this combination might bring into being a national movement of the urban
middle class, comparable in power, perhaps, to the agrarian
movement which has hitherto determined the direction of our
trade policy, but is now more or less played out. Such a movement would adopt the constitutional conceptions of liberalism
and therefore, as in England, work not in opposition to the
government, but along practical business lines in accordance
with the interests of the country. It would demand a more
decisive share in the government than the right wing of our
middle parties, and would there defend the interests of the
urban middle class against those of feudalism, narrow agrari-
anism and orthodoxy. . . . It would support the moderniza-
tion of the state, and would take a wide view in connection with
business relations abroad, whether with the Colonies or the
Great Powers. In the long run the country cannot do without
a bourgeois evolution of this type.'

How far Germany still was from such a bourgeois evolution,
even in the first years of the war, is illustrated by an anecdote

told by Dr Stresemann in his preface to a recent book, Theodor Eschenburg's *The German Empire at the Crossroads*. When he and his chief, Herr Bassermann, the leader of the National Liberal party in the Reichstag, were on a visit to Bulgaria during the war, King Ferdinand of Bulgaria asked Bassermann to come and see him, and discussed the political situation with him at length for an hour and a half. 'When Bassermann returned from the audience,' said Stresemann, 'he said to me: "The King of this country looks upon it as a matter of course that he should compare notes and discuss the situation with me as the leader of a German party. No party has ever been more loyal to the monarchy and the Kaiser than ours. But never has the Kaiser thought it necessary to speak one single word to me; and when, during the Kiel week, he visited the Hapag liner on which I was a passenger, he gave orders that none but ladies should be presented to him, so that he should not have to run the risk of speaking with me. That makes one feel bitter." And yet Bassermann would have recoiled from any decisive step, not merely because he realized the difficulties and dangers of the parliamentary system, but because, though he felt that he was at liberty to criticize the Kaiser, he yet remained fundamentally an officer of the Kaiser's army. That constituted the conflict during the war between Bassermann the politician and Bassermann the major.'

Bülow who wanted to give a liberal tinge to his naval and clerical *bloc*, which had just emerged victoriously from the polls, and who probably saw in Rathenau nothing more than a young millionaire dilettante of liberal tendencies with a footing in Society, sent for him and offered him the opportunity of accompanying the Colonial Secretary, Dernburg, as his right-hand man on a tour of inspection to Africa. Rathenau accepted the proposal and thus for the first time occupied an official post. It would be fascinating to know what he who gave and he who accepted the post, the actual and the future Foreign Ministers, said to themselves when they met officially for the first time. Each doubtless considered the other a dilettante. Both were good conversationalists, both were brilliant, apt at quotations, aphorisms, and metaphors, both were cynics in the sense that, not having a very high regard for the person with whom they were conversing at the time, but rather fearing him, they strengthened their inner certainty by an assiduously disguised contempt. Unfortunately nothing is preserved regarding this historic conversation. And the post itself did not produce anything of direct significance. Rathenau accompanied Dernburg, who would probably have rather had a Christian for a companion, to Africa on two occasions, in 1907 and 1908. As is evident from his letters, he enjoyed the vast African landscape, but seems frequently to have found his subordinate position painful. Both journeys were more or less in the nature of agreeable holidays, which brought Rathenau nothing, interfered with his other activities, and left him otherwise unaffected.

To be sure they did have the indirect effect of turning his attention more closely to England and her relations with Germany, which were even then a source of justifiable anxiety. After returning from his second journey in 1908 he handed Bülow a memorandum on *England's Present Position* which, as time has shown, correctly diagnosed England's attitude and the effects of German naval policy without falling into the illusions that then prevailed. The memorandum begins by sketching out the foundations of England's vast power—her industrial and colonial supremacy—and describes in detail the dangers which were threatening it, showing how 'both sources of anxiety, the industrial and the colonial, serve to concentrate English attention on Germany. . . . England looks into the racial cauldron of the Continent and beholds a people of unceasing activity and enormous capacity for expansion, hemmed in by nations that are rapidly becoming effete. Eight hundred thousand new Germans every year! Every five years an increase almost equal to the entire population of Scandinavia or Switzerland! How long will anaemic France be able to resist this pressure? Germany becomes the embodiment of English fears. . . . It would be foolish and superficial to believe that small acts of friendship, deputations, or press campaigns can still a disquiet which flows from such deep sources. It is only by our policy that we can create the impression in England that on Germany's part there is no ill-feeling, no fear, no need for expansion or for an offensive.'

As is well known, this policy actually took the form of accelerating the building of the fleet with the help of the new Reichstag, fostering the quarrel with France over Morocco, driving Russia into the arms of England through a virtual protectorate over Turkey, and offending Edward VII. by imperial indiscretions which amiable relatives were only too ready to pass on.

But, in contradistinction to Harden, Rathenau refused to hold the Kaiser solely responsible for Germany's decline. He saw as a second and more profound cause the Prusso-German system of government which, by showing a fatal predilection for a few families, restricted the choice of talent for the service of the state. In *The State and the Jews* (p. 199) he says in answer to a Herr von N.: 'A people of sixty-five millions has the right to demand that the leading posts in the state shall be filled by the very best talents, and positions of responsibility by competent specialists. A thousand ruling families, whatever their natural or technical accomplishments, cannot cope either in numbers or character with the enormously increased demands on the administrative machine. No right-thinking man will wish to belittle the services these families have rendered, or to lose their decisive co-operation in the highest matters of state. But if they wish to monopolize the machinery of state permanently, conditions will go from bad to worse and the way be open to

those makeshifts which have several times, though by hard
knocks, brought the obstinate conservatism of Prussia to reason
and which may therefore well be described as dispensations of
Providence.'

He repeatedly alluded in his writings, in conversation, and
in letters to the dangerous consequences of this arbitrarily restricted method of selection. In his *Criticism of the Age* (1911,
p. 121), he deals with this point in detail. I quote only the
following passages: 'Although the Prussian aristocracy has the
gift of producing much remarkable talent from a small number
of men, its equipment is not really intellectual. Its great advantages lie in an infallible sense of honour, a sharp eye for
the practical, in its courage, endurance and frugality. . . .
When mechanized industry converted whole fields of state administration into pure business enterprises, and changes in outlook and in function called for daily reorientation and continuous resource, it became clear that even the very best sort of
mediocrity was sometimes inadequate by itself to solve problems which had no precedent; nor could it compete with the
best foreign talent. For meanwhile other countries had consciously or unconsciously arrived at the conviction that supreme
responsibility should only be borne by conspicuous talent, and
that there is no excuse for a great state if it fails to discover
such talent. Thus without the help of legislation, but as the
result of a freer practice in those countries, independent methods of selection of the greatest variety have been evolved,
which all, however, have this in common, that they sift out the
gifted from the mass of mediocrity, and entrust them with the
responsibilities for which they are designed by nature. This is
not the place to analyze these methods of selection; it is enough
to point out that Prussia ignores them and is consequently
obliged to recruit its leaders after the antiquated custom, from a
field a hundred times smaller. Hence the doubly onerous task
of discovering superior talent falls upon three royal "Cabinets,"

and it may happen that owing to the exaggerated demands for wealth, birth, a good appearance and personal charm, the most serious responsibilities in peace and war do not always fall on the strongest shoulders.'[1]

In 1912 he wrote to a diplomat: 'What concerns me is not so much the fact that government posts are occupied by aristocrats, as the absence of an independent method of selection. It is a matter of complete indifference to me from what social stratum competent people are recruited. But what is necessary is that there should be some guarantee that only the most fitted— and these in the largest possible number—should be entrusted with responsibility.' (Letter No. 77.) To Captain von Müffling he wrote during the war (1917): 'It is my belief that as time goes on political and administrative tasks become more and more complex and difficult and call for correspondingly higher talents, talents which the hereditary system is less and less able to provide. . . . As I see the matter, talent is not among the privileges of heredity. It must be continuously generated anew from the ranks of a healthy people. A lack of suitable talent and an excessive reliance upon inherited qualities have led to the policy of the last thirty years and to inevitable conflicts resulting from it.' (Letter No. 244.)

But his point of view is most clearly formulated in the book which he published during the war, *In Days to Come* (p. 344): 'Energy and fixity of trend are the two most important weapons in the struggle for existence among nations. They are the concern of the peoples themselves. Neither reigning families nor castes can provide these essentials, for one of the rules of the struggle is that all the available powers of a nation should be

---

[1] All appointments in the Army, the Navy and the Civil Service were made by the Kaiser as Emperor or as King of Prussia through his three private Secretariats (called 'Cabinets') the 'Militär-Kabinett,' the 'Marine-Kabinett' and the 'Zivil-Kabinett,' who thus exerted a paramount influence in all personal matters and were responsible to nobody but the Kaiser himself. Their members were members of the Kaiser's personal suite and neither the Reichstag nor even the Ministers had any say in their councils or any direct influence on their decisions.

utilized, including all its forces of spirit and of will. Fixity of trend arises as the distillate of all possible thoughts, energy as the essence of all conceivable manifestations of human genius. If we restrict the possible sources of supply to a narrow circle of a few hundred or thousand souls, we deliberately impoverish the spirit and the will of a nation, and that nation will perish as soon as its neighbours stake the whole wealth of their possessions against it. A people numbering many millions has the duty, metaphysically speaking, at all times and in all spheres of activity, of generating a vigorous trend of will and a galaxy of highly gifted persons. Should it fail to do this, or should these forces be diverted to the pursuit of gain, mechanical invention, or a life of idle comfort, or, should they remain undiscovered owing to political indolence and an inadequate sense of responsibility, then this people has passed its own death sentence.'

Thus it is not surprising that Rathenau's views very soon became even more pessimistic than those then usual; from the combination of two such fateful causes as the Kaiser's abnormal mentality and the inadequate basis of selection for government service he divined the inevitability of a catastrophe. As early as the autumn of 1906, I had casually remarked in conversation with Rathenau that the general mismanagement had already lasted so long that one might begin to hope that it would run its course without disaster; to which he replied: 'You are mistaken. A bank like the Deutsche Bank can be run for five years by quite incompetent directors without the public becoming aware of the fact; but after that its position will gradually decline. With a state like Germany, misrule may perhaps continue for twenty years without any great damage: then suddenly the consequences become visible on every hand.'

After his second journey to Africa Rathenau held no further official post until the war. His activities in connection with the

A.E.G. and dozens of other undertakings continued to increase, as also did his literary activities. In 1908, by way of making a clearance, he collected a number of articles and aphorisms which had appeared anonymously in the *Zukunft* under such pseudonyms as W. Hartenau, Walter Michael, Renatus, and Ernest Reinhart, and published them under his own name with the title of *Reflections*. The book appeared in the form of a huge Bible-like quarto and was printed in two colours on expensive paper. Its pretentious get-up deceived many people into regarding it as the mere whim of a millionaire; it seemed to flaunt the wealth of its author and his vanity. I well remember the impression it made: it was not favourable. People glanced at it casually, and put it down with a smile.

Perhaps it is from this unfortunate literary venture that we must date the atmosphere of faint contempt, almost impalpable, rarely expressed, but increasingly perceptible, which enveloped Rathenau like a cloud, obscuring his image for the majority, doing him an obvious injustice and causing him much bitter pain. For to one who was so ready to erect a barrier between himself and others, this emergence from anonymity had been no light matter; he had produced something which he knew to be of value, he had given of his very best, and the result was that people refused to read him, or listened to him only with a smile. Some years later, after he had published his third book, he summed up the attitude of the world to his works in the following letter to a friend: 'You want to write about my book? My friend, I must warn you. If you depart an inch from the stereotyped judgment: "witty, cold, a dilettante in sixteen subjects, and a tolerable business man," you will be laughed to scorn. This is what people will have me to be, and I am content to be tolerated as a harmless fool. They ask me: "How do you find time for such nonsense?" and if I told them that that is my life, they would send for the doctor. Be prudent, dear friend;

it is not considered good form to treat me kindly.' (Letter 65, January 20th, 1912.)

It was now that Rathenau's tragedy came out, so to speak, into the open; the duality of his nature, which had until then been a personal matter, suddenly became a weapon with which he was attacked from without. His enemies acted according to the immortal recipe of Bartolo in *The Barber of Seville:* 'To begin with a faint rumour which skims the ground like a swallow before a storm—pianissimo: whispering tones—and a poisoned arrow falls in its flight! Some ear or other catches it and deftly conveys it—piano, piano—to your ear. Now the trouble is sown; it germinates, crawls along the ground, sets out on its journey, hastens—rinforzando—with infernal speed from mouth to mouth. Suddenly, you cannot tell how, calumny has made its appearance: it whistles shrilly, puffs itself out, and in a trice it has the form of a giant. It takes a run, spreads its wings, flies up, strikes with thunder and lightning and becomes, with the help of God, a general clamour, a crescendo, a choir of vengeance and damnation. Who the devil could withstand it?'

The stages which led from the indifferent reception of Rathenau's *Reflections* to the bullets in the Königsallee can be arranged in a practically continuous series. At first he was ignored. But when he continued to court publicity with the *Criticism of the Age* and the *Mechanism of the Mind*, whispers and irritation arose among his colleagues at the fact that a man who was a director of eighty companies should also write books. People found it comic that a business man should preach the birth of the soul; compromising, that a rich man should attack luxury; shocking, that at the same time he should build a villa in the Grünewald; grotesque, that he should let the Chamberlain wheedle him into buying the royal pleasance of Freienwalde. However, these were petty offences, which one could

132

laugh at. But it was unforgivable, if not pathological, that a leader of industry should advocate the nationalization of monopolies, the abolition of the right of inheritance, the ruthless taxation of the wealthy, the liberation of the proletariat, a society without classes, and other Red impossibilities; that stamped him as a dangerous subject, against whom any steps were justified.

Without doubt he was himself aware of the paradox of the situation: that he, the great industrialist, should come forward as the protagonist of a policy which was more radical than that of the agitators in his own factories. He always saw himself quite clearly, and certainly realized how unconvincing and dangerous was the part he had assumed. He has been accused of vanity, and Lord d'Abernon, in his memoirs, repeats the accusation. But this does not seem to me to go to the roots of the matter; the real springs of his actions lay deeper. He was under the compulsion at least to *think* out to the end, even though he should not live to see it completed, the process by which the soul can be freed from the shackles of mechanization; or, putting the case in other words, he was in subjection to his intellect, which, kindled by imagination, continued without respite to illumine like a flare the conditions of inner freedom down to their smallest details. It would be unjust to Rathenau not to keep constantly in mind this irresistible power of his intellect, which in the complicated workings of his inner life raged like an element unchained—and which he therefore hated like a secret vice, while regularly succumbing to it. And over and above this pressure of the intellect, there were at work in him the same motives which led him later in spite of all warnings and in the face of manifest danger to his life to accept the post of Foreign Minister. These were a peculiar fatalism which he had perhaps inherited from his Jewish ancestors, and the transmutation of the inhibitions due to caution into their opposite, into a stimulus to restless action;

this transmutation being due to the glamour of 'courage' in the eyes of a 'fear man' who despised nothing in himself so much as fear and had striven to eradicate it by a ruthless discipline. For spiritually he belonged to those whom Nietzsche has described in his *Fröhliche Wissenschaft* as 'men on the way to courage: men who have an inner impulse to seek in all things something to be overcome'; and whom he goes on to describe as 'endangered men, fruitful men, joyful men! For the secret of getting what is most fruitful and enjoyable from life is to live dangerously!' (Nietzsche, *Works*, V, p. 215.) Finally, merging all these elements into an irresistible impetus, there was spiritual pride, which has nothing in common with vanity: the sin of Milton's Lucifer, 'what time his pride had cast him out from Heaven,' the determination not to bow spiritually to any one.

And yet the extent of the hostility which he aroused surprised him. In his *Apology* he says: 'This hostility became positively passionate after my writings began to deal with economic problems. Powerful groups and associations of trade and industry considered their interests affected, and spent an enormous amount of money and labour in fighting by press campaigns, lectures, political agitation and literature those of my ideas which they considered to be dangerous' (p. 72). And in a letter written in 1918: 'So much hatred has been, and will continue to be, stirred up against me by the campaigns of interested parties, by the *Hansabund* and all the others, that I need no little will-power to defend myself. I have never expected thanks for my work; but no German for decades has been subjected to the amount of enmity which has come instead.' (Letter No. 439.) Thus a man who in the afternoon had met him at a board meeting or for a confidential discussion perhaps financed a meeting that very evening to protest against his 'double life.' For it was his 'double life' that provided the weapon of attack: 'This man does not practise what he preaches.

His principle is: Judge me by my words, not my deeds.'
(*Apology*, p. 83.) 'To others he preaches abstinence; he himself
lives like a prince. Others are to work for their souls without
any thought of reward; he allows himself to be paid hand-
somely by a dozen companies. He wishes to abolish the inequality of wealth and the right of inheritance, so that every
one can have an equal chance; but he does not hesitate to take
advantage of the privileges which his father's position gives
him. You are to become humble Christians again; he remains,
needless to say, the cunning Jew!'

Every one who has studied Rathenau's personality will reject
as the opposite of the truth the degrading reproach of hypoc-
risy, dishonesty, and deception which lies behind these charges.
For in reality the contradictions with which he was charged
grew from the depths of his personality with the relentlessness
of fate. It was true, however, that in his actual life his two
natures did conflict with each other, and so gave an easy opening to demagogues to incite against him crude persons to whom
such contradictions were inexplicable. The villa in the Grünewald was not simply, as he says in his *Apology*, 'respectably
bourgeois'; it was far above the middle-class standard in style,
cost and extent. His expenditure was not, as he believed, 'more
or less appropriate to the junior partner in an industrial concern,' but, for all his precision where money was concerned, to
that of a leading industrialist. He had bought the pleasance of
Freienwalde not merely to save it from destruction, but because
it pleased him to pass a few weeks in the summer in an
historical and charming old Prussian country seat built by his
favourite architect, Gilly.[2] Outwardly, there was nothing to
prevent him from giving up his directorships, reducing expenditure to the level of the purely necessary, and living by the
light of his work and his soul in modest bourgeois style. If we

---

[2] Friedrich Gilly (1772-1800), the leading Prussian architect of the classicist
period.

must impute some tragic failing to Rathenau, then it lies here: not in what he did or neglected to do, but, as is the case with every tragic figure, in what he was. It followed inevitably from the complexity of his nature.

But his ideas also followed from this complexity, and their value lay just in those contradictions in which they were rooted. For they were rooted in the same contradictions as is the world of the twentieth century, and for men who belong to this world the ideas that are valuable and redemptive are not those that come from simple souls. We cannot provide the soil of divine simplicity in which the ideas of St Francis would blossom; at the best we cultivate such ideas like exotic plants which may perhaps bear a few sickly blooms on alien soil, but no ripe fruit. Only those ideas are fruitful for us which are born in men whose souls are of our own type; only such ideas can find their accustomed climate and can develop to maturity.

Thus Rathenau is saying too little when he writes in his *Apology:* 'What gives power to my writing, the one quality which it possesses, is that it does not reek of the midnight oil. It is experienced and lived.' He is saying too little, because immediately afterwards he denies a part of his life by attempting to gloss over actual contradictions. The truth is that it was only because, like Conrad Ferdinand Meyer's Ulrich von Hutten in a similarly agitated period, he was 'a man with his contradiction,' that his ideas are a serious and fruitful challenge to us—who are also 'men with our contradictions.' Had Rathenau resigned his directorships, moved into a slum, lived in poverty, and devoted himself entirely to the salvation of his soul, he might perhaps have become a saint; but he would have solved the great problem of the age only for himself, for his solution would have left the outside world as cold as does the continuance of mendicant friars or yogis. But that with all his inconsistencies he strove for a solution—whether practical or not; that he passed old and new ideas through the filter of his

136

contradictions; that fate compelled him, as it compels but few, to be completely that which he was—these things exposed him to the hatred and bullets of his enemies, but they also give him an authority which saints and theorists can no longer command. He has accurately indicated the point at which he was obliged to turn his back on Tolstoy, whose teaching had moved him deeply: 'Tolstoy's mistake was that, instead of following the law which he divined in his own nature, he bowed to a theory which suppressed his creative spirit as artist and thinker, in order to give strength to the weak forces of his "enthusiasm." . . . But he who embraces the enthusiastic life, not from the beginning and from his own unconscious necessity, but strives for it consciously, or worse still, with a definite purpose—he does himself violence and sins against the light.' (*Apology*, p. 92.) It may be accounted a form of 'tragic guilt' in the Greek sense if a man grasp for a crown that he has not strength enough to hold, but those alone are entitled to look down upon him who have striven for the same object and who, with an equally complex nature and without denying its complexity, have achieved the unity that was denied to Rathenau.

And now in the course of the next few years this tragedy of Rathenau the man and Rathenau the millionaire-revolutionary was merged into one still greater—the tragedy of a world rapidly nearing catastrophe. The background gradually assumes an uncanny clearness. There is still a distance, a breathing space; but slowly the background moves up and approaches him, draws him into itself and swallows him up.

1911: Agadir, the first warning flicker of the Great War. Germany makes a panther-spring on Morocco and finds England at the side of France ready to fight; Italy goes to Tripoli and throws a fire-brand into the Balkans, destined shortly to set Europe and the world alight. In Germany, Bülow is in disgrace, Bethmann-Hollweg Chancellor in his stead, Kiderlen Secretary of Foreign Affairs, Jules Cambon cautiously watching events from his Embassy on the Pariser Platz. Agadir causes a panic on the stock exchange; but it turns out to be a false alarm, after which trade goes on booming. For in all the great capitals, Berlin, Paris, London and Petersburg, the dance before the guillotine is about to begin.

Talleyrand said of the last years before the outbreak of the French Revolution: 'He who has not lived through them does not know what life is.' And now again the world seemed in the throes of a delirium, shivering with apprehension and yet intoxicated with a sort of ecstasy, reeling headlong in a revel to its doom; and wherever that was at its wildest, there Nijinsky, the genius of the dance, appeared in its midst. But Rathenau writes, 'Wherever I turn, I see shadows before me. I see them every evening as I make my way through the shrill noise of the Berlin streets: I see them when I consider the insane way we flaunt our wealth; when I hear the empty, sabre-rattling speeches, or read the reports of pseudo-Teutonic exclusiveness which collapses before newspaper articles and the casual remarks of court ladies. It is a mistake to think all is well simply because the lieutenant is spick and span and the attaché optimistic. Not for decades has Germany known a more critical time.' (*The State and the Jews*, 1911. *Collected Works*, Vol. I, p. 206.)

Rathenau, who for the last three years had devoted his energies wholly to business and literature, now returned to politics. Freienwalde is not far from Hohenfinow; the Chancellor was Rathenau's neighbour, and friendly relations developed between them. At a dinner at the Chancellor's in February, Bassermann, the leader of the National Liberals, invited Rathenau to become one of the Party's candidates for the Reichstag. The outcome was that in May he was asked to stand for Frankfurt an der Oder. Rathenau accepted on condition that he should be nominated jointly by the National Liberals and the Freisinningen (Radicals) as the first step in the di-

ROOM IN THE SCHLOSS FREIENWALDE

rection of a great liberal bourgeois party such as he had advocated in his article in the *New Era* in 1907. After some weeks of disappointing negotiation he withdrew his name. His decision seems to have been determined by reports from his constituency: the name Rathenau was like a red rag to a bull, because he was a Jew and because of his well-known opinions. It was the first time that Rathenau really felt the practical effects of his unpopularity and his particular views. He was spared the experience of a public rebuff; the episode remained secret. Most people, including his closest friends, knew nothing of it.

Meanwhile the Agadir affair was maturing. During the spring there was increasing tension with England over the naval question. Germany had to choose between two courses: either attempt an understanding with England over the Naval Estimates without any beating about the bush, or else pursue the same object in a more roundabout way, by first bringing pressure to bear on England and disintegrating the Entente, and only afterwards negotiating about the fleet. The German Government chose the second course: in a speech in the Reichstag Bethmann made an evasive reply to the English feeler towards a direct understanding. Rathenau himself was in favour of such an understanding. In an article entitled *Politics, Humour and Disarmament,* published in the *Neue Freie Presse* of April 12th, 1911 (*Collected Works,* Vol. I, p. 173 *seq.*), he put forward practical proposals in the matter, introducing into the discussion the notion of a quota of armaments. Once again, as in his article in the *New Era,* his point of departure was the view that armaments do not constitute a decisive factor in a state's position. 'The part which a state is justified in playing on the world stage is conditioned at every moment by geographical, physical and moral factors. Its actual sphere of power may temporarily extend beyond these limits, or on the other hand it may not reach them; but in the end power and the justification of power, expansion and the iustification of expansion, will hold the scales.' On this assumption it is 'certainly a difficult but not a hopeless task to find a means of relieving the military tension and keeping it at a tolerable level along the lines of the quota system, and in this sense the idea of disarmament is no mere Utopia.' Practically, as he goes on to explain, the task falls into two parts: the correlation, firstly, of material expenditure with national resources, and, secondly, of man-power with population. The first part of the task could be accomplished by an international agreement to the effect that 'the annual estimates for land, sea and air forces should not exceed a fixed proportion of the total expenditure of the state. The figures would have to be checked by an international bureau.' Without perhaps himself realizing it, Rathenau was here running far ahead of public opinion; for an international bureau empowered to check the expenditure of the various states would be a super-state organization such as no responsible statesman had advocated before the war. The second part of the task, the correlating of man-power with population, would be relatively easy. 'For the census of the population can be—and for the most part has been—exactly ascertained, so that it would indeed be singular if no international proposal were put forward for determining the maximum proportion of military strength to size of population.'

The German Government, however, persisted in its policy; the *Panther* made a demonstration in front of Agadir—more on the fleet's account than on Morocco's, and with an eye to England rather than to France. If a state of tension arose between France and Germany it had been supposed that England would hold prudently aloof; but she stood firm on the side of France. Germany was obliged to save her face by negotiations regarding compensation for Morocco; and a year later Bülow, in conversation with Rathenau, summed up the result by saying: 'They know well enough abroad that Germany gave way in July, 1911.' Tittoni had said to him: 'What a change in the behaviour of France compared with 1905! It is difficult to believe that that was only seven years ago.' (Rathenau, *Diary*, October 4th, 1912.) [3]

1912. January. In Paris, Society is mad for war against Germany at England's side: journalists, bankers, men about town, poets, dowagers are militant. In the cheap cabarets of Montmartre, where the petit bourgeois sips his cherry brandy after supper, the theme which goes down best is Agadir and the German climb-down in face of England's cruisers. Musset's answer to *Die Wacht am Rhein*, '*Nous l'avons eu votre Rhin allemand*,' becomes a music hall success, applauded frantically by the gallery. From Paris D'Annunzio bombards Italy with war odes—one every ten days as punctually as an artillery barrage; a million and a half copies are printed of each, to be posted up in the barracks, distributed amongst the regiments fighting in Tripoli, recited publicly by enthusiastic students in cafés and squares. Italy is wild with excitement. Giolitti, the Prime Minister, has to resort to artifice in order to seize a French ship, alleged to be smuggling arms to Tripoli, so as to divert some of the Italian war fever from Austria on to France.

Meanwhile, in England the agitation was deeper though less perceptible. On February 8th Haldane, the Secretary of War, appeared in Berlin and for the last time made overtures for a naval agreement. The negotiations broke down owing to the opposition of the Naval Secretary, von Tirpitz. Still worse, Haldane left Berlin with the impression that Germany was less to be feared than he had previously imagined. He had ascertained that chaos reigned at the top: the Kaiser told him one thing, Tirpitz another, the Minister of Foreign Affairs something else; and each made complaints about the others. And in addition he had found—and this had deeply impressed him—

[3] Rathenau's Diary, which I have been allowed to use, is still withheld from publication.

that the spirit which had made Prussia and Germany great, the high philosophical and ethical culture that stood at the back of all great German achievements, had withered at the summit, where it no longer counted for anything. When Haldane, himself a philosopher, deplored the neglect of the graves of Fichte and Hegel, the Kaiser replied: 'In my Empire there is no place for fellows like Fichte and Hegel.'[4] Seldom has the remark of a monarch on a historic occasion been more unfortunate. It is true that a few days later the Kaiser observed to Rathenau that 'the French were at present uneasy; all that was necessary was for him to go to Cowes; then he and the King of England would put everything straight again. His plan was: A United States of Europe, including France, against America.' (Rathenau, *Diary*, February 13th, 1912.) The French uneasy! George V. against his Cabinet! England against America! These words express the spirit in which German policy was pursued; credulous, optimistic without adequate grounds, and without any precise idea of the forces that were actually at work.

Rathenau's conception of the international situation was somewhat less naïve, as he shows in two articles he wrote for the *Neue Freie Presse*. The first, which was clearly written with one eye on the Kaiser, was published on April 6th, 1912, under the title of *England and Ourselves. A Philippic. (Collected Works*, Vol. I, p. 209.) In it he again considers the quota system and tries to make it palatable to the Kaiser by adding as a corollary that 'England should offer Germany a treaty of neutrality' (*i.e.* a promise, embodied in a treaty, to remain neutral in the event of a war between France and Germany). 'If England prove willing to come to such an understanding, it will be up to us to arrive at some agreement in the matter of armaments which will give both nations a breathing space, whether it be on the lines of Churchill's proposals for a naval holiday, or the adoption of the quota system on the basis of

[4] Lord Haldane himself repeated these words to me.

142

keels or tonnage.' It must be admitted that this proposal revealed a lack of understanding, unusual and remarkable in Rathenau, of the psychology both of English political circles and of the German Admiralty. To the latter the idea of a quota in any form was unacceptable, no matter what corollaries were attached; for the English a promise of neutrality would have brought about precisely that which England was ready to go to war to avoid—*i.e.* it would have given Germany a free hand against France, after which she would have been in a position to build as many ships as she wanted. In his diary for February 14th Rathenau notes: 'For several days past a very great strain; busy almost every minute.' And under April 3rd: 'Slack and exhausted for several days.' Perhaps the psychological weakness of his first article is to be explained by this physical state.

In the second article, *Political Selection*, published on May 16th, Rathenau makes another attempt to trace the responsibility for Germany's present position, and finds it to lie, as in his *Criticism of the Age*, published a year earlier, in the inadequate methods by which German diplomats and statesmen are recruited. Formerly the Prussian nobility were also the economic leaders of the state, and in the much more simple conditions then prevailing were quite able to recruit the necessary material from their own ranks. 'Today, however, the nobility have lost their ascendancy, and the industrial intelligence of the world lies with the middle class; the international situation is one of utter confusion; in other countries it is the best brains that lead . . . our competitors confront us with their finest talents and most experienced fighters. Now if only we can mobilize our mental forces in like manner we shall have nothing to fear from the contest; but failure to do this will leave us exposed to a constitutional weakness of a kind that has repeatedly proved fatal in the long run. . . . It is not the workers that threaten Prussia's greatness, for modern socialism lacks the strength of positive ideas; no, the danger, a twofold one, lies in another quarter: the lack of adequate leaders and the unequal distribution of burdens. Our age bears a remarkable resemblance to that of Frederick William II.[5] This time, let us hope, internal equilibrium may be restored without serious convulsions.' (*Collected Works*, Vol. I, p. 223 *ff.*)

In the autumn of the same year, 1912, in the October number of the *Zukunft*, he wrote a strangely sombre *Festal Song for the Centenary of 1813*, which was permeated throughout with a sense of impending catastrophe. The underlying note of this remarkable *Festal Song*, which was in reality a desperate protest against the organized and false enthusiasm on the occasion of the centenary, is indicated by the terrible text from Ezekiel which Rathenau put at the head of his work under the title of *Oppression*:

> Also, thou son of man, thus saith the Lord God unto the land of Israel; An end, the end is come upon the four corners of the land.
> The end is come: it watcheth for thee; behold, it is come.
> (Ezekiel vii, 2, 6.)

Meanwhile Rathenau had suffered severely at the hands of fate. A few days after the appearance of his article, *England and Ourselves*, his friendship with Harden came to a sudden end as the result of a personal difference—an event which both from the human and the political points of view amounted to a catastrophe. Long negotiations and unsuccessful attempts at reconciliation led to Rathenau's challenging Harden to a duel, which the latter refused on principle; this was followed by an endless succession of reconciliations and further breaches which continued up to the Revolution and after. Finally on Harden's side friendship gave place to an implacable hatred, in which, however, up to the very end one could detect a certain desire for reconciliation and for the affection that had been lost. After

[5] The King whose slackness was held responsible for the collapse of Prussia before Napoleon at Jena.

Rathenau's death he not only wrote the well-known article dictated by hate, but also and at the same time a letter to Rathenau's mother which showed very real feeling. Yet the details of this quarrel cannot yet be revealed; it must suffice to note that their relationship, which passed from friendship into mutual contempt and hostility, was for both of them a profoundly disturbing experience.

Soon afterwards Rathenau met with a still severer blow. His father, who was suffering from diabetes, returned from Vienna in the middle of May with a gangrenous wound in his foot. It was amputated, and as his condition at the time and his natural violence of temper precluded the possibility of asking his permission beforehand, Walther had to assume responsibility for the operation. He could not help fearing that his father, in his headstrong passionate way, would never forgive him. And in actual fact when Emil Rathenau learned what had happened he was so beside himself that he struck with his crutch, as if demented, at his daughter who was standing by the bed. The extent to which Walther was shaken by this illness and the serious responsibility it entailed is shown by the handwriting of his diary, which during these weeks becomes irregular and agitated for the first and only time.

The clearest light on his life, intellectually so honest, humanly so lacerated and so tossed from pole to pole, is thrown by the letters written during these years to his friend. Since he could never get away from himself and was always looking into himself, and since he used his friend as a mirror, these letters are a series of self-portraits, and reveal with terrible clarity his seclusion, his growing isolation, his restlessness, and the manner in which his nature was concentrated on himself and his problems.

I have suffered no less than you, and I feel far from well. I hoped that you would make us some sign earlier and then detain me. (Perhaps that was impossible.[6]) He [Harden] called on me in order to fetch a book, and came into the house to stay five minutes.

I had much to tell you which has now perhaps no further interest, and I also wanted to ask you about several things; but now I feel utterly crushed and exhausted. I am sitting with burning eyes beside the lamp.

Affectionately yours,
W.

You have not hurt my feelings; on the contrary, you have helped me. True, as far as details are concerned I still think I am in the right; these literary questions I have thought out carefully, and in this matter I do not recognize any of my contemporaries to be a judge. *'Humble si je me considère, fier si je me compare.'*

But it is true: there are too many people worrying and plaguing me, although I neither want anything from, nor plague any one myself. Is it really weakness? Or is it just human and perhaps even something better? Let me for once suppose the worst; then two things only will help: either flight or rudeness. Which, remains to be considered.

Whether it would be right for me to retire from business I dare not decide. My last three jobs, the African ones and the transport one, which all had their value, would never have been if I had not been living the life of this world.

The greatest mistake I have made in the last few years of my existence, a mistake moreover which is really quite alien to my nature, has been my communicativeness. My fate is loneliness and I accept it. Just as I have no brother, so there is nobody who can place himself in my position; from time to time

---

[6] Refers to Harden's intervention—equally unexpected and undesired by both parties—during a visit of Rathenau's.

a sort of parallelism seems to occur, and then suddenly everything seems infinitely distant again. If I were to measure myself by other standards, then I should be a failure in good and ill. If I were an eccentric—and why am I not? because I fight against it—then people would leave me to my whims. But because I go part of the way with others, peaceably and sociably, they all want to model me to their taste, which however they do not succeed in doing.

Au revoir till Sunday, and with warmest greetings,

Your W.

I shall expect you on Wednesday. I am free from six o'clock onwards and thankful that you are coming.

Since midday on Saturday I have been suffering from your message which you repeated on Sunday. It makes me doubt my reason if I am to believe—as I am now trying to without success—that I have only dreamed the terrible scorn of your lines. You only wish to see me in the presence of a third party? And this is your answer to my readiness to meet you in a free and friendly spirit after this difficult experience? And it was not enough to give me your decision, which was in itself sufficiently appalling; no, you must needs repeat it, clearly, distinctly and in writing.

It is beyond my comprehension. I feel one thing only, that whether deliberately or not you have done me the most terrible wrong. And now you actually speak of scorn and thereby seem to mean me, who merely said that I must try to get over what I felt about all this before I saw you again. Do you really think that I could so far forget myself as to come to you now when you would have everything prepared for a meeting in the presence of a third party?

I can only repeat that I am completely unable to understand

it, although I have been trying for hours now to see it from your point of view; it would seem that you yourself have forgotten what you arranged and wrote to me.

Farewell. I feel no bitterness, but I am very worried.

W.

VICTORIASTRASSE 3

The only thing about your letter which gave me pleasure was P. . . .'s tranquil, rich Venetian poem. Hauptmann's influence has had a good effect on him.

Harden's affairs do not concern me. But your cold injustice hurts me most deeply. Again I have to see myself in this cursed light and everything that has been and is hard for me, that human considerateness and inner decency demand of me, is branded as a crime. I often ask myself: is your view of me really so superficial, or do you wish to destroy me or confuse me completely? You have much; I have nothing; but you want to take from me even what little peace of mind I have, for again and again you put your finger on this one point, in amused wonder as to what I shall be able to bear—and yet you express surprise when I speak of your thirst for power.

That you put me on a level with him (H.) and contrast me invidiously with everything which is in keeping with your nature—this wounds me doubly as the conclusion and end of such thoughts.

These words of yours, written in perfect calmness—the handwriting shows me that—do more to estrange me than a whole year of absence. For you it is only the obvious present that lives (for your will is to dominate); to me the inner image is equally valuable. And that you smash to pieces like a child, for the pure joy of it.

Your W. R.

THE PATH TO THE ABYSS

'Soothingly into the heart.' It is out of the *Chino-German Days and Seasons*. And two lines further:

> In you vision and faith unite;
> But the seeking soul strives and struggles, never wearying,
> To find the law, the reason, the Why and How.

Warmth and affection! You know I have often put my affection into words and you know too what my real feelings are. But because it is sometimes possible for me, the inwardly dumb, to say things to you which are at other times inexpressible—you therefore take them as mere half utterances, because they are not *more*; is then what is spoken more than that for which language can find no words?

No, you have no right to doubt me; I say this in a higher sense than that in which you wrote it. What you call 'the element of uncertainty' lies not in me but in your image of me. To satisfy yourself that this is so you have only to compare your present conception of me with that of a year ago. [Even in this letter what motivation!] You should have known that my depression was deep and not merely momentary by the fact that—for the first time—I did not answer your letter! There are two things you cannot get over: distrust and the suspicion that I am vain. And this failure in discernment corresponds—forgive me, I certainly don't want to hurt you—to the weakest point in your intuition, which is otherwise so clear.

Both in my good points and my bad you will not look upon my like again. For with me the Lord God has set going an experiment which even if it proves a failure—and that seems to me more likely than the opposite—will at least have been an interesting one. And the best of it is that I am honestly and earnestly awake to the position and follow the threads in all their windings, whithersoever they lead. You know that in this game you have much influence; I warn you not to abuse it.

My warmest thanks for your letter of today, for it is again

149

you yourself writing; and if this answer too seems to you cold and heartless, then ask yourself for a moment why I have written it.

Your W. R.

Very many thanks for your two dear letters and the charming flowers. Their scent and colour surround me now. Just think! Yesterday I came across the vase made sixteen years ago expressly for your semi-circular recess; I have packed it up with the drawing showing how it should be placed, so that it may bring you my Christmas greetings.

Today I am going to do what I never do; I am sending you a book, and what is worse a sad one.[7] I don't suppose you will read it, and perhaps the second half is not worth reading anyway. Goethe sent this book to Charlotte von Stein and said that it was as if by a younger brother, but an unfortunate one. I have not got the right to say this; but there is much that the book would make clear to you. You would see the danger which attends the man to whom youth means oppression. To find one's way into freedom out of such a labyrinth is a difficult, almost superhuman task. And to succeed in this is, I think, a greater achievement than any external triumph. The author did not quite succeed. He remained broken and floating on the surface his life long. The capacity for love was lost. Things might have been quite different; but in reality he was only stubborn, not strong. But there is one thing that you would understand: what, that is to say, the action of demoniacal forces can do to men. Fallen angels and liberated demons: the principle involved is the same. Even about education there is something to be learned here.

I was very pleased to see you again at last, and in a world to which you belong and which is able to do you justice.

[7] *Anton Reiser* by Karl Philipp Moritz, a friend of Goethe. This autobiographical novel was published in 1785-1790.

THE PATH TO THE ABYSS

I am thinking of how you looked standing at the head of your little staircase—it was just as I should have wished. Farewell. I have a great deal of work to do this winter and shall be egoistic and shut off from the world. Give me a little light in my solitude.

Affectionately,
Your W.

Your letter has disconcerted and disarmed me. So that I now feel myself entirely to blame. I seem to myself unjust and hardhearted and yet I know that what I wrote and said was not from any coldness of heart.

But there is one thing that you should know: what is it that continues to hold me together in this world, me, the loneliest man I know, whose only choice lies between passionate flight from the world and dismal seclusion in the midst of the alien tumult? You know well what it is: I cannot do without you. And if there come hours of forgetfulness when I know nothing of myself and feel myself to be only a mechanism—at the first return of consciousness I find myself on the old road again.

I must expend myself, not only on the things I love and dream of, but also on many others—things that make me hard and cold. I must do this, because men of my type are responsible for all that nature has given them to do and be; I have no right to live a life of imagination and contemplation without spiritual conflict and exertion. Nor must I ask the reason why. Nature has united in me heterogeneous elements; and she must answer for it. And I must do my work conscientiously, without knowing for whom. I know that this must make you suffer. You do not possess me completely; but nobody will ever possess me to the extent that you do. There has been a certain change in my feelings in the last few years, but not in the deeper spheres. I am more at peace, but also more confident. And you must believe me when I tell you that in the distance there is

151

always that which calms my heart, a certain feeling between us, your feeling for me and mine for you.

I say this with reluctance, for I have remained silent about other things which I consider highly to my credit. And yet one other thing: can you really believe that this mood of returning to my thoughts, speaking out, revealing—so rare and so unprecedented in my life—can be a thing of the moment and of chance, a mere superficial gesture? And if you do not believe it, then you *must* know and feel that of all the things you give me there is one above all others that simply must not be taken from me; the certainty I have of finding in you something that belongs to me and that I cannot be deprived of. If I have reproached you—perhaps unjustly—at bottom it was due to the fact that in the midst of doubt and change it was not I but my sense of security that felt threatened. I have suffered too much in my life from worry, doubt and trouble, so that nowadays renunciation comes easier to me than despair. If you were able to picture to yourself the nature of my life—which you do not really understand (and perhaps rightly) because it is dualistic but not divided against itself—you would be less anxious and also cause less anxiety to me, who have the unfortunate quality of receiving and condensing rays like a concave mirror. Thus if the mirror trembles ever so slightly the image swings up and down.

Can you understand me? I am afraid that very little will be clear amidst all this confusion. But I mustn't spend the whole night writing. My car is at the door. Tomorrow I shall be in Westphalia and the day after in Munich at the Continental. I think it would do me good to find two words—not more —from you there, otherwise your last letter will ring too long in my ears, and there is a note in it which makes me uneasy.

Yours affectionately,
W.

Now at last I can and must write to you again, for I have just finished my summer's work.[8] Though small in size, it is large in content, for it contains a man's whole life. For that reason it may have some human interest for you, though I find it difficult to picture you finding your way through this mountainous region; it is a sort of history of mankind. I don't know whom I ought to give it to as a whole, and so I am hesitating as to whether there is any sense in printing it.

I have tried to be as clear as if I were addressing children, but now I have got to the end I feel it should have been grandchildren rather than children.

Don't be alarmed! This is not arrogance, but loneliness. You have often prophesied that this is what must happen. But you were wrong in one point: only now do I feel completely myself; my wishes become ever quieter, and when I look out through the pouring rain over the restless sea to the far green-gold expanse of sky beyond, I have a sense of deep peace and freedom. It is as though this book, which has meant so much to me, had liberated a part of my very self—a beautiful foretaste of a happy death.

Don't be alarmed! I don't want to hurt your feelings, yet I cannot keep silence or speak of anything else. Only an hour ago my thoughts were entirely centered—as indeed they have been for the last two and a half months—on the past and the future. Now the sheets lie in front of me as if they had fluttered down from the sky, almost alien, no longer my own, and it is as if years had passed.

I have nothing much more to say. I have been here since Saturday—there is an autumn sea, Nature is all rain, waves, banks of cloud, while the sun breaks through at intervals (it is actually doing so as I write). I think I shall stay here till the

[8] *Criticism of the Age.*

153

end of the month; there is no hope for staying longer; work is piling up in Berlin.

Farewell. Warmest greetings. W.

Thank you for your words of reconciliation, and for so delicately drawing back the veil that had begun to cover unforgettable memories. . . .

This winter it has become clear to me as never before that a man's life signifies nothing unless all his powers of mind and sense of responsibility are exerted to their utmost. There is something half-wrong in receiving gifts, even from Nature.

All good wishes for you and yours; may they bring happiness to your home and your countryside and your life!

Yours affectionately,

22.12.11 W.

1913. Poincaré. On January 16th Poincaré is elected President of the French Republic; Pams, whose election slogan had been 'Peace,' is defeated. All Paris responds with the cry: '*Poincaré c'est la guerre.*' The period of compulsory service is lengthened to three years. To popularize the army, Millerand, the Minister of War, institutes a great weekly tattoo; late every Saturday the troops, gay with flags and music and Chinese lanterns, march in procession through the streets of Paris, accompanied to right and left by the patriotic songs of the mob who march along with them. Society flocking to Nijinski at the Châtelet and to Caruso at the Opera stop their cars when the troops come past and during the intervals step out into the streets to applaud them. In the East the Second Balkan War is raging. Russia raises a loan of 665 million francs in Paris for strategic railroads. The Grand Duke Nicholas, Russian Commander-in-Chief, pays an official visit to the French army; the Grand Duchess, a Montenegrin princess, publicly salutes 'the lost provinces of Alsace-Lorraine.' In England, Lord Haldane, after his abortive visit to Berlin, is quietly organizing the British Expeditionary Force. In Germany the Government has put before the nation a scheme for an 'emergency loan' of a milliard marks for new armaments. In order to start it off and as a prelude to the 'Great Age' that is to come, an 1813 centenary celebration is held on the grandest scale.

On March 23rd Rathenau counters this agitation with a passionate warning in the *Neue Freie Presse—The Sacrifice to the Eumenides. (Collected Works*, Vol. I, p. 253 *f.*) It would be worth while to reprint every line of this article, which is the most powerful and convincing he ever wrote, but I shall quote here only the more essential passages:

'The German empire is asking its citizens for a loan of a milliard marks and the interest on some further milliards in order to strengthen its defences in the east and its army in the west. It is a question, they say, of averting a doom, and we are asked to recall the voluntary sacrifices of a hundred years ago. Six months ago fourteen millions for special troops seemed beyond our power; today a thousand millions seem to come of their own accord. It is the psychology of the annual company meeting: a wretched embezzlement on the part of a bank messenger causes an uproar, but the loss of half the company's capital is met with a determined resignation which seems to say "Thank Heaven it is only half." . . . The last generation looked on quietly and without surprise while two worlds were being parcelled out, the African and the Mohammedan. . . . Nine-tenths of the plunder went to France and her allies; Germany got her colonies by private initiative, but by exploiting the strength of her position politically or diplomatically she got nothing whatsoever. And yet the German Empire entered the Concert of Europe as the undisputed paramount power, as an umpire and guarantor. . . . It has raised a fighting force such as this planet has never seen before, and passed an equally unprecedented defence estimate of one and three-quarter billion marks. No Continental power has a fleet that can rival it in size; none is so prosperous, or has so many civilized inhabitants. And the result is—nothing. Indeed less than nothing, for the voice of Germany, which was more powerful than any in Europe thirty years ago, has now ceased to matter, or at least matters less than that of France . . . . In such a situation, politically starved, with declining self-confidence, and torn by internal difficulties, we have now to face the prospect of being encircled on the East. . . . Hitherto the Entente and the Triple Alliance have never measured their respective strengths; now they have done so and, behold, we have the sun against us—but for the moment only the sun. So we quickly take stock of our forces, *personnel* and *matériel*, and make out the account. A milliard is needed; produce it and the account is balanced. . . . The sacrifice should and will be made.

'But it is misleading to compare the taxes proposed by the Bundesrat with the national sacrifices of 1813. The finest thing about that period was not the sacrifice nor the victory, but the heart-searching that preceded them. . . . Money and armaments alone will not avail to avert our doom. Material forces only call up material forces in reply. . . . If the extension of the military service in France becomes a law, war is assured. . . . The double tension—that, more dangerous than outspoken, between England and ourselves, and that, more outspoken than dangerous, between France and ourselves—is now acquiring full explosive power, reinforced by the sensitiveness of Russia, who sees the seed of our milliard loan sprouting in a ring of fortresses about her borders. By this sacrifice to the Eumenides, demanded in the name of the hundred years' cycle, our doom will not be averted; it will be hastened. . . . Class rule and its concomitants, inadequate personnel and weak policy; the conservatism of the ruling elements, and its concomitant, the unequal distribution of burdens: that is the double injustice and the double danger of our country. . . . Perhaps it

156

is not yet too late to apply the true lesson of that great epoch and abolish the injustice. But the most crying injustice of our age lies in the fact that the most efficient industrial nation in the world, the nation most rich in ideas and with the greatest capacity for organization, is not allowed to control its own destiny. . . . The weakness this two-fold evil causes Germany, year in, year out, cannot be made good by any number of brigades. . . . It is not the physical power of the battalions in themselves, but this power multiplied by the degree of business capacity, that decides a nation's position in the world. . . .

'Wars and national destinies are not the product of the will; they spring from natural laws which lie at the root of differences of population, national energy, and physical factors. Yet above these mechanical laws stand others which are ethical and transcendental. When inner strength grows slack, when the formulas, morals and ideas of a nation lose their significance, then external destiny takes control. It is not outer conditions and political constellations, but inner laws, moral and transcendental necessities, that forcibly determine our fate. Our sturdy people has been educated by the same method that it likes to use with its own children—by blows. Formerly the obstinate pride of the ruling caste was responsible for our catastrophes, but now this pride is accompanied by the indolence of the nation, which is not prepared to fight for its responsibilities and so will be compelled to fight for its security. But when the hour of fate arrives, people will realize that all effort which does not rest on the double foundation of a strong policy and a just constitution is like chaff before the wind. The passion which at present serves the interests of material life will then be transformed into real concern for the welfare of society and the state, and obsolete rights and privileges will meet the same fate as the bloated carcass of our present industrial system. One single hour will see the crash of what was believed to be secure against the ravages of time. . . .'

At the end of the year Rathenau followed up this powerful challenge with a further article, *German Dangers and New Aims*, which appeared in the *Neue Freie Presse* on December 25th, 1913. (*Collected Works*, Vol. I, p. 267 *ff*.) It was a final attempt to offer a solution which should find for Germany a way out of her desperate situation and at the same time guarantee peace to Europe: 'There is one possibility left: an industrial customs union, of which sooner or later, for better or for worse, the states of Western Europe would become members. . . . The problem of securing Free Trade for Europe is difficult, but not insoluble. Commercial legislation must be co-ordinated, companies indemnified, receipts from tariffs must be distributed, and some substitute provided to make up for them; but an industrial unit would be created which would equal and perhaps surpass that of America, and within the league there would no longer be any backward or unproductive regions. At the same time the most potent cause of international hostility would be removed. . . . What prevents the nations from trusting one another, mutually supporting each other, exchanging and enjoying in common their possessions and strength, is only indirectly questions of power, imperialism and expansion; the root of the matter is industrial. Fuse the industries of Europe into one—and that will happen sooner than we think— and political interests will fuse too. This is not world peace or disarmament, nor is it general debility; but it is an alleviation of conflicts, an economy of power and the solidarity of civilization.'

Meanwhile Rathenau's most important book, *The Mechanism of the Mind*, had appeared in October, dedicated 'to the young generation.' At first it caused less stir and had a smaller sale than his *Criticism of the Age*, which appeared in January, 1912. It was three years before the first three thousand copies were sold, whereas the first edition of the *Criticism of the Age* of the same size had to be reprinted after a month. The basic idea of the *Mechanism of the Mind* had been expressed by Rathenau in his *Festal Song*, in the words:

> 'Man! The folds of the deceptive veil
> Obscure the vision with vanities,
> And hide from you the ways of God.
>
> .   .   .   .   .
>
> Man, O man, think of thy soul!'

This conception was, to be sure, irreconcilably opposed to the sabre rattling and the riotous orgies of the period. Rathenau was well aware of the contempt with which his appeal to the soul was received by public opinion in general, and of the definite hostility it aroused among his colleagues. The blows of fate which fell upon him had momentarily disorganized the delicate mechanism of his soul—as his handwriting shows. In the self-analysis of his letters to his friend a new note can be detected: a certain serenity, the first signs of exhaustion, a renunciation, an inner stillness like the lull after a storm. One feels the evening drawing near.

I found your kind beautiful letter, and the red roses, on my return home early today; thank you! I will thank Paul for his thoughtful and friendly information tomorrow. Now it is night.

No, the soul is not to be gained by battling for it! But it does not rest in peace, like the gift of the blue sky; it grows, like all living things, according to its own law. Nor is it hostile to life like the distorted kind of ascetic Christianity; it is wholly free, courageous and joyful, like the true sayings of the New Testament. It does not separate the body and spirit; it demands no renunciation, service or cult; its most inward expression is a certain moral disposition.

This disposition, however, is as much Franciscan as Goethean, as much pagan as Christian; it is the disposition that lives for the thing and not for the person, which deifies creation rather than the ego.

It is not only those who have come out of the darkness who walk this path. There has never been a true spirit, gay or sombre, happy or suffering, who has not trod it. The spirits who are chained to the ego all look the same, however various the faces they bear. Therefore I am not afraid of giving this book to the young; if it leads them to sentimental enthusiasm this will mean that they have not understood it. But they *will* understand it! And they will understand, too, the way that leads from the ego to the thing, to the idea, to being; and this same way will also lead to the greatest deeds.

It is not a forerunner that I wish to be, but a sort of signpost at the cross roads, who will watch with joy all who take the right road. But I will not again change my direction; the thin compass needle is fragile, but every little piece of it points to the pole.

You think that nothing in this book belongs to you? When you have mastered it, and you will master it, you will feel that it is not only a confession, but also the transmutation of an experience.

Affectionately yours,

27.11.13 W.

GRAND HOTEL QUIRINAL
ROME

What can I do but take the hand you offer me? You must believe me: even in those most difficult days you never ceased to mean a great deal to me, and in these last years of difficulty and disillusionment and anxiety about my father, your image has always been with me. Your image—for our actual meetings are no longer a success.

When we meet among other people I feel a tension and embarrassment which make every word constrained. For a few

160

moments you control yourself—with effort—I feel it—and then comes a movement, a look or a word which wounds me to the quick, which—forgive me for speaking so freely—infuriates me. And then against my own nature I become suspicious and prone to take offence; I can no longer believe wholeheartedly in the kind things you say to me; every word seems to bear a double meaning.

When we are alone, on the other hand, other things are blown aside like a breath as if they were lies and foolishness. I remember your once saying to me: 'But come, we can't talk about botany'—and then nothing remains but the I and the Thou; however, even then we are not united, and the atmosphere remains troubled and threatening. I ask you: 'How am *I* to understand this?' You say you feel constrained in my presence. Isn't it rather undignified to expose ourselves to such situations? Ought we to destroy the best that is in us and between us by such influences? In me they tremble and vibrate for weeks afterwards, even though I have something of my father's strong constitution. I wrote and said to you a year ago: It depends on you, not on me. What is the use of trying to find out now the reason for this unfortunate state of things? If we cannot now muster strength to gain our freedom, then we are not worthy of freedom. And if this freedom dies, all trust, security and confidence die with it. For how can I feel you by my side as the inspirer of my life and work when I know that you never have a moment's ease in my presence, and when, moreover, every friendly word is drowned in a thousand shades of contradiction and opposition? I feel frankly—forgive me once again; I am going to say something very unkind—that there is a false note, whenever you take a step towards renunciation, companionship and mutual understanding; I realize that you are prompted by the kindest motives, but I also realize that you are demanding a sacrifice from your nature which it is humiliating for me to accept. And in any case what is to happen? It isn't a question of sacrifice. Freedom will only be possible when you can bring yourself willingly and fearlessly to recognize things for what they are. I know what this means—not to me—but to your free-born nature. I shall never again bow to your will; but neither shall I desert you. I shall always come when you call, but I shall hold back in silence until I am wanted.

But in the meanwhile I take your hand and hold it with deep affection, whether we are near or far apart. I know that we cannot completely lose one another; this I know, even at this distance, from the feeling I have when I see your dear handwriting which your own hand has formed and on which your arm has rested. But from people such as I life demands strength and freedom and sometimes even sternness.

Farewell. I should like to have told you something of Rome and your own dear land along with my Christmas wishes and greetings, but after all it is more important that we have at last cleared the air between us.

Affectionately,

21.12.1913   Your W.

1914. The times are out of joint. A peculiar atmosphere is abroad, something intoxicating, a mixture of brutality, unbridled sensuality and mysticism, slowly permeated by the smell of blood. Extraordinary events are happening everywhere, which in this atmosphere seem like the signs and portents that precede Caesar's death in Shakespeare's play. In Berlin, Court circles, usually so hopelessly matter-of-fact, take to attending spiritualistic séances; spirits are raised from the dead in the very study of the Chief of the Imperial General Staff, Moltke. In Paris the wife of the French Minister of Finance, Caillaux, assassinates a famous journalist. Russia, having secured a loan of six hundred million francs in January for the construction of strategic railways, becomes brutally outspoken; on March 12th the *Petersburg Stock Exchange News* publishes a threatening semi-official announcement: 'Russia is prepared for War,' which soon proves to have been written by the Russian Minister of War, Sukhomlinoff, himself. This is followed in June by an article in the *Prussian Year Book* on *The Motives and Aims of Russian Policy* by a Russian professor, Mitropanoff, which without making any bones about the matter offers Germany the choice between the withdrawal of her military mission from Constantinople and war. On June 28th the Archduke is assassinated at Sarajevo.

In London the season is at its height, such a season as London has not seen for years. Again the Russians are leading the dance: the Russian ballet, Chaliapin, Prince Yusupoff (who was afterwards to murder Rasputin) and his bride, a Grand Duchess —he remarkably handsome, she remarkably lovely, and still almost a child, weighed down like a Russian ikon by a mass of jewels. All Europe, half America and half Asia are in attendance! Indian Maharajahs flaunting precious stones worth the labour of ten generations, American bankers with gorgeous yachts anchored off Cowes, the most fashionable of Parisian beauties, great artists like Rodin, Richard Strauss, Debussy and Stravinski—London the cynosure of the world!

Then suddenly a transformation. It looks as if the feast might end like that of Belshazzar. There is a mutiny of British officers in Ireland, and the Government dare not punish them. In London the soldiers of the Irish Guards on duty at the Palace jeer at Mr. Asquith on his return from a meeting of the Privy Council. At the luncheon party at his house, which he is delayed from attending, the rumour of this demonstration precedes him and the former French Premier, Jules Roche, draws me aside and says: 'How tragic to watch the collapse of a great empire at such close quarters!' The sister of Lady Randolph Churchill is said to have left suddenly for Ireland in order to distribute rifles hidden in her park. When the German Ambassador, Prince Lichnowsky, rather rashly inquires of Lady

Randolph about this journey and asks her what it means, she raps out sharply just one Italian word: 'sangue' [blood] and then, with a flash of her remarkably fine dark eyes: 'But if we are attacked we shall all stand together like one man.' [9]

Meanwhile Mr. Winston Churchill was assembling the Grand Fleet. On July 15th the Third Squadron began its 'Test Mobilization'; on the 17th and 18th 'incomparably the greatest assemblage of naval power ever witnessed in the history of the world' was reviewed at Spithead, and all London thronged to see this stupendous spectacle. Finally, on the morning of the 19th, says Mr. Winston Churchill in his book *The World Crisis*, 'the whole fleet put to sea. It took more than six hours for this armada, every ship decked with flags and crowded with bluejackets and mariners, to pass, with bands playing and at 15 knots, before the Royal yacht, while overhead the naval seaplanes and aeroplanes circled continuously.' Such was the response of the British Government to the situation on the Continent, while in their minds, as Mr. Churchill records, 'the squalid, tragic Irish quarrel' was uppermost. But six days later the Austrian ultimatum burst on the world; instead of civil war, War!

Rathenau wrote in his diary for 1914: 'At the end of January or the beginning of February a memorable conversation with Bethmann in the presence of Winterfeldts. He inquired (perhaps rhetorically) whether one should be consistent or opportunist in national affairs. I replied: "This alternative does not exhaust the matter. What the country demands above all else is a clear lead." ' On March 12th he breakfasted with the Kaiser at the Minister of Transport's house. The Kaiser seemed peculiarly nervous about Alsace: 'We can no longer feel secure about the concentration.' The wife of Moltke, the Chief of the General Staff, having made Rathenau's acquaintance,

[9] I happened myself to witness this scene and hear the words at a tea party in the garden of the Prime Minister's house in Downing Street.

asked him to attend a lecture of the mystic and prophet, Rudolf Steiner, in his community, of which she was a patron.

Rathenau's letters this spring show a new and tender preoccupation with Nature; the realm of the soul hovers only just below the surface. On March 22nd he writes to Fräulein Fanny Künstler: 'If your picture of me mounted on the easel of your dear memory has brought you help and strength, it is now time to take it down again. I am not this creature of clarity and harmony you seem to think I am. Like all of us, I suffer from worry and passion, from fear and desire, from misery and foolishness. If I have gained anything out of the conflicts I have been through, it is the possibility of finding my bearings when the cyclone has died down. Today is the first day of spring. I went for a walk along the banks of the Havel; a rainstorm came up, and passed over the distant waters and the red and yellow of the young tree tops.' (Letter 120.) To Fritz von Unruh in April: 'The four of us were sitting in the Freienwalde Kurhaus when the news came, the Hauptmanns, Ekke and myself, and we all thought of you. It was one of those cloudless summer days we have been having lately; the blossom just coming out, the garden a carpet of flowers, and a clear view of the distant hills.' (Letter 132.) The next day to Fanny Künstler: 'I love to think of your beautiful home; it reminds me most pleasantly of my South German relatives' charming houses. They have lived for generations in the same spots in Mainz and Frankfort, in sweet-scented rooms thick with memories; great pear-trees grow in front of the windows and bear enormous fruit which used to enchant us when we were children. At Freienwalde yesterday there wasn't a cloud in the sky all day, so clear was the atmosphere that one seemed to be able to see an almost infinite distance; the first fruit trees were in blossom on the hills in the summer-like warmth." (Letter 124.) Then again to Fanny Künstler at Whitsun: 'I came here yesterday, but unfortunately cannot stay long, for there is work awaiting me in Berlin. I still feel that I can't shake off the winter. I have hills and trees around me again, but I am too dull and stupid to understand their language; I can only breathe irregularly and with difficulty in the long pulsations of Nature. Yet the sky is streaming peacefully from west to east; cloud columns, gloom and sunshine follow one another; and now with the last banks of clouds the night is here in all its silence.' (Letter 131.) At the end of June again to the same person: 'The roses are in bloom here now, or rather they are like a river of colour. I have to close the window at night, so overpowering is the scent of the limes. I cannot work.' (Letter 135.) The middle of July: 'The roses are making elaborate preparations for their second bloom. The trees stand heavily laden in their blue-green foliage; they already have their fruit and are beginning to dream of autumn. Hot days dim the horizon, and evening comes, still late, with the clouds aflame with colour. By the time I get up it has been broad daylight for hours: I wake up in sunlight.' (Letter 136.) Finally, at the end of July, when the war was already close at hand: 'The last few days I have had to be in Berlin, and I now return to find the chill of autumn, and the rich foliage shivering in expectation of summer's end. Alas, the end is here, the days are drawing in; in all one's thoughts there is something of farewell.' (Letter 140.)

This is the turning-point, also, in Rathenau's life; and it may therefore be well to make clear in what respects the policy that he propagated both in writing and by word of mouth differed from that of the Kaiser. For this policy, which was even at this date quite clear in his mind, is the key to his actions and outlook during the war, while it is also the foundation on which he built up a new foreign policy for Germany after the catastrophe. The material for this survey is to be found in his political articles in the period preceding the war, and it is for this reason that I have dealt with them in such detail. In one of these articles, *Politics, Humour and Armaments,* he puts the question: 'What does business or political genius really amount to?' He replies: 'It seems to me that it resides in nothing else but the fact that in the camera obscura of the mind an image of the world takes shape which reflects all the essential laws and relationships of reality, and which thus can always to a certain extent be rearranged experimentally, so that within human limits it can even show the image of the future.' (*Collected Works,* Vol. I, 174.) That is true; but one should add that not only political genius, but any sort of political activity—no matter on how small a scale—if it is to be successful, presupposes a conscious or unconscious, but certainly precise and consistent, picture of the world. What struck one about the Kaiser, who determined the general lines of Germany's pre-war policy, was the contradictions, the lack of precision, the arbitrary assumptions, the superficiality, of his picture of the world. He operated upon the body politic as a surgeon of the Middle Ages operated upon the human body, with a conception of its anatomy which was derived in part from the Bible, in part from a patchwork of the latest pet ideas of those professors who were in favour at court. Rathenau, on the other hand, had before him an altogether precise and consistent picture of the world, the details of which might be incomplete or disputable in places, but which taken as a whole reproduced the actual state of affairs, and not merely its surface but its real depths. The world of today presented itself to him as a single industrial and intellectual mechanism which was only superficially divided by political frontiers. Armaments, which only serve to strengthen political boundaries, are therefore incapable of maintaining a state permanently above the level which the interplay of its industrial, intellectual and moral forces assigns it. It is these last, and not armaments, which determine a nation's true standing in the scales of fate, and in the long run its actual position in the world. And these deep forces are bound up with one an-

167

other all the world over, for the whole world is a single machine, and any industrial, intellectual or moral force which is lost at any point diminishes the amount of power available for driving the whole machine and each of its parts. On this account the mobilization of all the industrial, intellectual and moral forces and talents of a people, by means of an unprejudiced and democratic system of selection, is more decisive for the international standing of a state than any number of armoured cruisers could ever be. And finally, as every state is only a part of the one great machine, it is doomed to perish if it isolates itself, or is isolated from the others. Thus in war the most deadly weapon is the economic blockade; and if the war should be a long one intellectual and moral isolation is no less dangerous.

The remoteness of Rathenau's picture of the world from the old imperial policy is shown by the paths which the latter actually took: for thirty years it persisted in regarding as its most important, indeed almost its sole, task the solution of the armaments problem: how to increase the German fleet without coming into conflict with England; it precluded a third of the nation, the social democratic workers, from any sort of participation in the affairs of the nation on the ground that they were 'fellows without a fatherland'; it preferred to tolerate a hereditary lack of talent in diplomacy and in the highest offices of state, a lack which it actually admitted itself, rather than open leading positions in the state to middle-class talent, such as during these years was appearing on all sides in commerce and industry; it failed, to take only one example, in that province which was most its own, the preparation for war, because it overlooked the significance of industry in war and so confined its industrial measures to a vague project which was never taken seriously and therefore never carried out. And thus at the beginning of the war Rathenau had to spring into the breach in order to fill this fatal gap in the German front.

CHAPTER VIII

IN DAYS TO COME

RATHENAU's first work of historical importance—of international importance in its effects—was the organization of German raw materials at the beginning of the war. As early as July 31st he had protested in an article in the *Berliner Tageblatt* entitled *On the Situation* against the policy of the government in following Austria blindly and stupidly into the war: 'The government has left us in no doubt of the fact that Germany is intent on remaining loyal to her old ally. Without the protection of this loyalty Austria could not have ventured on the step she has taken. The government and people of Germany have the right to know both what Russia has asked and what Austria has rejected. Such a question as the participation of Austrian officials in investigating the Serbian plot is no reason for an international war.' (*Collected Works*, Vol. I, pp. 305, 306.) The article discloses a trace of hope, the hope of one who stands at the bedside of a dying man; but it shows little confidence in the judgment and stability of the German government, and still less in Austria's desire for peace. And rightly so: for we know that the Austrian demand which Rathenau mentions was put forward with the express intention of making war with Serbia inevitable.

And so the war came; and Rathenau seemed completely overwhelmed. Witnesses testify that while the people were seized with a delirious excitement that has never been paralleled, Rathenau was wringing his hands in despair. An old friend, Frau von Hindenburg, describes how he came to her and sat in silence, while the tears rolled down his cheeks. How

differently he had sat opposite Bülow a few years before, sceptical, yet eager, accepting without much ado his first official
post, displaying without doubt the gentle magic of his conversation. Now he was suddenly silent, old, broken. He writes to a
friend in September, that gloriously beautiful St Martin's summer, which will always be remembered for its mildness by all
who spent it under the open sky: 'The year has lost its colours
and seasons; I feel winter.' (Letter 145.) He shuddered before the death shadow which he felt to be spreading over his
beloved land. He saw—what practically no one else did—the
stupendous world machine which was being set in motion
against Germany. He knew its inexhaustible sources of power,
against which those of Germany were small and strictly limited; he realized the inadequacy of our political leadership, to
whose importance in war people were blindly indifferent; he
saw the fragile nature of the political structure in which the
storm had overtaken us, and the insufficiency of our armament.
He said to the deputy, Conrad Haussmann, in the autumn: 'Do
you know, Herr Haussmann, what we are fighting about? I
don't, and I should be glad if you could tell me. What will
come of it? We have no strategists and no statesmen.' (Conrad
Haussmann, *Schlaglichter*, pp. 13, 20.)

But what most distressed him was something else: he felt
that the moral strength which had been ours in former wars
was now lacking. He wrote to Fanny Künstler in November:
'Apart from this obvious pain there is another, a duller pain,
more mysterious, which benumbs everything within me. We
must win, we must! And yet we have no clear, no absolute right
to do so. . . . How different it was in 1870 with the ideal of
unity before us! How different the demand for our very existence in 1813! A Serbian ultimatum and a mass of confused
precipitate telegrams! Would that I had never seen behind the
scenes of this stage!' (Letter 199.) And in December: 'There
is a false note about this war; it is not 1813, nor 1866, nor 1870.

Necessary or not, superior might or not—it shouldn't have happened as it did. . . .' (Letter 157.)

This mood remained. The outbreak of war was a blow from which Rathenau never recovered. It was the crisis of his life. And the way in which he reacted to it throws more light on the real relationship between his two natures than all his writings put together. It was only in his letters that he took flight into the realm of the soul; in practical life he reacted as a 'fear man' with his intellect, in that he threw his whole personality into the breach, in the attempt to ward off future dangers of which at that moment practically nobody but himself was aware. 'Even if everything else deceives, life itself does not deceive. Consider my life,' he had written to his friend. *Ecce Homo!* Here was a choice between two attitudes, a choice which involved not only his life, but his whole spiritual existence. And he chose that which the intellect, not the 'soul,' dictated to him. 'Soon after the outbreak of the war,' he wrote in his diary, 'I took two steps:

'1. I offered the Chancellor my services and worked out for him a project for a customs union between Germany-Austria-Hungary-Belgium-France.

'2. I went to Colonel Scheuch at the War Office and sketched out to him my ideas for the organization of raw materials.'

It shows the depth of his insight that even at the beginning of the war he envisaged the dangers of the post-war period correctly, and instead of proposing an allied customs league, as Naumann did later in his *Central Europe*, suggested the inclusion of enemy countries, France and Belgium, as well—*i.e.* an industrial union of the whole of Europe—a state of affairs which is being brought ever nearer by developments since the war.

But it was only his second idea, the organization of raw materials, which could be put into practice at this date. In an address on 'The Organization of Germany's Raw Materials,' given at the 'Deutsche Gesellschaft' on December 20th, 1915 (*Collected Works*, Vol. V., p. 23 *ff.*), he explained with classic simplicity his guiding principles and the methods he applied. 'Raw materials, organization! An abstract, colourless phrase like so many others of our time, for modern speech lacks the creative power to evolve vivid words for strong concrete ideas; a lifeless phrase, and yet a great conception if one really tries to picture it. Look around you: everything you see, buildings and machinery, clothing and food, armaments and traffic—all contain some foreign ingredient. For the industrial life of the various nations is indissolubly connected; by land and sea the riches of all the countries of the earth flow together and unite in the service of life. . . . Every day we hear about the difficulties of providing food for the people. And yet this provisioning is based upon a productive capacity which can deal with more than eighty per cent. of the demand. A blockade can restrict our supply, but it cannot annihilate us. It is a different matter with those materials which are indispensable for carrying on the war; here a blockade may mean annihilation. . . . On August 4th last year, when England declared war, the appalling and the unprecedented occurred: our country became a beleaguered fortress. Cut off by land and sea, we were thrown on our own resources; and the war lay before us, unpredictable in duration and expenditure, in danger, and in sacrifice. Three days after the declaration of war I could not endure the uncertainty of our position any longer; I went to see the Head of the General War Department, Colonel Scheuch, and was received by him on the evening of August 8th. I put it to him that our country could probably only reckon on a supply of indispensable war materials for a limited number of months. His estimate of the duration of the war was not less than mine, so I felt I had to ask him what had been done and what could be done to save Germany from strangulation. . . . Very little had been done. . . . On returning home anxious and dispirited I found a telegram from the Minister of War, von Falkenhayn, asking me to come and see him at his office next morning. It was Sunday, August 9th. The conversation lasted for some time, and by the end of it the Minister had decided to set up an organization, no matter how large, no matter by what means, provided it was effective and solved the task that was imposed upon us.'

The 'War Raw Materials Department' was instituted by ministerial decree. It was directed by Walther Rathenau and a retired colonel, who was attached as an observer. Rathenau's other colleagues were Professor Klingenberg of the A.E.G., and Wichard von Mollendorf, afterwards Under-Secretary of State, who, as Rathenau pointed out in his address, 'in the course of friendly conversations with me was the first to put his finger on this serious breach in our industry.' At its foundation the department consisted of five people in all. And since the War Office had no clerical staff to place at their disposal, they were obliged to spend several hours a day in addressing envelopes. Also, the number of materials with which the Department had to deal was at first small. Foodstuffs and liquid fuel were excluded; but everything which could be described as war raw materials was included. The official definition ran as follows: 'Such materials as are needed for the defence of the state and which are not obtainable permanently or in sufficient quantities within the country itself.' To begin with, only about a dozen came under this definition, later the number grew from week to week, and finally there were a good hundred. They began with metals, then came chemicals, then jute, wool, rubber, cotton, leather, hides, flax, linen, horsehair. All these materials were seized in accordance with the new 'commandeering' regulation devised for the purpose on Rathenau's suggestion; and they were then dealt with by another institution, the War Industrial Companies.

In order to collect the materials, or, if they were not forthcoming in sufficient quantities, to manufacture them and place

173

them at the country's disposal, four different methods were devised: 'Firstly, all the raw materials in the country were controlled [by commandeering]; they were no longer left at the
disposal of individual will and individual caprice. No material
or semi-product was allowed to be used for luxury or for subsidiary purposes. Secondly, we had to force all available materials from over the frontier into the country, either by buying them in neutral countries, or by requisitioning them in occupied territory. Thirdly, there was manufacture. We had to see
to it that everything indispensable or unobtainable elsewhere
was manufactured in the country, and that new methods of production were discovered and developed in cases where the old
methods were no longer adequate. Fourthly, the materials
which were difficult to obtain had to be replaced by others more
easily procurable.'

The opposition which Rathenau had to overcome would have
broken many a stronger man. Some of the military bureaucrats
regarded him, the civilian and the Jew, whom they had to tolerate because he was making up for what they had themselves
neglected to do in long years of peace, with a distrust which
they seemed to take pleasure in accentuating. One day his department was isolated by a wooden partition, which had grown
up overnight, from those of the other old-established gentlemen in the War Office, as if it had been a cholera station. Even
with his immediate colleagues his relations were not always very
peaceful; with industry, trade, and agriculture and with certain
deputy generals about the country they were at times positively
warlike. But the tenacity he had acquired through long business
experience and the superior attitude he had so skilfully maintained from childhood onwards proved even stronger than the
wooden partition behind which the guerilla war was waged
against him. Under their protection he was able to perfect his
organization and after nine months hand it over, to the vexa-

tion of his opponents, to a successor from the War Office selected by himself, Lieutenant-Colonel Koeth.

From two points of view this organization of Rathenau's was, and still is today, of exceptional significance:

It saved large areas of Germany from sharing the fate of northern France; for without it the German army could only have defended the frontiers for a few months. As early as October, 1914, the nitrogen question had become so urgent that General Staff officers at the front considered that the war could not possibly last beyond the spring, since the supply of nitrate, which is indispensable for all forms of explosives, would only last till then. For the military authorities at the front this question was a far more serious matter then than questions of reinforcements or even strategy. The catastrophe was only avoided by the unparalleled speed and skill with which Rathenau took the necessary steps to conjure away the threatening nitrate shortage—and this in those same days in which the spiritual and mystical side of him wrote the despairing letters to Fanny Künstler and told Conrad Haussmann that he didn't know what we were fighting the war for. Through 'commandeering,' all the supplies of nitrate in the German Empire (and later in occupied Belgium, especially in Antwerp harbour) were secured for the army; and as the War Office had made no provisions for a supply this chiefly consisted of an immense number of small and even minute quantities which the peasants had been hoarding for manure and which in a few weeks would have been spread over the soil and irrevocably lost as far as the army was concerned. By appropriating these supplies and deflecting them to the munitions factories (in the face of desperate opposition on the part of the farmers) he held in check the nitrate shortage until such time as this substance, which had hitherto been exclusively an imported article, could finally be produced in the country itself. To this end steps were taken to produce nitrogen from the air by the Haber-Bosch process. Rathenau commissioned numbers of factories with this object, and thanks to his energy and gift for organization they sprang up astonishingly quickly, in spite of bureaucratic interference, and were able to make up in time for the decreasing supplies of requisitioned material. By Christmas the crisis was over. This work did as much towards protecting the frontiers of Germany and frustrating the meeting of Cossacks and Senegalese under the Brandenburger Tor as the Battle of Tannenberg or trench warfare in France. It was one of the really decisive actions of the war.

Again, the organization had great significance for the future of industry. Rathenau touched on this as early as 1915 in his address. I refer to the War Industrial Companies, which were an entirely original and typical idea of his own. Their task was the commercial management of the requisitioned raw materials; that is to say, after these had been commandeered it was their business to get hold of them, to look after them, if necessary to collect and store them, to fix their price, and finally to allot them to industry at the right time and in the right quantity. No bureaucratic organization composed solely of officials would have been able to do this, nor would that free play of forces which we call private enterprise. Therefore, Rathenau invented and created a new, mixed type of undertaking, the 'War Company'; and it was these which first placed German industry in a position to supply the army's requirements.

Rathenau refers in his address to their 'paradoxical nature': 'On the one hand they signified a decisive step in the direction of state socialism . . . on the other hand they aimed at self-government in industry, and this on the largest scale. How were these opposing principles to be reconciled?' 'The War Companies are self-governing in character, but by no means unrestricted in their freedom. The War Raw Materials Company was instituted under strict official supervision. Officials of the government departments and the ministries have an un-limited veto, the companies are run for the public benefit and may not issue either dividends or profits from liquidation. In addition to the usual bodies of a joint-stock company, the board of directors etc., they have an independent Commission for Valuation and Distribution, directed by officials or members of Chambers of Commerce. In this way they occupy a position be-tween a joint-stock company, which embodies the capitalistic form of private enterprise, and a bureaucratic organization: an industrial form which perhaps foreshadows the future.'

Through the activity of these companies the whole of Ger-man industry was converted, according to the different areas of production, into a series of self-governing bodies, which, under the supervision of the central state administration, had all pro-duction and distribution in their hands: an industry regulated in accordance with the needs of society, carried through to com-pletion and functioning systematically, which for the first time in history took the place of an industry existing for the profit of the private capitalist. Rightly did Rathenau say in his address: 'Our industry is (already in 1915) the closed industry of a closed industrial state. In the future our methods will have a very far-reaching effect.'

It is worthy of note that the Allies, too, were compelled by the pressure of the war to replace private enterprise by a sys-tematic industry based on their needs. Sir Arthur Salter, who directed this transition from the one to the other and who realized like Rathenau its significance for the future, has de-scribed it in detail in his admirable book, *Allied Shipping Con-trol* (Oxford, 1921). The difficulties which confronted the Al-lies were different in character from those of the Central Pow-ers; they were not threatened with a shortage of foodstuffs and raw materials in themselves, but with the difficulty of being able to transport them both from overseas. Hence their system-atic industry did not, like ours, develop out of the requisitioning of raw materials for the army by a department of the War Office, but out of the requisitioning of cargo space for transport by a department of the Admiralty. But in order to adapt the production, transport, warehousing, distribution, and prices of raw materials and foodstuffs to war requirements, they, too, were obliged to form War Companies for the individual products—the so-called 'Programme Committees,' which, like Rathenau's, were mixed self-governing bodies under the control and direction of government officials and which also coalesced into an organized industrial system. But in the case of the Entente this systematic control of industry finally extended even beyond the national frontiers, because the sea was the common and indivisible line of communication between all the Allies and the source of their supplies: and towards the end of the war the national industrial systems of the various Allies—England, France, Italy, etc.—were united under an inter-state authority, the 'Allied Maritime Transport Council' in London. This welded more than two dozen states into one single international industrial area for producing the necessary supplies. In the last two years of the war the most urgent question was not the conflict between the two armies, but the struggle between the two industrial bodies, which had divided up the surface of the earth into two powerful state socialist organizations to the exclusion of all but a few small and rapidly dwindling enclaves of private enterprise. And what decided the struggle was not the defeat of the German army, but the defeat of the German industrial organization through the blockade and the convoy system. This succeeded in frustrating the German counter-attack—the attempt to cut the arteries of the allied supply organization by means of the unrestricted submarine war. Had this achieved its aim, the Allies would have been compelled to abandon the contest, not through a military defeat in the traditional sense of the term, but through the breakdown of their supply system. Sir Arthur Salter points out that in

April, 1917, when the U-boat campaign was at its height, this appeared to him, and to all who were in a position to review the situation, to be an imminent danger, and only to be avoided by the convoy system, which was employed as a last resort. It is, in any case, an established historical fact that industry systematically controlled by public bodies functioned on the whole satisfactorily on both sides for several years, and that both parties were thus led to recognize its superiority, at least in war emergencies, over the traditional type of private enterprise.

Rathenau summed up his war experiences in their relation to his main problem—the overcoming of mechanization through a 'realm of the soul'—in a book published in February, 1917, under the title of *In Days to Come*, which he supplemented in January, 1918, by another work, *The New Economy*. The ideas he develops here are to be found in essence in his *Physiology of Business*, published in 1901. In the meantime, however, the experience of the 'soul,' and then the war, had both served to extend and render more precise his original conceptions. For the experience of the 'soul' gave him an aim which lay beyond industry and politics; while the war, by calling into being new types of industrial organization, helped to foreshadow a new order of industry beyond the mechanistic plane, and hastened a change in outlook which appeared to justify the hope of a coming reform.

There are three tendencies of the age, furthered by the war, which seem to point to a stage beyond mechanization—in Rathenau's sense to a coming 'realm of the soul': in public opinion, a growing contempt for mere riches (often in the form of 'antisemitism'), which goes along with an increasing respect for responsibility; in industry, a progressive depersonalization of property, brought about by the extension of limited companies and the multiplication of communal undertakings (War Companies); and in politics, the development of the sovereign state into the people's state.

179

WALTHER RATHENAU

'How,' asks Rathenau, with regard to these tendencies, 'is the transcendental task to be converted into the pragmatic?' (*In Days to Come*, p. 64.)

The answer is: The first step should be the abolition of the proletariat as such. For the burden imposed on the proletariat is the greatest hindrance to the life of the soul today. But is the abolition of the proletariat—*i.e.* of a dispossessed lower stratum, compelled to work through want—possible without crippling the process of production? Would a classless society produce enough for its own existence? To put it briefly, can we do without slaves today? [1] Or is their existence necessary in the interests of the slaves themselves? If absolutely indispensable types of labour can be performed only by a dispossessed class, then the answer must be 'Yes.' The existence of the proletariat would then be justified, much as the subordination of the worker bees to the queen bee, or of the slaves in Plato's state, is justified. Hence Rathenau attempts to show that in view of the advances in technical science, public opinion, and private convictions since the war, a dispossessed lower stratum is no longer necessary for the maintenance of production.

Hitherto, the most important incentives to production have been hunger and acquisitiveness, ambition, and the desire for pleasure. The capitalistic world is the product of these stimuli, a product daily reproduced anew. These driving forces owe their power to the inheritability and inviolability of private property, and hence to the persistence of a ruling caste privileged by inheritance and inviolable in its legal foundations—

[1] Robert Owen, the great cotton spinner and founder of English socialism, tells in his reminiscences how, round about 1788, he had to work as many as eighteen hours a day, as salesman in a London warehouse, when he was only seventeen. This seems scarcely credible. Yet in the recently published industrial programme of the Liberal Party (*Britain's Industrial Future*, Ernest Benn, London, 1928) it is asserted that at the present time (1928) apprentices from sixteen to seventeen years of age work as much as sixty, seventy, or even eighty-two hours per week; in some cases from eight in the morning until midnight or 1 A.M., thus from sixteen to seventeen hours a day (*loc. cit.*, p. 388).

the so-called bourgeoisie. But so long as these impulses determine the process of production we are bound to have the counterpart of the bourgeoisie—a proletariat suffering from birth
from inherited disabilities. Yet even before the war Rathenau
had shown that these impulses were beginning to yield to others. And the war, which made short work of the sacredness of
private property, simultaneously favoured the rise of these
other impulses.

In the first place joy in labour began to return. The rationalization and infinite division of labour have made this a luxury,
a mere matter of hearsay, to most modern workers. But a
change is gradually taking place. As Rathenau showed in his
small book, *Autonomous Industry* (Eugen Diederichs, 1919),
p. 7, the process of production has 'a tendency to convert manual labour into supervisory work and thus make it a little less
soulless.' Certainly that alone would not suffice, for 'this transformation takes too long and is after all only partial.' But it is
being supplemented by giving the worker more responsibility
over his mechanical labour, a process which made great strides
everywhere during the war. 'As there is so little room for the
rise of responsibility within the actual limits of his labour, the
worker must be able to find this outside those limits by having
a share in the management. The provisional solution of the
problem is the co-operation of the workers and officials in the
conduct of the undertaking' (*loc. cit.*). The ultimate solution,
of which more later, is the 'New Economy,' the uniting of the
whole of industry into self-governing bodies, in which each
worker has a voice. It must suffice here merely to refer to this
and to insist that joy in labour in the form of responsibility is
destined to play an ever-increasing part as a driving force in the
process of production.

But it is not merely the division of labour which kills the joy
in creation; it is even more the necessity, the compulsion, to
perform a hated task. Thus the abolition of the proletariat

would remove one of the most serious obstacles to this joy in labour. For it is only when the struggle for existence has ceased to be a crude matter of life and death that 'there will be room for those pure forces which will be the moving impulses of the future. . . . We must have freedom from drudgery, freedom from want and free choice of occupation; we have spoken of these conditions; they can be fulfilled. If they are, then there will no longer be any need for ignoble impulses, for the despot's lash, for greed or fear.' (*In Days to Come*, pp. 207, 209.)

On this point Rathenau's views coincide with Kropotkin's, but run counter to Marx, whose Communist Manifesto, with its cynical view of human nature, demanded that 'everyone should be *compelled* to work, and that industrial armies should be instituted, especially for agriculture.' To the objection that without compulsion the majority or at least an impossibly large number of men would not work, Kropotkin answers that 'dislike of work may be common amongst savages, but for the great mass of civilized peoples work is a habit and laziness an artificial growth.' (Kropotkin, *Anarchistic Communism*, p. 31.) Which is right, Kropotkin or Marx? On the basis of Rathenau's assumptions—free choice of occupation, increased responsibility for the worker, increased pressure of public opinion (which would be equivalent to moral pressure), and elimination of disagreeable work by mechanical contrivances—it will, I think, be admitted that in an industry working systematically in relation to demand, and hence, like the war industries, without serious market crises, the total number of the unemployed and work-shy would scarcely exceed the average number of those who are out of work against their will in our existing society. Thus at least as much would be produced *without* the existence of a lower stratum which is compelled to work by hunger as is today *with* this stratum. In those Prussian families of the official and noble class which were in a position before the war to offer their sons an assured income, the number of idlers dwindled away almost to nothing under the influence of their class-consciousness which told them that it was no longer 'good form' to do nothing. And, indeed, with the progressive rationalization of industry and the increase of productivity, very possibly the most serious problem of the future will not be how to find the necessary labour supply, but how to deal with the surplus.

Moreover, the abolition of poverty would immeasurably strengthen another of these impulses: the feeling of solidarity. We have already discussed the growth of this sense and its root in the increasing interdependence of human relationships. Even before the war Rathenau's *Mechanism of the Mind* had laid stress on its significance for the new world order. And the war, which taught us all the absolute and ever-closer interdependence of people and nations, has done much to develop it. The elimination of want from the competitive struggle would so enormously increase the influence of this sense that we may with some confidence reckon it along with the joy in labour as an impulse of elemental power in the industrial life of the future.

Thus Rathenau's answer to the original question: Is a dispossessed lower class really necessary today? is an unhesitating 'No.' The second question, which is morally raised by this 'No': Will a time come, not incalculably distant, when it will be possible to abolish the proletariat? he answers with an equally unhesitating 'Yes.' And in *In Days to Come*, and especially in in *The New Economy*, he sets out to demonstrate this by his great constructive scheme for a classless society, in which there would be no proletariat, no hereditary oppression, no privileged ruling caste. This scheme is the very core of Rathenau's life-work, the residue of his whole personality, the final outcome of all his experiences; of the mystical, transcendental, religious, just as much as of those organizational, technical, commercial, and social experiences which were the result of a singularly

183

active and many-sided business career. Whatever one may think
of the details of this scheme, there are two things one cannot
deny: first, the sincerity of the transcendent will, the will to
free the soul, by which it is inspired; and secondly, the accurate
knowledge of all the facts of industry on which it is based. It is
not the project of an armchair theorist or demagogue, and still
less the bright idea of a prosperous dilettante; it is, rather, the
most serious part of the life-work of an unusually serious man,
of a man unusually conscious of his responsibilities, and with a
knowledge of the modern world and particularly of modern
industry equalled by few. A great organizer of industry speaks
on the revolution of industrial organization; that alone entitles
him to be listened to with respect.

The point from which Rathenau starts is this: that, partly
as a result of the war, it would today be technically and
psychologically possible to abolish the dependent condition of
the proletariat without violent revolution. Technically, because
taxation is ruthlessly set on equalizing differences in income.
Psychologically, because the change of attitude which the war
helped on has broken down the resistance to this process.

As Rathenau has shown, the war has brought about a new
way of thinking which may be summed up in the phrase:
'Property, consumption, and demand are not private matters.'
(*In Days to Come*, p. 74.) 'In days to come,' he says, 'people
will find it difficult to understand that the will of a dead man
could bind the living; that any individual was empowered to
enclose for his private gratification mile upon mile of land; that
without requiring any special authorization from the state he
could leave cultivable land untilled, could demolish buildings
or erect them, ruin beautiful landscapes, secrete or disfigure
works of art; that he conceived himself justified, by appropriate
business methods, in bringing whatever portion he could hold
of the communal property under his own private control; justified, provided he could pay his taxes, in using this property as

he pleased, in taking any number of men into his own service, and setting them to whatever work seemed good to him, so long as there was no technical violation of the law; justified in engaging in any kind of business, so long as he did not infringe a state monopoly or promote any enterprise legally defined as a swindle; justified in any practice, however absurd and however harmful to the community, provided always he remained able to pay his way' (*loc. cit.*, pp. 75, 76).

What follows? That it is possible even now, because it is widely recognized to be desirable, to introduce legal provisions for subordinating industry to the good of the community; that under these new conditions the dispossessed proletariat must disappear; that the fate of the new order should not be left either to the free play of forces, or to a revolution, and that therefore the state must intervene by legislation and devise some means of abolishing the proletariat. (*The New Economy*, p. 218.)

These means are, in the first place, the utmost restriction of the right of inheritance. 'Among those goods of humanity which are inviolable and beyond criticism, the moral concept of the inheritance of wealth and power can find no place. Custom may have made it acceptable to us, but it is nowise sacrosanct. . . . Yet the whole nature of our social stratification reposes upon this moral concept. . . . This is what condemns the proletarian to perpetual servitude, and the rich man to perpetual enjoyment. It binds the burden of responsibility upon the weary who would fain repudiate it, and chokes the creative impulse of the functionless, some of whom long for responsibility.' (*In Days to Come*, p. 110.) 'The restriction of the right of inheritance, in conjunction with the raising of popular education to the higher level, will throw down the barriers which now separate the economic classes of society, and will put an end to the hereditary enslavement of the lower classes.' He fully admits that 'the nature of the legislative enactment is a matter

185

of minor importance. It is of immeasurably greater significance that the coming transformation is preceded by changes in sentiment and ethical values' (p. 112). But yet he demands that a legislative reform should accompany this change of sentiment. 'All inheritance over and above a moderate amount of landed property should accrue to the state' (p. 117).

By restricting the right of inheritance to this extent one would radically affect that state of affairs which divides the nation into two camps. But other measures, already prepared for by the change of outlook, are also necessary. Thus there must be a thoroughgoing state regulation of consumption. 'Consumption is not a private matter; it is a matter for the community, for the state, for morality and humanity. . . . The years of labour requisite for the production of some delicate embroidery, or some textile marvel, have been filched from the clothing of the poorest among us; the carefully mown lawns of a private garden could with less expenditure of labour have grown wheat; the steam yacht, with its captain and crew, with its stores of food and coal, has been withheld for the whole term of its existence from the possibility of playing a useful part in the world's commerce. Economically regarded, the world, and still more the nation, is a union of producers. Whoever squanders labour, labour-time, or the means of labour, is robbing the community' (p. 78). 'The most obvious way of regulating consumption is an extensive system of taxes on luxury and excessive consumption. In certain spheres these taxes may have to be practically prohibitive. The purposes of such a system must not be fiscal. The revenues derived from the taxation of luxury are accessory. The primary, the exclusive object of taxation is to restrict consumption' (p. 113). And, indeed, consumption should be taxed in such a way that 'in the case of any expenditure beyond a reasonable minimum reckoned at so much per head of population [elsewhere Rathenau mentions three thousand marks as the reasonable yearly expenditure for one family] for each mark consumed a mark should accrue to the state' (p. 83). 'Tobacco and spirits . . . and, above all, manufactured (including home-manufactured) articles of luxury must be heavily taxed, to the extent of several times their original cost of production. . . . The occupation of space must be taxed. Large private parks, extravagant dwelling-places, stables, coach-houses and garages must pay their quota of taxation. Steeply graduated taxation must be imposed upon domestic service. Horses, carriages, and motors, in so far as these are used for purposes of luxury; excessive expenditure upon illumination; costly furniture; rank and title—all should be the objects of taxation, not as a source of revenue to the state, but in order to restrict consumption in these directions' (pp. 113, 114).

However thoroughgoing the taxation of consumption, it can only really touch the outer covering of upper-class privileges; but their very core is affected by Rathenau's proposals for an equalization of property, which amount, indeed, to a complete taxing away of private wealth. 'The distribution of property,' he says, 'is no more a private matter than the right to consumption' (p. 100). One is reminded of Proudhon's icy words—*La propriété c'est le vol*—especially as state interference with the rights of property is a revolutionary conception, associated, in fact, with class war. A multiplicity of owners will combine to form a class, especially when their rights are hereditarily transmissible. They think of increase as well as of security. They may struggle among themselves, but their chief opponent is the subject class, all the more when members of this class are not formally excluded from ownership, but can acquire property, or perhaps already possess a little. It becomes a matter of pressing interest to the owning class that the disinherited should be deprived of all power; that they should be excluded from access to the weapons of culture, organization, and ownership; that they should be allowed only such a modicum of rights and re-

sponsibilities as is essential to the maintenance of the existing
social equilibrium. . . . Two concomitants appear. . . . One
of these is power, which is inseparably associated with ownership, and which tends as time passes to come more into the
foreground. The other is inheritance, traditionally associated
with property, although the association is not perhaps destined
to be permanent. In conjunction, the two constitute the power
of the owning class' (pp. 87, 88). 'Economically considered,
the whole civilized world today lives under the dominion of a
mighty plutocracy' (p. 96). (A variation of the remark for
which he was so bitterly reproached: 'Three hundred men control the economic destiny of the Continent.') 'Plutocracy is
group dominion, oligarchy; and of all forms of oligarchy it is
the most objectionable.' 'Plutocracy does not rest on common
ideas, but on common interests.'

Rathenau now proceeds to examine the ethical and economic
justification of personal wealth. 'Where does personal wealth
come from? How is it acquired?' (p. 101). 'Is wealth savings?
In view of the brevity of human life, a moderate competence
is the utmost that can be saved out of the regular income from
labour. The income which can be heaped up to form riches
is not the reward of labour; it is the winnings of other
categories. The popular notion that any one can grow wealthy
simply in virtue of thrift is erroneous. . . . Any one who
desires to become wealthy must satisfy a widespread economic
demand. But this alone does not suffice, for competition plays
its part. Competitors appear to satisfy a portion of the demand,
and to secure a share in the profits derived from its satisfaction.
In the end the entrepreneur finds that, instead of the anticipated
wealth, he earns no more than average profits, receives merely
the average return for his trouble. The acquisition of wealth,
therefore, is only possible when the entrepreneur can restrict
competition, can raise the profits at pleasure, or can indefinitely
extend the circle of those who are willing to make the requisite

188

IN DAYS TO COME

sacrifice. Nothing but a recognized or an enforced monopoly will put him in such a position' (p. 102). 'Monopolies enrich their holders, and there is no other way to wealth' (p. 103). 'At the same time it is obvious that it would be a very simple matter for legislation to regulate all the sources of individual wealth, and if necessary to take them out of individual hands' (p. 104).

Now, the war has shaken to the roots the conception of the inviolability of private property. State interventions in rights of property, which amount at times to expropriation, are passed over almost without comment; it is taken for granted that the interests of the community take precedence over the economic right of individuals. 'The first step towards the kingdom of the future is the realization that industry is everybody's affair.' Thus the way lies open for the regulation of the conditions of property and the adjustment of differences of property by the state.

Of all the reasons which Rathenau brings forward for abolishing inequalities of property he lays the greatest emphasis on the monopoly in education enjoyed by the children of rich parents. 'Our age . . . cannot fail to recognize that every citizen who, from childhood onwards, is denied access to the cultural advantages of his day is being robbed. Not only is the individual robbed, but the state is likewise cheated' (p. 88). It demands, therefore, universal and equal education. But 'however well-meant this demand, its fulfilment is hampered by many restrictions. . . . From rich mansions and poor tenement houses the members of hostile classes are brought together as school-mates. The former have been well cared for, and possess the class consciousness of the well-to-do; accustomed to listen to the conversation of cultured parents, they have tolerable manners, express themselves with ease, and are already equipped with the elements of knowledge derivable from an environment of good books and works of art; they have gained

189

experience from travel, and have often profited by elementary tuition; they are vigorous and well-nourished, with trained bodies, refreshed by quiet sleep. The others, in all these respects, display opposite characteristics. Now there is demanded from them new behaviour, a new speech, and the adoption of a new outlook; they must leave the familiar circle of life, and while this mere change of scene is already dissipating part of their energy and will-power, they must laboriously acquire a new knowledge which comes so easily to their well-dressed school-mates, and which these already in large measure possess. Embarrassed and helpless, these little citizens often enough grow stubborn when obscurely and painfully they become aware of the great gulf fixed between themselves and their more fortunate companions. Nothing but exceptional strength of will and exceptional talent can bridge this gulf; and, even for the exception, talent and will-power may prove without influence upon the career. As for the others, after a brief contact they relapse into utter hopelessness, blaming not merely outward inequalities of fortune, but their own profound inadequacies' (pp. 88, 89). 'Equality in education can only bear fruit upon the soil of equality in the circumstances of life, equality in domestic conditions, and equality in civic origin. . . . Once again we find ourselves compelled by moral necessity to adopt a policy of economic equality' (p. 90).

Thus Rathenau demands that all private wealth be progressively taxed out of existence by taxes on property and income: 'Not, however, as of old will these be regarded as an ultimate resource for the levying of national revenue, imposed with fear and trembling, and paid with reluctance. Such taxes will imply a recognition of the fact that a person who acquires means beyond what is necessary for the ordinary amenities of civilized life is only the conditional owner of that which he acquires, and the state is fully entitled to relieve him of any or all of it' (p. 114).

This demand, if one takes it seriously, goes far beyond the programme of the Socialists, which, after all, does not exclude inequality of property; it approaches Communism. But did Rathenau mean it seriously? Is it not perhaps simply a red flag which he liked to wave over his ultimately capitalist industrial structure? The answer lies in his whole system. For it is just this demand for the furthest possible equalization of property which is most intimately bound up with his goal: the removal of all obstacles to the free unfolding of man's soul. In fact, under present conditions, it cannot be separated from this aim, in so far as in our civilization lack of education makes inner freedom impossible. Christianity, which also preached the kingdom of inner freedom in the soul of man, was able to dispense with equalization of property and communal ownership, but only when the civilization of antiquity had begun to decline, and when no education or knowledge were necessary to enable one to equal the best of the age in spiritual growth.

But if private property is to be completely abolished, where shall we be able to find another adequate incentive to work? To put it in another way, how is one going to persuade the leaders and pioneers of industry to step forth, to set to work, and accept heavy responsibility, without the enticement of wealth? No objection is so frequently brought up against far-reaching schemes of social reform as this one, that under an economic system in which personal profit is either rigorously restricted or completely forbidden all incitement to progress would be lacking, and hence stagnation or retrogression would be the result. 'May it not be that when society has been deprived of these motive forces, its mechanism will run down; may it not come to pass that the progress of civilization will be arrested; will not the physical and the spiritual goods of mankind fall into decay? Or will forces remain in operation competent to continue the planetary process under purer conditions?' (p. 162). Rathenau replies that there is no cause for anxiety, for the leaders no less

than the liberated proletariat would be moved by other impulses, by joy in creation, love for their work and the feeling
of solidarity, and moved not only to jog along with the others,
but to exert their influence as innovators, leaders, and pioneers.
And more important still, they would be moved by the true
driving forces of the born leader: the will to power and the
desire for responsibility, which impel him, quite apart from
considerations of pleasure and profit, to great achievements and
great risks. Thus the problem of economic leadership in a
society where the individual has no opportunity of enriching
himself does after all admit of solution, 'and that by distin-
guishing clearly the three effective forms of property: the right
to enjoyment, the right to power, and the right to responsibility' (p. 93). That is to say, the leader should be left the prospect of power and responsibility; then one can safely deprive
him of the prospect of personal gain, without making him any
the less creative or happy in his work.

One can count on this all the more confidently when the
forms of industry brought into being by capitalism in its last
stages induce of themselves a 'new way of thinking' in the great
industrialists. In his brilliant little work *Stocks and Shares*
(*Vom Aktienwesen*), published in October, 1917, soon after *In
Days to Come*, which is a sort of reconnaissance before the
break-through to new economic conceptions in *The New
Economy*, Rathenau maintains that 'the great undertaking of
today is no longer purely a system of private interests; it is
rather, both individually and collectively, a national concern
belonging to the community, which owing to its origin still
bears, rightly or wrongly, the marks of an undertaking run
purely for profit, but which for some time and to an increasing
degree has been serving the public interest.' (*Collected Works*,
Vol. V, p. 154.)
'Almost without exception,' he says in the earlier book, *In*

IN DAYS TO COME

Days to Come, 'these enterprises assume the impersonal form
of the joint-stock company. No one is a permanent owner. The
composition of the thousandfold complex which functions as
lord of the undertaking is in a state of perpetual flux. . . .
This condition of things signifies that ownership has been de-
personalized. . . . The depersonalization of ownership simultaneously implies the objectification of the thing owned. The
claims to ownership are subdivided in such a fashion, and are
so mobile, that the enterprise assumes an independent life, as
if it belonged to no one; it takes an objective existence, such as
in earlier days was embodied only in state and church, in a
municipal corporation, in the life of a guild or a religious order.
. . . The executive instruments of an official hierarchy become
the new centre. . . . Even today the paradox is conceivable
that the enterprise might come to own itself by buying out the
individual shareholders with its profits. . . . The depersonalization of ownership, the objectification of enterprise, the
detachment of property from the possessor, leads to a point
where the enterprise becomes transformed into an institution
which resembles the state in character' (pp. 120, 121).

Rathenau describes this state of affairs as the 'autonomy' of
the undertaking. For its juridical position and development he
might have pointed to the old German guild law, which conceived of the guilds not purely as fictive 'juridical' persons de-
riving their rights purely from those of their members, as was
the Roman conception, but as real institutions acting in their
own right, and maintaining their own existence independently
of their members. Gierke had already years ago called attention
to the juridical similarity between the modern joint-stock company and the German conception of the state modelled on that
of medieval German guild law.[2] Thus Rathenau is right in
saying that the depersonalization of ownership transforms the
undertaking into an institution which resembles the state in

[2] Gierke, *Das deutsche Genossenschaftsrecht*, 3 vols., 1868, 1873, 1881.

193

character. For there is no legal difference of principle between such an autonomous industrial undertaking and that association of all the nation's citizens which is known as the state. Naturally enough this objective development of the under-taking is followed by the subjective psychological development of the man in charge of it. 'In so far as leaders of private enter-prise on a large scale still exist, they have long been accustomed to regard their businesses as independent entities, incorporated objectively as companies. Such an entity has its own personal responsibility; it works, grows, makes contracts and alliances on its own account; it is nourished by its own profits; it lives for its own purposes. The fact that it nourishes the proprietor may be purely accessory, and in most cases is not the main point. A good man of business will incline to restrict unduly his own and his family's consumption, in order to provide more abundant means for the strengthening and extension of the firm. The growth and the power of this organism is a delight to the owner, a far greater delight than lucre. The desire for gain is overshadowed by ambition and by the joy of creation. Such an outlook is accentuated among the heads of great corporate undertakings. Here we already encounter an official idealism identical with that which prevails in the state service. The execu-tive officials labour for the benefit of times when in all human probability they will long have ceased to be associated with the enterprise. Almost without exception they do their utmost to reserve for the undertaking the larger moiety of its profits, and to distribute no more than the lesser moiety in the form of dividends, although to the detriment of their individual in-comes. . . . Covetousness, as the motive force, has been com-pletely superseded by the sense of responsibility. Thus the psyche of the industrialist works in the same direction as the evolution of the conditions of ownership' (pp. 122, 123). In other words, the power which a gigantic concern of this sort offers the industrialist is so fascinating that it constitutes in itself an incitement to the greatest efforts, even if it does not bring him much reward.

But here one encounters another objection: would not the result of the universal equalization of property simply be to make everybody equally poor? Rathenau calculates that on the scale of production in pre-war Germany, and making allowance for the necessary reserve for the renewal and extension of the means of production, each family would be entitled to an income of about three thousand marks. Even if one increases this to, say, four thousand marks present value, it would preclude all but the most modest style of living. And therefore the most pressing task of the new industry is 'so to increase its efficiency by internal reorganization that the produce of human labour if distributed fairly and naturally will ensure decent conditions of life to the individual and free cultural development to the community.' (*The New Economy*, p. 207.) And its economic goal would be 'to raise the standard of industrial activity' (p. 208).

Practically, therefore, perhaps the most important and incontrovertible part of Rathenau's programme of reform is that which relates to the heightening of productivity and the better satisfaction of demand. 'Theoretically,' he says, 'the extent to which the efficiency of an industry can be increased is quite unlimited. One can imagine factories so completely mechanized that one man would suffice to keep the whole clockwork of production going. In fact, there are certain works, particularly in the chemical and electrical industry, which have very nearly reached this state already. Now suppose we had a country equipped with a thousand such works; the amount of goods it could produce is beyond calculation, and the individual's share of the consumption, in so far as the system of distribution was tolerably just, would be as large as he liked. And as for a shortage of raw materials throughout the earth, that is such a remote possibility that we need not let it worry us here.

'But we shall not arrive at complete mechanization of the

195

means of production all at one blow. All we can do is to speed up the process to a certain point. For all mechanization demands reorganization, and this is the result of a stupendous sum of stored-up labour and inventive skill, of living capital. . . . It cannot proceed more quickly than the world's annual saving of labour, which is of equal significance. . . . All saving of labour helps to further the reorganization of world industry, and its progress in the course of centuries will mean the heightening of the effectiveness of labour, the increase of goods available for consumption, the shortening of working hours and the raising of the standard of living. . . . Hence every hour wasted owing to imperfect technical development is a national loss' (p. 208 ff.).

From the standpoint of wasted labour Rathenau criticizes our present economic system root and branch. Its basic defect is 'the wrong turning given, wittingly or unwittingly, to the whole process of production' (p. 211). This is the outcome of unregulated competition and the concentration on profit and nothing but profit, which means satisfying the demand for luxuries before dealing with the demand for the necessities of life. 'We spend from two to three thousand millions yearly on intoxicating liquors, we squander hundreds of millions on show and all manner of rubbishy trifles, we allow tens of thousands of able-bodied men to lurk behind the shop counters of our great cities, and hundreds of thousands virtually to live in railway carriages the whole year round fighting out the competitive struggle for business orders, with the result that at the end of the year each firm has sold neither much more nor much less than last year. Now all this betokens not merely a loss in national saving, but a positive misdirection of the whole process of production, through which labour and materials are wasted to an incalculable degree, factories lie idle, the cost of production is heightened and the power to compete with other countries sensibly diminished' (p. 212).

196

IN DAYS TO COME

Thus the organization of industry is wrong in general; but it is also wrong and wasteful in particular. Rathenau enumerates its defects in organization under four heads:

1. With the same resources and the same working hours, different factories produce an astonishingly unequal quantity of goods. The causes of under-production in many works are: wrong situation, antiquated machinery, and failure to utilize new technical devices for saving power and labour. Germany's coal consumption alone could be diminished by half if all factories were run on scientific lines and all sources of power made accessible. And this saving would itself be completely eclipsed by the gain in labour, materials and transport, and the increase in productivity and turnover, if this reorganization were extended simultaneously to plant and situation, to equipment and the running of the concern (p. 216 ff.).

2. Splitting up of production in factories and types, which gets in the way of a systematic and scientifically thought-out division of labour between the different factories, and hence prevents mass production. 'The entire modern system of production is based on the idea of mass control and division of labour. . . . But whereas within the individual factory the division of labour is carried out consciously and to an increasing extent, from factory to factory and between the various groups it is still left in the main simply to tradition and to the chance workings of the principle of equilibrium. The group division of labour, if I may so call it, has made the greatest progress in England and America, where consumption is at its highest and production at its most uniform. The English cotton industry owes much of its world supremacy to this fact. There are important English factories which spin no more than two or three different qualities; whereas with us infinitely smaller concerns find themselves compelled to undertake both coarse and fine spinning at the same time.

197

· WALTHER RATHENAU

'It is impossible to foresee the extent of the economy and increase in production that would result from a scientific allotment of labour between the different groups. But the specialist can get some idea of what would happen if he reflects that all intermediate factories would be transformed into specialist factories, always working full time at the one kind of work, with staffs of picked specialists devoting all their energies to the development of their own particular province, without having to be responsible for any odd piece of work that happened to turn up' (pp. 217, 218).

This division of labour between the different factories in the same branch of industry presupposes, of course, an extensive standardization of production. 'If Germany succeeds—and it will succeed, though perhaps not under private enterprise—in carrying normalization and reduction to type to the point demanded by a really scientific labour system, then with an appropriate division of work between factory and factory one could be sure of at least doubling one's productivity, though equipment and working costs remained the same' (p. 221).

3. If what may be termed the horizontal division of labour between different factories dealing with the same stage of production is thoroughly uneconomic, so is that vertical division which exists between factories which handle raw material in its progress from intermediate product to semi-product and final product, and then on its way from the last manufacturer to the wholesale dealers, large and small, the retailer, and the consumer. 'The time spent on commercial travelling and the distribution of trifling luxuries and articles of consumption, such as tobacco, stationery, soap, involves the loss to industry of whole armies of young and able-bodied men, whose numbers easily run into six figures' (p. 224).

4. Finally, we lack adequate protection for the country's industry: protection against competition from without and waste from within. So long as economic nationalism rules the world,

198

we cannot, to our cost, employ foreign workmen or officials, or pay interest on foreign loans. This state of things 'will ultimately help people to realize that the industry of the world is and ought to be a communal industry' (p. 226). But 'above all we cannot allow the old and absolute right, dating from the time when there was a surplus of resources, to remain intact— the right of every one who can afford it to employ the labour resources of the nation for his personal comfort and show, or for any supposedly industrial purpose he thinks fit. . . . Hitherto every heir or recipient of a dowry has been at liberty to surround himself with a swarm of lackeys; or, if he wanted to engage in industry, to employ workmen, foremen, and officials, with the help of whom and of the machinery he had raked together he was free to start on any sphere of industry which interested him or seemed likely to prove profitable. In future the needs of the community must be the deciding factor. This question of objective, scientifically demonstrable, and verifiable requirements will form the central point in all scientific decisions' (p. 228).

The eradication of these mistakes, the reorganization of industry along proper lines, the progressive increase of production with a view to heightening the general standard of living, the supersession of private enterprise by a communal industrial system based on demand—these things cannot be left to the play of *laisser faire*. With a blunt directness which is a little difficult to reconcile with his contempt for 'technical organization' as contrasted with changes of mental attitude, Rathenau advocates a systematic 'New Economy' carried through with the necessary powers and afterwards consolidated by definite regulations. 'The division of labour according to groups can no more be left to the free play of forces than the internal technical reform of individual factories; this task, like the others, can only be accomplished by a comprehensive reorganization of industry.

199

For good intentions alone, unless they go hand in hand with supreme authority, are helpless in the face of the arbitrary splitting up of markets' (p. 218).

His own experiences in connection with Germany's war industry must have convinced him of the necessity for some authority strong enough to overcome all obstacles to a thorough reorganization, and for some means of consolidating the new system once it had been introduced. The consideration of what this authority should be and how it should come into being naturally raises the question whether a dictatorship of the proletariat or of some other group, say a Fascist dictatorship, which could avail itself of the resources of the state, would be necessary for this purpose. When Rathenau wrote *The New Economy*, the Russian Revolution had already taken place. Yet he himself had no belief in the success either of a sudden revolutionary transformation or of one brought about by over-hasty, though peaceful, means; because both the necessary increase of the means of production on the basis of economy, and the equally necessary change of mental attitude, must needs be slow to take effect. Thus the only transformation possible is a slow one; one which follows in the wake of increased production and changes in public opinion, though at the same time one which is consciously directed by its leaders and supported by the resources of the state.

Having dealt with the necessity for a change of attitude and for adequate authority, Rathenau then proceeds to depict in detail that new organization of industry for which he is striving, the ultimate product of which would be his New Economy. 'Let us imagine,' he says, 'that all factories of the same kind, whether industrial, commercial, or mechanical, are co-ordinated, say, all cotton spinning mills, all iron rope factories, all joiners' works, all wholesale dealers in goods, all in separate units; imagine further that each of these associations is co-ordinated with the other businesses connected with it, and thus that the whole of

200

the cotton industry, the iron industry, the timber industry, and the linen industry are amalgamated in separate groups. The first of these organizations we may call functional unions, the second industrial unions. . . . Associations of this type already exist in large numbers and in every field, but they serve only private interests, not industry in general. Functional and industrial unions would be corporations recognized and supervised by the state, enjoying extensive rights of their own' (p. 231).

Actually the most important element in the foundation on which Rathenau is building is not simply the combination of works of the same kind into unions, but over and above this the object for which they are combined: for they are not to be simply representative of private interests, but, like the War Companies, are to serve the community. Rathenau rightly insists that it is this fact which fundamentally distinguishes them from those industrial unions, combines, cartels, and trusts which are becoming increasingly common even under the present system of private enterprise. The value of the new order of industry to be built on them would therefore depend before everything else upon the means by which, and the degree to which, they could be brought into relation with these communal aims.

'The most important of the two types of organization,' says Rathenau, 'is the functional union. . . . It is not only closely related to the neighbouring groups, but also to the workers, the public and the state. . . . In form, the functional union most resembles a limited company, in its activity, a combine. The individual undertakings are interested in the company (*i.e.* in the functional union as company) according to their productive capacity; they elect the management, which in its turn nominates the directors. . . . Each undertaking delivers its goods to the combine (*i.e.* to the functional union as combine) in so far as they belong to the industrial circle of the union; those goods which require further treatment are taken at a discount.

... The union is responsible for selling the goods at prices which are graded for the small and large consumer, the trader and those who will work upon the goods further, respectively; the person who uses the goods himself also has to pay the price for the completion of the manufacturing process.

'So far there has been little to distinguish either the structure or the activity of the union from that of any other syndicate. The differences begin with the co-operation of the state. . . . The state grants the functional union important rights, sometimes almost amounting to prerogatives: the right to accept or reject new participants, the exclusive right to purchase home and imported goods, the right to close down unproductive factories with compensation, the right to purchase concerns for the purpose of closing them down, converting or developing them. . . . In return, the state demands a share in supervising the administration; it demands also that the union shall work for the common good; and finally it demands a proportion of the profits. . . . The state is represented on the management . . . in addition to the workers' (p. 231 *ff.*).

What are the activities of the functional union? Rathenau mentions among others:

'The organization and handling of sales and export, and extension of markets.

'The procuring, and, if necessary, the importation, of raw materials and other materials with the assistance of commerce; the importation of manufactured goods, in so far as, and so long as, home production is inadequate.

'The increase and cheapening of production through the dissemination of technical experience, the improvement and reequipment of factories, the closing down of unproductive works and the purchase of those that are obstructive or badly managed; if necessary, the erection and maintenance of its own model factories and the extension and, when required, the financing of suitably situated and productively run concerns.

'The preparation and execution of a large-scale and scientifically thought-out scheme for the division of labour between factory and factory, and between district and district. The distribution of quotas for production, and the deciding voice and co-operation in the erection of new factories.

'The introduction of uniform types, norms, and models; the cutting down of the quite superfluous types for show purposes.

'Negotiations and relations with the neighbouring unions of the same industry, with unions of officials and workers; representation of the interests of the union before the government and legislature' (p. 234 ff.).

Thus it is not the state, nor any official department, but the functional union (in the administration of which the state co-operates through its representatives) which effects the transformation of industry, and which, in conjunction with the other functional unions, works out its scheme, rationalizes and standardizes production, is responsible for technical progress, and regulates import and export. Behind it, but with extremely self-restricted powers, stands the state.

But, it may be objected, will not these unions of carpenters, cotton spinners, weavers, printers, hat makers, glove makers, will not all these unions become modernized guilds in the spirit of the Meistersinger period and relapse into red tape and nepotism? Rathenau answers, 'No.' For the functional union is not an association of small and individual autonomous concerns, formed to protect individual interests, 'but rather a community of production, in which all the members are organically bound up with one another, to right and left, above and below, in which they are welded into a living unity, possessed of a common vision, judgment, and will—in fact, not a confederation, but an organism' (p. 235). He might have added that the co-operation of the community, and especially of the consumers, in its management would alone preclude the danger of a relapse into the fossilized condition of the medieval guilds.

203

The functional unions would thus become the nerve centres of the new industry. 'The activity of the industrial unions is more simple and fundamental than that of the functional unions.' The main tasks of the organized industry as a unit consist in adjustment and mediation between the functional unions. Generally speaking, there is no profit-making community within the industrial union, and it need not therefore have the outward form of a company run for profit; it is sufficient that it should have the form of a union formed to promote an object (p. 238). Negotiations between different functional unions take place within the framework of the industrial union over questions of demand, times of delivery, mode of payment, complaints of the workers, development, limitation of output. 'Every one who is well acquainted with industry will appreciate the enormous advantage which is obtained from a review of one's requirements if possible every year. When one knows at regular intervals the quantity and quality of rails, yarn, kettles, motors, accessories, chemicals, or panes of glass that will be required, it is possible to draw up far-reaching programmes for manufacture and distribution of work, with the result that all factories work permanently at top pressure, production is enormously cheapened, large warehouses are no longer necessary, traffic is diminished, work speeded up, capital and interest saved, and efficiency raised generally. Each industry in its entirety can estimate the extent of the demand both at home and abroad. . . . Trade between union and union does away with the middleman, and there is no further need for the countless branch depôts, the hundreds of thousands of commercial travellers, and the dead warehouses, dead stock, doubtful credit, and surreptitious financing. . . . But trade still has its function, though in a new form. Goods have to be collected from the various sources into repositories, they have to be sent from the repositories along various channels, and overseas and inter-state connections have to be kept up' (p. 238 *ff.*).

Who will finance the new industry—*i.e.* who will take the financial risk of developing existing undertakings or creating new ones? 'If we consider,' says Rathenau, 'the actual functioning of large-scale private property, looking at the matter in a purely mechanical way and leaving aside ethico-social implications, we see that such property performs a duty which . . . is of great importance from the economic point of view. Private property shoulders the risks of the world economy.

'All the enterprises of the capitalist system share common characteristics; they all require large means, and they are all risky. The revenue department of any properly organized community can supply the requisite means. Much more difficult, however, is it for a municipality or a state to engage in bold ventures. These corporations lack the passionate stimulus of private enterprise; the sense of responsibility renders them timid; they are devoid of that autocratic and instinctive judgment which makes the prospects of success outweigh the possibilities of danger. Onlookers are apt to imagine that specialized skill can provide a substitute for the aforesaid incisive powers of judgment, but the desiderated substitute will not prove effective when the risks of great enterprises are under consideration; the experts will differ among themselves, and by the time they have settled their differences, the favourable opportunity will have been lost.

'Private capital secures ample funds by the joint-stock method; it encounters the risks of enterprise by indefatigable endeavours towards success and profit; it overcomes the uncertainties of the future by exercising the greatest possible care in the choice of its agents, and by the number and variety of its enterprises.

'Hitherto this demand could be met only by means of the surplus capital which, accumulating in the hands of the well-to-do after these had consumed all they considered requisite for daily life, clamoured for reinvestment and increase. The smaller savings were satisfied with increased security and less risk.

'The question now arises, what new capitalistic forms will replace private enterprise, when the superfluities of individual wealth have disappeared owing to the diffusion of a general and equalized well-being?' (*In Days to Come*, pp. 119, 120.)

To this Rathenau replies that almost all big concerns are constituted in the form of companies, and directed by officials who have to bear at least the moral risk for all new ventures or developments of existing ones. And if these undertakings become communal in the sense of the New Economy, very little alteration will really be necessary. 'If the constitution [of such an undertaking] be wisely drafted, the enterprise will be able to provide for all future requirements of capital, however extensive these may become. Its first resource will be to lay hands on the revenues which hitherto from year to year it has distributed to the shareholders. Next, temporarily or permanently, it can issue debentures. In case of need it can retract a step and issue new shares. Above all, if under the protection of a state whose wealth is inexhaustible (the state of the New Economy is such a state, because it acquires by taxation all the wealth of private individuals and practically the complete revenue of all undertakings) and if subjected to the control of this state, it has a right to expect that in case of need the state will provide it with funds in return for sufficient guarantees. Nay, more, the state itself will wish and demand that autonomous enterprises shall be willing at any time, under proper supervision, to take over and to invest surpluses from the state treasury' (p. 122).

In actual fact a very considerable proportion of big undertakings all over the world today are financed by these methods, for the participation or supervision of a state or community has transformed them into communal industrial concerns. In Germany, according to Professor Julius Hirsch, the capital of all such big undertakings amounts to fifty-two thousand million marks. (*Report of the Berlin Chamber of Industry and Commerce*, March 10th, 1927, p. 224.) According to the *Report on Britain's Industrial Future*, which the British Liberal party recently compiled with Professor Keynes's help, the capital of the big undertakings in Great Britain which are more or less socialized in this sense amounts to four thousand million pounds, which the Report estimates to be about two-thirds of the total capital invested in large British undertakings. (*Britain's Industrial Future*, 1928, p. 74.)

In other words, in the New Economy the state in its capacity of banker, the state bank, will absorb almost the whole net profit of the country's industry by taxing consumption, income and property; and thus, together with municipal bodies and the like, will acquire what is practically unlimited power over the maintenance, development and foundation of undertakings. But the risk involved in founding and developing these undertakings will have to be borne in the main by the functional unions with the financial support of the state or the municipality. Hence it is not surprising that no provision is made in the New Economy for a body which shall protect the industrial unions, regulate the relations between them, and in fact have control over the industry as a whole. Nevertheless the functions of such a body Rathenau considers indispensable—*i.e.* 'the determining of what materials, by what means, and to what ends both the individual and the community shall carry on production.'

For the regulator of the whole industrial structure is in fact the state. 'Every one of the changes which we have demanded on moral, social and economic grounds will strengthen the powers and completeness of the state. The state will become the moving centre of all economic life. Whatever society does will be done through the state and for the sake of the state. It will dispose of the powers and the means of its members with greater freedom than the old territorial potentates; the greater part of

the economic surplus will accrue to it: all the well-being of the
country will be incorporated in the state. There will be an end
of economico-social stratification, and consequently the state will
assume all the powers now wielded by the dominant classes.
The spiritual forces under its control will be multiplied. . . .
The state in which the popular will has thus been embodied and
made manifest cannot be a class state. . . . We are faced with
the demand for a People's State.' (*In Days to Come*, p. 203.)

From his first political article *The New Era* (1907) onwards Rathenau had consistently advocated the effective participation of the people in the affairs of the nation and the right of
their leaders to hold important state positions. Thus the fact
that during the war he put forward these same demands with
redoubled vigour did not imply any change of faith. For the
'People's State' simply means a state in which the most gifted
personalities from the ranks of the people are free to rise to the
highest offices of state and in which each individual has a voice
in all decisions which affect his interests or outlook. The opposite
of the People's State is the feudal state, in which rank and
property alone lead to the top and in which momentous decisions
lie entirely outside the control of those they concern. The German Empire under William II. was no longer the complete
feudal state; it was a mixture, a mongrel incapable of survival.
For whereas the outstanding positions in the industrial world
were open to fairly wide sections of the people, the leading
posts in the army and administration were still filled in accordance with feudal principles; and the people's right to control
their own destinies in political questions was merely theoretical,
while in practice they were deprived of this right by the astute
manoeuvrings of the ruling class, the servility of the people's
representatives and the indifference of the middle classes.
We know what importance Rathenau attached to free selec-

tion from the broad masses of the people for political and administrative office, not only after, but long before the war. In this connection the particular form of the constitution does not matter very much. Under a monarchy of the English or Swedish type the method of selection may be on the broadest possible basis, whereas a republic can put all sorts of formidable obstacles in the way of talent. 'These things,' as Rathenau once said, speaking of political corruption, 'are not matters of the form, but of the essence; they are psychological traits of the peoples from which they spring.' Hence those who refuse to recognize Rathenau as a true democrat, because he subordinated the form of the state to its spirit, misunderstand the real depth of his conviction. He was not satisfied with the mere name, but demanded the thing itself.

He considered the best apparatus for the selection of political talent to be Parliament through the agency of political parties. 'The parliamentary system,' he says, 'is indispensable, because it is a school for, and a means of selecting, statesmen and politicians.' That is 'the real meaning of the parliaments of our age.' (*In Days to Come.*) At the same time, they still fulfil their original function of providing a means by which the people can exercise its control, even though in a very inadequate and partial fashion. And in view of this inadequacy Rathenau adopts the new conception which has arisen in France, America, and England in the course of the last generation on the basis of Gierke's guild idea, the conception of councils—*i.e.* the view that each group of men who fulfil a common function act in their own right, and that the state merely exists as the supreme arbiter between these various groups. It follows from this that, owing to the impossibility of doing justice to the enormous variety of interests in the modern state, the individual can exercise his rights in a reasonable, genuine, and effective way only through the medium of these groups. The autonomous joint-stock company, which has cut itself loose from its shareholders and become an independent organism, may have predisposed Rathenau to this conception; though it is hardly necessary to point out that the idea of councils which he adopted is far bolder and more revolutionary than this, since this new form of association demands far-reaching independence even in relation to the state; in fact, it almost amounts to a state within the state.

In *The New State* (*Der Neue Staat*), published in May, 1919, Rathenau proceeds from the principle that 'the purely political conception of the state no longer reigns single and supreme; there is room for new types of organism.' (*The New State*, p. 269.) He considers it a 'paradox' that the modern man readily allows 'all his faculties to be subordinated to politics. . . . Not that I believe that these purely political questions will cease to have any meaning in the future. They will exist along with others. . . . But they will lose their supremacy; in fact, they have already lost it. . . . While the imperialism of the ruling classes was reaching its height, the state had already become an adjustment of various interests, a mechanism for organization and administration with incomplete autonomy. . . . But the centralistic conceptions remained, though they had lost all meaning' (pp. 270, 271).

Today, however, 'it is becoming clear that the idea of the wise, central power and parliamentary self-government is nothing but a fiction. It is assumed that even though great political questions no longer determine the fate of nations, one single body of mediocrities must know, understand, judge, and decide all fundamental questions relating to the different departments of national life. . . . Not only must it; it actually believes that it can' (p. 272 *ff.*). The reality is the very opposite of this fiction. Rathenau's point of view coincides with that of Léon Duguit, Professor of Constitutional Law in the University of Bordeaux, as expressed in his masterly book, *Les Transforma-*

tions du droit public. In this he argues that the supposed
sovereignty of the state is continually being resolved into small,
individual sovereignties of specialized groups which actually
(since the state is no longer in a position to survey them effec-
tively) exercise sovereignty by taking ultimate decisions in the
most varied departments of modern life. Rathenau says of the
modern state: 'It has already become a collection of imaginary
states, a multiplicity of slanting cones on the same level, the
points of which are lost in the parliamentary clouds. Strictly
speaking, in addition to the political and juridical state there are
the military, the ecclesiastical, and the administrative state, the
educational state, and the commercial and industrial state. All
these states are autonomous, even though they are subordinated
to the supreme, political state in some cardinal respects. Though
they are almost independent, they are individually and collectively stunted. For they lack a foundation in the soil of the
people, even though certain of them, especially the ecclesiastical
and the administrative states, have, as it were, thin, tenuous
roots in local self-governing institutions. They receive their
popular admixture solely through the medium of the communal
and completely inadequate central organism of the political
parliament' (p. 287). 'The first thing to be done, I maintain,
is to separate these interwoven states from one another and then
to build them up in a realistic spirit and give them an independent existence, subordinated though they must be to a political head. Thus we should create the new state, the state of the
future; thus we should create the true democracy' (p. 289).

Hence the ideal is far-reaching decentralization, according
to functions, not geographical areas; self-determination, not of
the country, but of the function. Only in this way will each
individual win a real share, and not only a paper one, in determining the infinitely involved circumstances of his life. It is
true that apart from a few mutilated remains, such as the
National Industrial Council and Factory Councils, Rathenau

failed to secure the embodiment of these proposals in the new
German constitution for which they were intended. He was as
unsuccessful as I had been some time before with the proposals
I had worked out for the German League of Nations scheme;
proposals which started from the same standpoint as Rathenau's, and which, though advocated by the then German Foreign Minister, Count Rantzau, and by his legal adviser, the
then chief of the legal department of the Foreign Office, Dr.
Simons, were ultimately turned down by the German Cabinet.
The course of development, however, is bound to proceed along
these lines. Symptomatic of it are the new constitutional laws
of Russia and Italy, which, although proceeding from opposite
poles of thought, nevertheless agree in subordinating the
regional to the functional principle. We have here the beginnings of a counter-movement to nationalism, before which both
nationalists and internationalists must bow, for it is an inevitable
product of the extreme complexity of modern life, and hence it
is bound finally to triumph. Rathenau was right in feeling that
only a functionally decentralized state and a functionally organized world could provide the appropriate framework for the
New Economy, the New Society, and the New Commonwealth
of Mankind.

The success of *In Days to Come* and *The New Economy*
was sensational. After the semi-failure of *The Mechanism of
the Mind* the sudden success of these two books put even the
most successful novels in the shade. The first edition of 5,000
copies of *In Days to Come*, published in February, 1917, was
followed by one of 8,000 in March and by another of 11,000 in
April. In little more than a year, by the middle of 1918, 65,000
copies of *In Days to Come* had been sold, while 30,000
copies of *The New Economy* were disposed of in the first
month after publication, January, 1918. Walther Rathenau be-

came the most widely read and most passionately discussed of German writers.[3]

Looking back upon the entire field and the probable effects of his proposed reforms, Rathenau says: 'These measures would have a more far-reaching effect on the whole sphere of moral and social relationships than any other revolution of modern times.' (*In Days to Come.*) True. But can we number among these effects those for the sake of which the whole reform was demanded—that is to say, the increased freedom of man, the broadening and progressive enlargement of the region within which he can develop his soul? Would they succeed in transforming into men again the millions of beasts of burden that work the industrial world machine? This is the touchstone that Rathenau applies to every proposal for political, industrial and social reform. Not whether it strengthens the state, increases production, or effects a more just and uniform distribution of the products of labour. All these things are important, but not decisive. What is really vital is whether it makes men finer, deeper, spiritually richer, and freer from external and internal inhibitions. 'It is not a question,' he writes in a letter, 'of searching out hidden talent from the masses of the proletariat, or of making ministers out of trades-union secretaries; that is all very well, but of quite minor importance. What does matter is that what you call the mob should be able to grow into men and children of God, should become, in spite of all their weaknesses and vices, free men, not good menials or loyal subjects.' (*Letters, New Series.* Letter 142 of 29.11. 1919.)

Whether a state of society is attainable in which such things are possible depends, as Rathenau himself points out, on a num-

[3] These figures, like those previously quoted, are taken from the admirable Bibliography of Walther Rathenau's Works, compiled by Dr Ernst Gottlieb of the Ministry of the Interior, which he has been good enough to place at my disposal.

213

ber of considerations: on whether solidarity and the sense of responsibility prove to be sufficiently powerful, without the pressure of poverty or the stimulus of wealth, to maintain, in fact to increase, the process of production; on whether this heightening of production is always and increasingly in advance of the growth of the population; on whether a new attitude of mind makes it possible to utilize this increase of production, not for the greatest profit, but where it is most needed; on whether democracy (the People's State) is sufficiently powerful to go on adjusting the differences in wealth by constitutional methods, without occasioning any violent convulsion. I have already given Rathenau's reasons for believing that these conditions can be fulfilled. He has himself emphasized the fact that this will be a slow process and that therefore the New Economy and the New Society will only gradually come into being. Are his plans, and in particular his New Economy, for that reason Utopian? The development which has taken place in the course of the last few years proves, I think, the contrary—namely, that they were essentially an accurate forecast of what is actually, though very slowly and gradually, taking place.

A beginning, a not yet fully grown branch of the New Economy, has been in existence since 1919: the organization of the German coal and potash industries. By the laws promulgated by the National Assembly on March 23rd and April 24th, 1919, the management of the coal and potash industries was transformed into self-governing corporations under the supervision of the state. Their constitution and functions more or less correspond to Rathenau's 'industrial unions,' though there is no socialization—*i.e.* no direct or indirect expropriation of the owners. It is, however, definitely laid down—and this is the decisive point—that these associations do not merely represent private interests, but discharge their functions 'under the supervision of the state according to communal industrial principles.'[4] The state has confined its intervention to this super-vision, except for reserving the right to reduce, in the interests of the community, the prices determined by the self-governing corporations. It is the latter which direct the business. At the head of the coal organization is a National Coal Council, which comprises representatives of the coal owners, miners, coal mer-chants, consumers, and the separate states; the Reich is repre-sented by the Minister of Labour. This 'coal parliament' di-rects the entire German fuel industry, including export and im-port, according to communal industrial principles. Under this parliamentary controlling body all the coal owners are united into geographical groups, 'coal combines,' according to districts, for administrative purposes, and particularly in connection with the selling of coal. The 'coal combines' in their turn are united into a 'National Coal Union,' which is a functional organ, the executive of the 'National Coal Council,' and is particularly concerned with the periodical fixing of prices.

This organization has many important defects. But the fusion of the German mining industry into one state-controlled self-governing body has proved in practice to have such advantages over the English method that, after studying the German sys-tem, a British Conservative, Mr. Robert Boothby, M.P., in a speech in the House of Commons on February 10th, 1928, ad-vocated a similar fusion and organization in the case of the thousand and one mutually competitive English undertakings, which were all conducted on the basis of profit alone, without consideration of the interests of the public; only by this means could they render themselves able to meet competition and be capable of acting as a unit.[5]

[4] Par. 2 of the Law relating to the Coal Industry of March 23rd, 1919, condi-tions, Par. 47. Conditions for the application of the Law regarding the regulation of the Potash Industry of July 18th, 1919, Par. 51.

[5] Boothby repeated his arguments in a more precise form in an article in *The Nation* of March 10th, 1928, entitled *An Economic Locarno.·*

215

Another element of the New Economy has been realized in the National Industrial Council, which, though crippled at the outset by those responsible for its birth, represents in its electoral body—composed of employers, employees and consumers, divided according to industrial groups—the skeleton of what is manifestly a functional organization of the entire system of German industry.

But the main way in which the New Economy is taking shape is in the concentration of whole branches of industry into national and international combines, cartels, and trusts. At present, in Germany, as we have just shown, coal and potash have made the greatest strides in this direction, but other great industries are following their lead. Iron and steel, electricity and chemistry, are already far on the way to fusion into national associations. These certainly only represent the private interests of business enterprise at present, but they will inevitably bring along with them communal control and a communal industrial organization, and are helping forward the functional, as against the regional, principle of administration, in that they find themselves compelled to amalgamate with similar functional organisms in other countries.

These, then, are the first steps towards the New Economy. They are finger-posts along the path to which Rathenau pointed. Another indication that he sketched out the lines of future development in an essentially accurate fashion is afforded by the fact that his proposals coincide with those of the most influential and progressive thinkers in the two great industrial countries of Europe, Germany and England. His views approximate most closely to those of the English Guild Socialists, who, like him, have laid the emphasis throughout not on wages, but on freedom, and who seek to obtain this freedom by similar means. From its earliest beginnings English Socialism has been distinguished from its Continental equivalent by the

IN DAYS TO COME

emphasis it has laid on human freedom and dignity. Its fore-
runners and its founders, Robert Owen, John Ruskin (*Unto
This Last*), William Morris (*Signs of Change*), Oscar Wilde
(*The Soul of Man Under Socialism*), its most important philosopher, Bertrand Russell (*Principles of Social Reconstruction
and Roads to Freedom*), have always consistently held to the
principle that the chief concern of social reform or revolution
should be man as such and his soul, not his greater or smaller
share in the products of his labour. This English socialism
found its most characteristic expression shortly before the war
in Guild Socialism. One of the leaders of· this movement,
G. D. H. Cole, inquires in his book, *Self-Government in Industry* (London, 1917, p. 110): 'What, I want to ask, is the
fundamental evil in our modern Society which we should set
out to abolish? There are two possible answers to that question,
and I am sure that very many well-meaning people would
make the wrong one. They would answer POVERTY when they
ought to answer SLAVERY. . . . Poverty is the symptom; slavery the disease. The extremes of riches and destitution follow
inevitably upon the extremes of licence and bondage. The many
are not enslaved because they are poor; they are poor because
they are enslaved. Yet Socialists have all too often fixed their
eyes upon the material misery of the poor without realizing
that it rests upon the spiritual degradation of the slave.'

There is no need to point out how nearly this passage expresses Rathenau's fundamental attitude. And in their schemes
of reform the guild socialists are equally near him. They, too,
desire the organization of industry and the state according to
'functional' groups. They, too, want each group to be self-governing within the limits of its function, and every circle of interests therefore to have its own representation in the political
parliament. They, too, contemplate functional and industrial
unions, the so-called 'Guilds,' which amalgamate the different
callings and trades into self-governing bodies under the super-

217

vision of the state. In return for the privileges which each
functional group enjoys, it would be incumbent upon it to perform its functions as efficiently as possible, to increase its functional energies to the utmost, and hence open the path to all
talent that exists within the group, in order that this talent
might find free expression without being inhibited by the limitations of the function which the group serves.

Thus, through its conception of function, Guild Socialism arrives at a new and broadened foundation for human freedom.
Man must be free, not merely in general, as an individual, as a
'contemporary,' as like among like; he must be free also in a
special sense as an *active* individual, specifically, as unlike
among unlike, as one who performs a function along with others, as the member of a group engaged on some specific function within human society, in order that his energies may contribute in their full force to the strengthening of that function,
to the strengthening of the group in its functional activity.
Thus we have a conception of democracy which extends far beyond the political province in that it embraces all spheres of human life and must, in course of time, transform them. That is
the conception of a universal functional democracy, which com-
pletes the one-sided purely political democracy, and whose aim
can be summed up in Nietzsche's stirring words: 'To win freedom for renewed creation.'[6]

Meanwhile similar views have gained a footing in German
Social Democracy under the influence of Otto Bauer and the
present German Minister of Finance, Dr Hilferding, and have
pushed the earlier State Socialist schemes into the background.

[6] I have taken these remarks almost word for word from my article on 'Guild
Socialism' in the Sunday edition of the *Vossische Zeitung* for August 8th, 1920.
The idea of Guild Socialism was first mooted by Arthur J. Penty in his book
The Restoration of the Guild System (London, 1906). The best account of the
aims of Guild Socialism in its later development is given in G. D. H. Cole's *Self-
Government in Industry* (London, 1917) and *Chaos and Order in Industry* (Lon-
don, 1920), S. G. Hobson and A. R. Orage's *National Guilds* (London, 1919),
and Bertrand Russell's *Roads to Freedom* (London, 1918).

218

In fact, the leading Social Democrats in the Socialization Commission, Kautsky, Hilferding, and Lederer, rejected in the most emphatic terms the proposal to nationalize the coal mines. The reason they gave was that 'the absorption of the coal industry in the normal state machine, with its bureaucratic constitution, would seriously interfere with the economic working of the mines.' (Report of the Socialization Commission, p. 32.) They formulated their aims in the following terms: 'Democracy in the factories with unified control of the whole industry, the elimination of capital as the dominant factor, the basing of industry upon the personalities who perform the creative work' (*loc cit.*, p. 35, Majority Report). The only fundamental distinction between them and Rathenau is that the Social Democrats propose to expropriate the owners of those concerns which are ready for socialization with compensation, while Rathenau's scheme secures the same object in practice by slowly but progressively taxing away property without compensation. From Rathenau's point of view, however, this difference is fundamental, for the progressive taxing away of property and income over and above a certain modicum would abolish for ever the distinction between rich and poor, whereas expropriation with compensation would not; the expropriated owners could always invest their wealth either in non-socialized concerns or else abroad. This abolition of differences in wealth was, indeed, Rathenau's particular aim, for by this means everybody would be assured the same opportunities for education, inner freedom, and the choice of a career. And this end can only be attained by socialization without compensation, as in Russia, or, perhaps more surely, by the way which Rathenau has indicated.

The points of contact between Rathenau and English Guild Socialism on the one hand, and the most recent tendencies in German Social Democracy on the other, raise the question of whether and how far he derived his ideas from others. It is well known that some time before the war an illustrated paper offered a prize to any one who could discover a single new idea in Rathenau's works, and that for some incomprehensible reason he himself entered into the stupid joke and provided the prize money out of his own pocket. The question in this form was absurd, for probably no completely new ideas have come into being for several thousand years past—as La Bruyère pointed out two hundred years ago. A thinker's originality does not consist in what he thinks, but in how he thinks it, in the form he gives his thoughts, in his manner of applying them, in the way in which he relates them to others, and still more in the depth of the experience which has caused them to be reborn within him. And what is really striking about Rathenau is the fact, which appears again and again, that he could only turn to account that which had become, so to speak, glowing and malleable within him as the result of a personal experience. It was only through such personal experience that a philosophical view, or even an industrial scheme, became of service to him. He points this out himself: 'The things men have to say to one another, even when they seem mere opinions,' he writes to a friend, 'are really *experiences*. Dialectic is childish and leaves one cold.' (Letter 96.) Reality—and in his case the reality had to be very personal and actually experienced—selected and sifted out for his personal use and for the workings of his mind the incalculable amount of material which he bore within himself. In his last years he read little, waiting for the experience which had to be caught like a fly in the intricate mental net of his mind, if it was to provide him with a grip on reality. Often he would have long to wait, and then he would complain of unproductiveness, hopelessness, emptiness, exhausted by the barren energies of his inner self. For, all in all, his experiences were few in number. Yet there was one here and there, and when this happened the effect was so profound that the ideas it engendered never afterwards grew dim. 'The law of my existence,' he wrote to his publisher, S. Fischer, 'lays down that

I must not call up my thoughts; I must listen for them. This leads me to wait and see whether problems will not still present themselves to which I can do justice.' (Letter 590.) To raise questions of priority with such a man is like reproaching a landscape painter with lack of originality because some one else had painted the same scene before him. What is important is not that this or that had been thought or put forward before; nor even that Rathenau, in his War Companies, invented a new model for communal industrial undertakings. The really important fact is that through being brought into a new relationship by their intimate association with his inner experience, certain economic forms of fundamental importance for the future development of industry and society acquired a new significance, a new direction, a new power. It is like the distinction which he himself makes between the Old and the New Testament in a letter he wrote in answer to a certain rabbi. (Letter 307.) He admits that most of the ideas in the New Testament are not new, but are also to be found in the Old. But in the Old Testament the emphasis is different, and 'it is this radical difference in tone and essence which concerns me.' Through the fact that in Rathenau's writings over all his ideas and proposals the experience of the 'soul' hovers like a light, and because he insists throughout that the goal is human freedom, not the state nor industry, nor any sort of material advantage for any one but man and man alone—because of this, there exists between his system and others which embody similar ideas and proposals 'a radical difference in tone and essence.' And it is in this that Rathenau's true originality consists. He is the man who amid the confusion of an aimless civilization, amid the stress of selfish conflicts, and in the face of political parties, his own colleagues and his own unregenerate self, held aloft with fanaticism and with pathos the banner of man, the banner of the Kingdom of Heaven that is to be found in every human soul, the banner that bears the words: 'In this sign shalt thou conquer!'

CHAPTER IX

ISOLATION

'I WRITE these words on the afternoon of July 31st, 1916. Tomorrow is the second anniversary of the opening of the European war. . . . For two years now I have felt myself to be distressingly alienated from my fellow-countrymen's way of thinking, in so far as they looked upon the war as an ordeal which would bring redemption. . . . Rejoicing in the July sunshine, the prosperous and happy populace of Berlin responded to the summons of war. Brightly clad, with flashing eyes, the living and those consecrated to death felt themselves to be at the zenith of vital power and political existence. . . . I could not but share in the pride of the sacrifice and the power. Nevertheless, this delirious exaltation seemed to me a dance of death, the overture to a doom which I had foreseen would be dark and dreadful—but not accompanied by rejoicings and therefore all the more terrible. . . .' (*In Days to Come*, pp. 184, 185.)

From the very first day Rathenau stood almost alone in his attitude to the war. He realized this, and felt it with all the depth of his longing for companionship, though at the same time with a suspicion of the feeling: 'I thank thee, God, that I am not as other men are.' While the Entente as well as Germany were indulging in the first unbridled orgies of annexation mania, while Erzberger was demanding Calais and Poincaré securing pledges for the Rhine frontier from the Tsar, Rathenau wrote on October 10th, 1914, to Gerhard von Mutius, who was at the centre of things in his capacity of Foreign Office representative attached to his cousin the Chancellor:

ISOLATION

Dear Friend,

Now that Antwerp has fallen I should like to think that the time had come for a declaration of a reassuring nature about the future of Belgium. This would help, I feel, to make the eventual peace negotiations more easy. For in view of Wilson's statement and the whole preliminary history of the war, in so far as it concerns England, it would appear that the Belgian complication will prove the most difficult point in any future international settlement. My thoughts will keep recurring to the difficulties of the peace, which seem to me almost greater than those of the war. Here the expectations of what victory will bring exceed all belief. No change of territory is great enough, no indemnity severe enough, to satisfy irresponsible opinion. To my mind the only peace worth having is a real peace, and one that will give a new and secure foundation to our policy. . . . What I should most like to see would be the conclusion of a peace with France which would transform our enemy into an ally. . . . For this reason I recur to my point which I should like you once more to urge on the Chancellor: by building up a central European economic system, we should gain an internal victory far surpassing all external achievements. . . . The Austrian programme needs the Franco-Belgian to complete it; and I should like again to draw attention to the fact that economic alliance with a neighboring country includes future political alliance also. (Letter 150.)

A few days later he writes again to the same friend: 'We must never forget that no nation can stand alone in the world. While there is war we must work for peace: and the peace must be a real one. And therefore it will be the chief task of the peace to try to mitigate the hatred on all sides.' (Letter 153.)

Had Rathenau's advice been followed the war would probably have taken a different course. For it was just this question of Belgium—Belgium and Alsace-Lorraine, but Belgium still

223

more than Alsace-Lorraine—which shattered the last hopes of a reasonable peace in 1917. But the advice was highly remarkable apart from this; for the underlying ideas are the same as were forced upon an intensely reluctant world by dire experience only ten years later, after Rathenau himself as Foreign Minister had first made them the basis of German foreign policy. It is, as I have said, highly remarkable that he should have clung steadfastly to these views—though they certainly followed inevitably from his view of life, and were real convictions and not just vague opinions—while all about him were losing their heads in the tumult of war. True, the result—both then and long afterwards—of holding these views was that, as he confesses in the above-quoted sentences, he 'felt himself to be distressingly alienated from his fellow-countrymen's way of thinking,' that he was to an uncanny extent the victim of loneliness. So long as he controlled the Raw Materials Department of the War Office his work and his official relationships served to keep from him the extent of his isolation. But when this work came to an end, and he grew aware of the ingratitude with which it was rewarded, he felt that he stood completely alone and unbefriended. A few days before he resigned he wrote to his friend:

WAR OFFICE
RAW MATERIALS DEPARTMENT
BERLIN, 25.iii.15

Thank you for your words and good wishes. I feel no inclination to do anything for myself. I dare not describe to you my thoughts and feelings; how I shall get through these many months, I simply don't know. Hitherto my work has kept me busy night and day, but now the void begins; for my power to influence things is now at an end. Perhaps my best course would be to go to the Front. I feel equally indifferent to Lugano or the Mendel; in fact, if I were not afraid of seeing people, I should stay on here.

The burden of making a decision weighs on me like a cloud. Like a flock of sheep, understanding nothing, we are driven into the Unknown.

I find that I can no longer listen to music with pleasure. The other night I was thoroughly bored by a performance of the Mass in B minor; it was, certainly, an unpleasant, exaggerated performance. But I cannot stand being in a large crowd of people. Thank you for your kind wishes.

Farewell. May the mountains give you a new lease of hope.

W.

And again, six weeks after he had resigned:

65 Königsallee, 9.v.15

You must forgive me, but at present I find any but the most casual conversation impossible. I feel so sore at heart that every word which goes beneath the surface causes me pain. I try to concentrate my thoughts on some more or less distant subject and perform a few unimportant daily tasks.

I hope we shall see each other when I am in the country. I was there yesterday—blossom and blue sky, and death over all.

Your R.

In addition to the distrust which falls to every outsider who accepts office Rathenau was also the victim of anti-Semitism, which now that he had become a public figure was aimed at him personally for the first time since his year of military service. In May, 1916, he writes to Emil Ludwig: 'That I, a private citizen and a Jew, have rendered the state a service of my own accord, this neither of the two parties concerned can forgive, and I believe this attitude will continue to the end of my days.' (Letter 200.) The absurd lengths to which even at this time certain young men of so-called 'nationalistic' circles went in

their attitude to him is illustrated by the remark of a certain
'Lieutenant G.,' of which Rathenau was informed: 'If this man
Rathenau *has* helped us, then it is a scandal and a disgrace.'
(Rathenau's letter of August 16th, 1916, to Wilhelm
Schwaner. Letters I, p. 219.)

In the course of his social career in Berlin Court society
Rathenau had worn his Judaism like the coat of a diplomat,
which gave him, the distinguished stranger, the key to closed
doors. At that time he had refused with a kind of bravado to
remove the difficulties which his faith put in the way of his
political career; and he had proceeded to discuss the question
theoretically and at a distance, as it were, in his essay on *The
State and the Jews*. But now for the first time the fact that he
was a Jew was brought home to him as a personal and cruel
fate. This is illustrated in the public discussion with a certain
Herr von T.-F. in the *Polemic on Belief* (published in 1917),
and even more clearly in that remarkable correspondence with
his nationalistic friend Wilhelm Schwaner, the editor of a 'Teutonic Bible.' These letters gave Rathenau the opportunity of
seeing himself, the Jew, exactly as he appeared in his opponents'
eyes, and are remarkable for the extreme consideration which
they show for the nationalistic feelings of Schwaner and his
followers. Rathenau could be very brusque in his replies to attacks which were not anti-Semitic in origin. In personal intercourse he was by no means always easy to get on with; on the
contrary, he was easily irritated by contradiction, and when he
let himself go he could be extraordinarily unpleasant. But the
letter in which Schwaner conveyed to him—why, one doesn't
really know—the above-quoted remark of the nationalistic lieutenant—a remark distorted by the crassest hatred—this letter
he answered not only in detail, but with an almost pathetic refusal to defend himself; in fact he actually thanks Schwaner
for his 'kind letter.'

He certainly did not deceive himself into thinking that he

226

could disarm his anti-Semitic foes by a friendly and conciliatory attitude. That he humbled himself before them out of fear is unthinkable; his whole life contradicts it. In order to understand his attitude, which always remained the same in spite of the ever-growing strength of the anti-Semitic attack, one must recall his ideas on Aryans and non-Aryans, on blond and dark races, and on 'men of fear' and 'men of courage.' 'The epitome of the history of the world, of the history of mankind, is the tragedy of the Aryan race. A blond and marvellous people arises in the north, etc.' The passage has been quoted already. Long after he had abandoned his theory of race intellectually it continued to influence him instinctively. To the last he could not withhold from his anti-Semitic antagonists a certain measure of approval—of their principles, if not of their animosity. As a 'man of fear' he felt himself inferior in relation to them. But this feeling of inferiority, which was fed by the growing anti-Semitic agitation, did not prompt him to defend himself; it only plunged him deeper into his inner loneliness, which to him was more painful than the outer one.

Even before the war he had written to his friend: 'Consider my life. Do you know of one more lonely?' (Letter quoted in Chapter VII.) In the *Mechanism of the Mind* he sings the praise of loneliness. 'Loneliness is the school of silence. The creative power of events lies in recollection. In the stillness . . . things and actions lift up their voices and express themselves; the event becomes experience. . . . The silent spirit awakens the echo of the essential.' (*Mechanism of the Mind*, p. 212.)

His father's death on June 20th, 1915, severed the most intimate and perhaps the last really close bond between himself and another. It is true that so far as his mother was concerned he now carried out his filial duties more tenderly than ever. Every day, no matter how busy he might be, he lunched with her at the Victoriastrasse. He knew, too, how to give her the proud feeling that she was indispensable to him. But in reality

227

there was much conscious reserve in his relationship to this mas-
terful lady, whose influence he feared either to oppose openly
or to submit to. His sister, who was much younger than he was,
he continued to regard as some one for him to educate. But of
his father he writes in a letter to Wilhelm Schwaner eight days
after his death: 'We were a long time in discovering each other,
my father and I; first came respect, then friendship, and finally
love. And now we are truly united; I feel that the last bars to
complete understanding are gone, and I have peace and security in his presence. . . . My life grows more tranquil and the
evening is at hand.' (Letter 169.)

His funeral speech had the effect of intensifying for some
time the campaign of vilification against him. It was pure vanity, so people said, to have delivered the speech himself instead
of getting a clergyman to do it—an address moreover which
was carefully prepared and written out beforehand. The echoes
of these criticisms penetrated as far as the Front. In reality he
spoke quite spontaneously, and not from vanity but because a
conventional speech by the grave of the man he loved more
than any other was to him an intolerable idea. Several years
later he could still write: 'Since my father and brother died—
for me they are not dead—there has been no one of whom I
could say, in the highest sense, that he was my friend.' (Letter
180.)

The glass wall which as a child he had begun to erect between himself and others now began to lose its transparency
even for him. Or to be more accurate: only the distance was
clear to his vision. The foreground, when it had ceased to have
any further meaning for him, tended to be more and more un-
cannily hidden from him by the image of his own personality,
his problems, his destiny, and above all by the workings of his
intellect, which completely blocked his range of vision. The reflections of his ego, the swarm of his involuntary thoughts,
thronged like ghosts about him. He writes to an acquaintance

soon after the beginning of the war: 'I feel nearer mankind than before; but to the individual I have nothing more to give.' These reflections of himself became for him a kind of second ego, which broke loose from him and came between him and the world. 'It is as though there were two people living within me, one growing and the other dying. The dying one is moved by passions and desires and love of pleasure, and with him dies much of the vigour and colour of life, much of its joy and friendliness; but the other grows, that other whom I can scarcely call "I" any longer. For my fate seems no longer to concern it; its ends are impersonal; it makes me the servant of forces over which I have no control. This other is like an alien power, which avails itself of my humble existence for a period in order to carry out its own purposes. . . . What I create, what I have to give others, is no longer my own. I can no longer give it; it breaks away as it pleases. On whose behalf? I must not ask.' (Letter 147. To Fanny Künstler, 23.ix.1914.) And some months later he writes to her again: 'What is there left for me to take an interest in? All is shadow and dream.' (Letter 161.)

His underlying mood became more and more one of weariness. The blows which had been dealt his once so vigorous and tenacious nature by personal conflicts, the serious cares and disappointments of the last years before the war, his despair about the war and his fears for Germany's future, all combined to bring about a weakening of his vital energy, a dulling of his enterprise and of his joy in practical creative work. When his father died he succeeded him as chairman of the A.E.G., but of his directorships in various companies he only took over those which were in difficulties or else still in the developing stage, or else those whose interests his father had had particularly at heart; the others, in contrast to his earlier insatiable energy, he refused. Shortly before relinquishing his post at the War Office he wrote to Fanny Künstler: 'You will notice a change in me, for I have become old and tired. We must see

whether country life can give me back my strength. . . .
Sometimes I want to live to see the peace, sometimes not.' (Letter 164.)

From the depths of his loneliness he clutched like a drowning
man at any hand that offered. Chance acquaintanceships blossomed overnight into gushing friendships, only to fade away
again as quickly as they had come and sink back into the shad-
owy world of their predecessors. He writes to Wilhelm
Schwaner in September, 1915: 'I have been a victim of inner
loneliness too long to be able to change things now. Up till
lately I have been wont to lament that the passionate experiences which filled my middle years did not lead to domestic
and family life. But that is past. My present wishes are very
few in number: to complete, if possible, the series of my writings and to fulfil the—probably only temporary—task of helping my father's work over the difficult period of our industry.
What will happen after that I do not ask. In this war year I
have become pretty grey—within as well as without.' (Letter
176.)

Nevertheless he was still anxious for practical activity—perhaps less so than formerly, and yet prompted to it irresistibly
by the 'purposive' half of his nature. One of the forms which
this inactivity now took was the assistance he gave to new clubs
whose object was to secure a cessation of inner political strife
by promoting social intercourse between representatives of different political parties. Foremost among these were the
'Deutsche Gesellschaft 1914,' which owed its existence to the·
author of *The Miracle*, Carl Vollmöller, and the 'Mittwochs-
Gesellschaft,' which was founded by Professor Ludwig Stein
and the leader of the National Liberal party in the Reichstag,
Herr Bassermann. Both these clubs played a not unimportant
part behind the scenes. They established connections in what
was for Germany a completely new form, between the government on the one hand, and members of parliament, journalists,

leaders of industry, bankers, and people from every department of public life on the other; and by means of these easy and unceremonious relationships they often exerted more influence on German policy and the direction of the war, especially in critical moments, than did the censored press or 'public opinion,' or even the houses of parliament, which after all sat within hearing of the Entente.

This was especially true of the 'Mittwochs-Gesellschaft,' a carefully selected and relatively small private club with only 70 members, which met weekly in the Hotel Continental for a confidential discussion of vital questions of the day. All shades of opinion from the ultra-conservative Count Westarp to the Social Democrats Heine, Südekum and David were represented in it. Herr Bassermann and Professor Stein began by asking twelve prominent personalities of different schools of thought to join, and each of these—of whom Rathenau was one—then co-opted four others. Among the regular attendants at the meetings were Field-Marshal Moltke, General Kluck, Prince Guido Henckel, Dr Stresemann, representatives of big business, such as Hugo Stinnes and Dr Hugenberg, and a number of well-known newspaper men, amongst whom the most prominent were Professor Hoetzsch and Herr Georg Bernhard. Leading Allied politicians, such as Counts Apponyi and Andrassy, came as guests when they happened to be in Berlin. In this small assembly, which was conducted on parliamentary lines, Rathenau found for the first time a platform for his oratorical talent.

For a short time he seems to have hoped that through the influence of Ludendorff, who had now become the real ruler of Germany, making of the Kaiser a mere figurehead, he might find an opportunity for launching his great reforms. Ludendorff's elasticity, his power of rapid comprehension, the enthusiasm with which he welcomed other people's ideas, provided they did not clash with his own, a certain childlike quality, a sign one could mistake for genius—all these made a deep impression on Rathenau, who was in every respect his opposite. In his essay *Schicksalsspiel* (*The Game of Fate*) [1] he says: 'I got to know Ludendorff in Kovno at the end of 1915. I felt that he was the man to lead us, if not on to victory, at least to an honourable peace, and from that day on I was one of those who did everything in their power to smooth his path to the Supreme Command.'

His high opinion of Ludendorff and his hope of being able to further his own ideas through Ludendorff's influence are certainly in large part responsible for the one serious mistake which Rathenau made in the war: his letter to Ludendorff of September 16th, 1916, in which he supported the Belgian deportations—*i.e.* the forcible transportation to Germany of seven hundred thousand Belgian workers to assist in the 'Hindenburg industrial programme.' In practice, as every one knows, the step was a failure; humanly considered and from the point of view of international law it was indefensible, and most seriously jeopardized Rathenau's particular war aims: international reconciliation, mitigation of hatred, and the economic unification of Europe. To explain his bewildering attitude in this matter one must take into account other psychological motives besides his regard for Ludendorff: a clouding of his judgment, not by war psychosis—for from that he was immune—but by his Prussianism, his deep desire to be German to the core, which always disarmed him in the face of anti-Semitic attacks, and in this case proved stronger than the dictates of reason. The conflicting moods from which arose this and perhaps other tragic self-contradictory situations (he used to reproach himself afterwards for the part he played in the war by his organization of raw materials) are partially revealed in the words in which he wrote to Fanny Künstler soon after the outbreak of war:

[1] Published on November 23rd, 1919, in the *Berliner Tageblatt*. Reprinted in *Was wird werden?* (*What is to Come?*) p. 5 ff.

ISOLATION

'We must win, WE MUST! and yet we have no clear, no absolute right to do so.' (Letter 155.)

His opinion of Ludendorff, however, was soon shattered. He has himself given a clear and convincing account of the dramatic end to their relationship in his essay *Schicksalsspiel* from which I have already quoted. 'In the spring of 1917 Headquarters were in Berlin for some days. . . . I called on Ludendorff and reported to him about the carrying out of the industrial side of the "Hindenburg Programme." I also told him that from what I knew of them, the views of the experts on the submarine question were wrong; it was out of the question that England could be defeated by the summer. Ludendorff did not agree, and the conversation was a brief one. In June, 1917, I reminded Ludendorff of my prediction by letter, whereupon he invited me to meet him at Kreuznach.'[2]

Rathenau carefully paved the way for his visit by an article entitled *Safeguards* in the *Frankfurter Zeitung* of July 5th, in which he objected on principle to annexations in the East, but—a concession to Ludendorff—did not 'in theory,' as he expressed it, reject them absolutely in the West.[3] The interview took place at Headquarters on July 10th. 'The submarine war was our chief topic. I discussed the monthly returns (which meant in fact the highest estimates), the small effect on English commerce, the illusory method of reckoning the total tonnage, the defensive measures, and above all the possibility of America's building more tonnage than we sank. . . . Ludendorff saw me again in the afternoon. He told me that there was only one point on which he could not agree with me and that was the question of the submarine war. When I asked him his reasons he replied that he had none to give me, that it was his instinctive feeling, that same feeling which had the decisive voice in his strategic measures. I replied that this would have

[2] *Loc. cit.*, p. 7.
[3] Reprinted in the pamphlet entitled *Zeitliches*.

233

settled the matter for me if it had been a question of strategy we were dealing with, but as it was a question of economics and technology I ventured to oppose my calculations and my feeling to his own. "I respect that," answered Ludendorff, "but you will admit that I have to follow my feeling." ' [4] When Ludendorff introduced his 'feeling' thus into a purely statistical and technical matter Rathenau gave him up as hopeless. He delivered a speech in the Mittwochs-Gesellschaft against the unrestricted submarine war, which made a deep impression on all who heard it. He objected to it on the ground that it was the kind of experiment which 'like a leap over the abyss only succeeds if its success is a hundred per cent. success. But this hundred per cent. includes both an unknown economic factor and a psychological factor which has never been properly appreciated here.' (Letter 228.) It was one of his most brilliant speeches, and in the end his estimate proved right and Ludendorff's wrong. But we now know from Sir Arthur Salter's book that in April, 1917, very little was needed to make up the hundred per cent.

The darker the situation became and the more difficult and painful the moral decisions involved, the more Rathenau withdrew into the loneliness of his inner self, out of the present into his own visionary future. He wrote *In Days to Come*, followed by the *Problems of the Peace and Industry* (*Probleme der Friedenswirtschaft*), *Stock Exchange Transactions* (*Vom Aktienwesen*), and the *New Economy* (*Neue Wirtschaft*). 'I write the whole day,' he says in a letter to Wilhelm Schwaner, 'but it is as when a widow bears a child; such children suffer much from weeping. I do not weep—but I do not laugh much either. Worry and anxiety I have often had, both for myself and those near to me; especially in 1903, when my brother died. But it was not like this.' (Letter 264, 2.ix.16.) The letters to

[4] *Loc. cit.* pp. 9-11.

his friend during the last two years of the war are permeated by a tone of both outer and inner loneliness.

65 Königsallee, 15.1.17

Thank you for your letter and the flowers. Faust? No. But I have been reading Nietzsche's letters to Overbeck with horror and dismay, including those terrible documents—the fossilized remains of his madness. So close to the abyss—and yet not over! How well I know the shadows that haunted this happily-unhappier I; only my loneliness is a peopled loneliness. And the greed and scorn of friends, not one of whom will ever come to one's aid. How well I know them! Smilingly they block the way in the path to the Abyss, and some must actually be forced to make room for the tottering waggon, till finally they succeed in breaking the spokes. How well I have known them, and know them still! Then with a smile and a shake of the head they will set up a stone to my memory to serve as a warning, and innocent young people will come and lay their wreaths on it.

Don't be alarmed; you will find me no less cheerful than usual. I will get the better of my mood as I do of other things. Good-bye for the present.

Your affectionate and ever faithful
W.

65 Königsallee, GRÜNEWALD

How am I to reply? You either do not know or do not respect the laws of production, at least not in my case. Do you really think that I get my inspiration from my fountain pen, like any Grub Street hack? I have never yet written a line which I did not have to write. But once written it belongs to me no longer. Without faith there is no responsibility and without responsibility no faith. To get through the task of production I must believe that it is imposed on me; otherwise I could not get through it. If any of my works are bad, this is not from lack of good will; I try, as hard as any one has ever tried, to make them as good as I can. If I have failed in this the world must take them for what they are. The world has always had more good will from me than I have had from it.

Or ought I to show more consideration for my readers? Lest I become, perhaps, too prolific? But when I have nothing to give I am silent for three or four years at a time. When I must speak, I speak. What impression it makes doesn't interest me.

You know how highly I rate your judgment; and it is at its strongest when dealing with some concrete problem. But what a man must do and believe, that no one can tell him; not even the person who shares all his life's experiences. These are the affairs of destiny; in face of them one must not and need not be afraid. They take their course. Wit can do no good, nor folly harm. If the will is good, tragic they may be, but neither false nor evil.

Affectionately,

13.6.17 W.

25.12.17

In these last days of the dying year I should like to send you one more Christmas greeting. In this year, in the midst of great suffering, you have found your true vocation and have worthily followed it. I have watched your fate with pain, but with joy and pride too.

I shall become more and more cut off from my fellowmen; but I keep the bridges open while I can. Please don't be annoyed with me! I know you have a kind heart.

Your W.

17.5.18

If I had to destroy your letters I should feel as though I were killing some living thing. Fortunately it is technically im-

236

possible. I must look through my drawers; there is scarcely one which does not contain some reminder of you. Thus I am afraid there is no chance of your getting Bettina's letter till the end of my days, as I have no idea where to look for it. It goes without saying that I have preserved nothing which could at any time be misinterpreted through malice or stupidity.

I have escaped here for a few days, feeling very tired; I arrived yesterday at noon in cloudless heat. Today I have been sleeping for hours on end, almost the whole day long. Here the lilac is in bloom, and apart from acacias and roses, which are late this year, it might be the middle of June. It looks as if we were in for a long drouth; this little district has had hardly any rain. It is evening now and the garden is full of nightingales once more. But things are not as they used to be. Something strange and indefinable has come between. Thoughts and moods come and go. I don't feel it is spring; there is no sense of awakening; everything is fully out, and decay is in the air as in August.

I now know that I shall not live to see the end of this confusion; perhaps none of us will. It is almost a comfort. Other men will gradually succeed us, and they in their turn will sink into the darkness. Everything we do is too early or too late. I feel a sense of freedom when I see the great spaces of the horizon and the daily round, the tyranny of time, disappears.

Twilight is fading away into the warm enveloping night; the meadows chirp and chatter. I could put on the lights and go on writing; but I am still so tired and troubled—everything keeps revolving in a painful circle. Don't be anxious, and above all don't think that I am ill. Tomorrow there are even some guests coming, two of my Swedish people. Early this morning I rang up Felix and said a few words on Raumer's behalf.

Farewell. My warmest greetings,

W.

No, . . . it is not right of you to touch again on that wish of yours; you know it distresses me. However, as it must be so, I shall arrange in my will for the letters to be handed over to you—or to whomever you designate—untouched.

I am delighted with your little picture. It is in harmony with the peace of your letter: peaceful and yet vital, slight, apparently trivial, and yet illuminating.

It is a strange thing, but though I have written much in my time I still find it as difficult as I did at the very beginning. I wrestle the whole day long, and in the evening four pages lie before me. How easy are words and how hard! The Greeks said that under the influence of music and song the Cyclopean stones of Troy built themselves into a wall. That is a bold image for a few pages of prose, but in this not outwardly bulky volume I have taken upon myself a serious responsibility.

I never leave the garden. The ground is still damp and the trees heavy from all the rain we have had. Throughout the day the clouds pile up in white masses in the sky, only to disperse again in the glow of evening. By night whole mountains of small half-invisible constellations float like snowflakes between the bright fixed stars, so clear is the sky. The day before yesterday I had to spend the day in Berlin. I came back bored and worried, and as I opened the garden gate and entered the cool quiet darkness under the trees I felt I had only one desire left. On my table lie books, scarce opened. Towards evening I often climb the little hill behind the house and bring back a few mushrooms for my supper. I have had few visitors. They find me dull and soon go again. Autumn is beginning.

Please don't think I am depressed or sad. Since the beginning of the war my best days have been spent working here.

Warmest greetings,

Your W.

When the collapse of Germany became imminent Rathenau made yet another—almost violent—attempt to break through the barrier that separated him from his environment. He turned *To the Youth of Germany* (it is the book referred to in the above letter): 'To you, Germany's youth, I address myself. To my contemporaries I have but little more to say. I have poured out my heart before them; my faith and vision, my troth and my troubles, I have displayed before their souls. Many have read my writings: the scholars to smile at them, the practical to mock at them, and the interested parties to grow indignant and rejoice in their own virtue. If warm voices have reached me, they have come from the lonely and the young and from those who neither grow old nor die.' (*To the Youth of Germany* [*An Deutschlands Jugend*], p. 6 *ff.*)

The style of his appeal is shrill, solemnly prophetic, and at times over-ornate. It often resembles a hand which is so heavily bejewelled that one forgets or overlooks the fine delicate fingers underneath. The ornament frequently obscures the idea rather than adorns it. One might almost call it modern baroque. But that would be unfair: for beneath the somewhat artificial pathos there is a glow of passion; only it is unnecessarily concerned with matters of expression; it is uncertain, like a voice which has too long held converse only with itself. Also perhaps the gap between feeling and expression had grown too great, and could now only be bridged by artifice. Yet in places his real feeling breaks through the elaborate words in unmistakable accents: 'Every night I remember in my heart those who have been killed and those doomed to die, and above all those in distress and those in fear. For all whom the war touches most deeply, old or young, live in fear and trembling, weeping tears that flow within and consume the heart' (*loc. cit.*, p. 1).

Much in this essay appears to be merely a repetition, in an

239

WALTHER RATHENAU

apocalyptic form, of ideas which he had developed elsewhere;
this is especially true of his re-proclamation of the 'realm of
the soul.' But here these ideas take solid form as actual needs
of the day. For the war is no ordinary war like those of the.
nineteenth century, no mere armed debate between governments. 'The crisis through which we are passing is the social
revolution . . . it is the funeral pyre of the social structure of
Europe, which will never rise again from the flames. . . .'
(loc. cit., pp. 10 and 76). It is the end of a dying, the beginning
of a new epoch of mankind. 'Our ways of life, our industry, our
social structure and our form of state—all are changing; as
are the relation of state with state, world communications, and
politics. Science, too, and even our language are in process of
change. Who has not asked himself when reading one of the
earlier authors of the vanished epoch, say Stendhal or Balzac:
How is that possible? Only thirty years ago the Gay Century
was at the height of its mother-of-pearl brilliance, and now
these drab-clothed men talk away in their new scientific jargon
of industry and the stock exchange, of steamships and parliaments, of bourgeois society and militarism, without giving a
thought to the newness of their world and with only a vague
idea of what went before them. And if perchance they mention
some old nobleman whose youth was spent in that age of gal-
lantry, it is as of a sort of fossil, dead and decayed, an antiquated ghost. So in your turn you [the new youth] will pass us
by' (loc. cit., p. 74 ff.).

Since the war is nothing but a symptom of the birth of a new
era, 'the time's ills' can only be remedied by the appearance of a
new type of man whose life is centred in the soul and not in the
greed of gain and subjection to material ends, and by replacing
the present condition of political and economic anarchy by a new
organization of mankind.

The new man is the more important of the two. 'No statesman or act of Parliament, no change in organization can help.

. . . Can you find the men and bring them together?' he calls to German youth. 'Do not forget: even if we could establish a German Earthly Paradise today, we should not have the men to administer it. . . . Look around you at these parliaments, these offices, these academies—everywhere. . . . And once again I lose heart and ask: Where are the men?' (*loc. cit.*, pp. 12-14).

This was indeed the problem which troubled Rathenau more than any other. Soon after the Spartacus revolt in February, 1919, he said to me: 'Bolshevism is an imposing system, and probably the future belongs to it; in a hundred years the world will be Bolshevist. But Russian Bolshevism is like an excellent play acted by some wretched company in a village barn, and when communism comes to Germany it will be the same thing over again. We have not got the men for so thoroughly complex a system; it demands a far finer and higher talent for organization than we can show. We—unlike perhaps the English and Americans—have no men of the requisite stature. We Germans can only organize à la sergeant-major; we cannot attain the high standard which Bolshevism requires. By night I am a Bolshevist; but when the morning comes and I enter the factory and see our workers and officials, then I am not—or at least not yet.' And several times he repeated: 'not yet.'

Just as he had once attributed the greater part of Germany's decline to the method of selecting candidates and had found the only hope of improvement in the introduction of a better personnel, so now the problem of the new order of things was to him above all a problem of character: whether, that is to say, it would be possible to find a new type with more backbone and a higher moral level to take the place of the mechanistic man broken in body and soul by his service to material ends. Hence his call to youth, from whom alone he could expect this new type of being, and especially to German youth, whom the war would seem to have made ready for some great spiritual transformation. He was probably thinking particularly of the circle of young men which gathered around Fritz von Unruh and his brothers.

The *new man* was the prerequisite; but Rathenau had an equally clear vision of the *new order*, 'the economic and social levelling, the moral and spiritual rejuvenation of industry.' He saw it in clear outline, like a plan that was certain to be realized sooner or later. 'I have an inviolable faith in these things, for they are already on their way; they have become an invisible destiny, for they are perceived, discussed and listened to, and have thus become a spiritual reality' (*loc. cit.*, p. 13). 'The coming peace will be nought but an armistice and the tale of future wars unending, the greatest nations will sink into decay and the world into misery, unless this peace succeeds in furthering the realization of these ideas' (*loc. cit.*, p. 86).

With a view to the prospective peace negotiations he is very much more precise than usual in his picture of a world organization whose object shall be the elimination of inter-state anarchy. True, his plan differs essentially from Wilson's League of Nations, which was based on the ideas of the eighteenth century. 'A League of Nations is both just and good,' he says, 'disarmament and courts of arbitration are both possible and reasonable; but all this will be in vain unless it is preceded by a League of Industry, a world economic organization. By this I do not mean the abolition of national industry, or Free Trade, or tariff agreements, but the distribution and common management of international raw materials, and the distribution of international products and international finance. Without these arrangements Leagues of Nations and courts of arbitration merely lead to the judicial murder of the weaker brethren by the correct method of competition; without these arrangements the existing anarchy merely leads to the violent struggle of all against all.

'This is what is meant by a League of Industry: the raw

materials of international trade are controlled by an inter-state syndicate. They are put at the disposal of each nation on the same original conditions, and at the outset in accordance with their current ratio of consumption. Later on the economic growth of each particular nation is taken into account.

'The same inter-state authority regulates exports on a corresponding basis. Each state can demand to have its export quota taken off its hands. This quota is reduced in proportion as the state refuses to accept the imports due to it. The states deliver their various products in the proportion in which they have been accustomed to do so; but they may freely enter into agreements to alter this proportion, and exchange of quotas is permissible.

'Each state in proportion to its export quota may demand a share in international financial operations that lead to deliveries.

'These would be the most important points to arrange' (p. 87).

He goes on to insist, however, that it must needs be a long time before the development of such a system can be completed. 'Decades must pass before this international economic system is built up fully. Further decades, perhaps centuries, will be necessary before the condition of inter-state anarchy can be replaced by one in which a supreme authority will be willingly accepted by all; and this authority must be, not a court of arbitration, but a sort of welfare centre—the most powerful of all executives, in whose hands the administration of the economic system must lie' (p. 88).

We may remember that even before the war Rathenau had mooted the idea of an international court. The business of this inter-state tribunal was to examine the various nations' expenditure on armaments and to see that they kept within the limits assigned by treaty. By this proposal he had consciously or unconsciously denied the absolute validity of the current idea of

243

sovereignty. In his appeal *To the Youth of Germany* he shows in discreet but unequivocal language that the whole complex of values connected with the ideas of state and nation is a matter for enquiry and not necessarily of universal validity. 'It is possible,' he says, 'that modern man will be forced by his despair to seek refuge in chaos. He may perhaps be driven to question all ideals, even to ask whether those values, which Christ, remember, did not recognize as values, fatherland, nation, wealth, power and culture, are really lofty and fundamental enough to justify the world in the hatred and envy, the injustice and oppression, the intrigue and violence and murder carried on in their name.' (*To the Youth of Germany*, p. 35.) Every absolute value is radical in its effect; it makes one sceptical of other values, eats into them like an acid, so that nothing is left of them but a residue—and this residue is at best only relatively valid. So it was in Rathenau's philosophy with his absolute value—the 'soul.'

But one must not over-estimate this radicalism of Rathenau's. For it was confined to the intellect; and in him the intellect worked according to its own laws and almost independently of the rest of him. His feelings lived in open conflict with this part of him, and his feelings were rooted in Prussia, in Germany, in German industry, and even in the 'blond' Prussian Junker. Thus in critical moments his actions sprang from a combination of, or often from a compromise between, these two impulses.

When Ludendorff's request for an armistice brought with it the collapse of Germany, Rathenau recognized at once the disastrous stupidity of Germany's declaring itself bankrupt instead of coming to an arrangement with its creditors ('the most disastrous piece of stupidity in history,' as he afterwards described it—and without exaggeration). Because a general exhausted by years of heavy responsibility had lost his nerve, Germany ran her head into the noose, thus ruining not only herself, but all Europe into the bargain, for it destroyed all possibility of a reasonable peace—a peace that might have healed the wounds of war. Feelings and intelligence alike were outraged by this crime. On October 7th, 1918, Rathenau published an article in the *Vossische Zeitung* entitled *A Black Day* in which he described the step as 'premature,' prophesied —what was indeed self-evident—that the reply would be unsatisfactory, and demanded that if it proved to be one that 'cramps and throttles our very existence, we must at least be prepared for it in advance. The people must be ready to rise in defence of their nation, a Ministry of Defence must be set up. These measures should only be resorted to if necessity compels it, if we meet with a rebuff; but there is not a day to lose. Such a Ministry should not be attached to any existing department; it should consist of both soldiers and civilians and have far-reaching powers. Its task would be threefold: first, to issue an appeal to the people in the ungarnished language of truth. Let all who feel the call present themselves; there will be enough elderly men to be found who are yet sound, full of patriotic fervour, and ready to help their tired brothers at the front with all their powers of body and soul. Secondly, all the "Field-greys" whom one sees today in our towns, at the stations, and on the railways, must return to the front, however hard it may be for many of them to have their well-earned leave cut short. Lastly, all men capable of bearing arms must be combed out of the offices, the guard-rooms and depôts, in East and West, at the bases and at home. What use have we today for Armies of Occupation and Russian Expeditions? Yet at this moment we have hardly half of the total available troops on the Western Front. Our front is worn out; restore it, and we shall be offered different terms. It is peace we want, not war —but not a peace of surrender.'

The article created a stupendous sensation. Prince Max, the Chancellor of the new People's Government, who had agreed

WALTHER RATHENAU

to the Armistice proposal, though most reluctantly and under persistent pressure from the military authorities, now began to hesitate. On October 8th he submitted the following question to the Supreme Command: 'Does the Supreme Command expect that an adequate reinforcement would be afforded by the *levée en masse*, as recommended by Walther Rathenau in the *Vossische Zeitung?*'[5] Ludendorff answered the Prince orally next day: 'No. In spite of our lack of men I have no belief in the *levée en masse*. It would cause more disturbance than we can stand.' And General Scheuch, the War Minister, supported this view.[6] Thereupon Rathenau went to see Scheuch and afterwards explained to him by letter on October 9th—what was as clear as crystal to every one except, apparently, the Supreme Command—that to evacuate the occupied areas as demanded by Wilson in his reply would be to 'make an end of our capacity for defence and thus put ourselves at the enemy's mercy.' (*Neue Briefe*, No. 50.) But the military authorities persisted in their refusal.

It would be idle to enquire whether the *levée* could have been carried out with success once Ludendorff had made his request for an armistice. As things turned out, the one result of the proposal was that Rathenau incurred the bitterest hatred of the masses for 'wanting to prolong the war.' And so when the Revolution broke out his position was indeed unique. For years he had been attacking the ruling system and all about it, its constitution, its policy, its economics, its social structure. He had never ceased to advocate its complete reorganization. And yet for reasons which were only too obvious—his position at the head of the A.E.G., his organization of raw materials, his connection with the 'Hindenburg Programme,' and finally and worst of all his appeal for a *levée en masse*—for all these reasons (all due in the last analysis to the double nature of his

[5] *Vorgeschichte des Waffenstillstandes. Amtliche Urkunden*, No. 36.
[6] *Loc. cit.*, No. 38.

246

personality) the Revolution could not but pass him by. This was probably the bitterest moment of his life. A year later he wrote to the socialist Prussian Minister Südekum: 'When the Revolution came, every one was agreed in wanting to get rid of me.' (Letter 580.)

And now Rathenau's real tragedy began, the tragedy which he himself felt as such. A series of mortifying experiences forced him to realize for the first time that his double nature imperilled his work, that it threatened not only himself, but his ideas as well, with extinction. Instead of looking on, as he had done till then, with a more or less studied detachment at the struggle of his theories, as set forth in his books, with the forces of nationalism, big business and organized Marxism, he now accepted the challenge to fight. Into the struggle he put all the energy that was left him. And finally he succeeded in saving at least a part of his ideas—but only at the cost of his life.

The first act in this final tragedy was Rathenau's desperate struggle to escape from his isolation and assist practically in the building up of the new Germany. Lectures, speeches, newspaper articles, pamphlets began to pour out in a continuous stream—first his *Apologie*, a sort of autobiographical justification; then *Der Kaiser*, setting forth the nature of his relationship to the former Kaiser; the *Kritik der dreifachen Revolution* (*A Criticism of the Threefold Revolution*), a virulent indictment of the lack of ideas in the German revolution; the small collections, *Nach der Flut* (*After the Flood*), and *Was wird werden?* (*What is to Come?*); his books *Der neue Staat* (*The New State*), *Die neue Gesellschaft* (*The New Society*) and *Autonome Wirtschaft* (*Autonomous Industry*)—all these are just incidents in Rathenau's struggle to gain first a hearing, and then a footing, in the councils of the new German Republic.

A month or two before the Revolution he had written an essay *Staat und Vaterland*, which restated in terms of the actual situation the aims which he had already described more generally in his great theoretical works: 'The World is in need of a Kingdom of Man which shall be an image of the Kingdom of God, the Kingdom of the Soul. The Kingdom of Man is the kingdom of Freedom and Justice. The Kingdom of Man is not ruled by wealth or inheritance, by tyranny or oppression, by violence or by anarchy; it is ruled by solidarity. Its leaders are no longer the privileged, the place-hunters and wire-pullers, but men of proven ability. The supreme law is not interest, but creation; the ultimate aim not wealth and power, but spirit. The slavery of man, the slavery of rank and sex and age is at an end.'[7] And in another passage in the same essay he declares it to be 'the clear and definite task of the German mind to base the state and industry on justice and morality, and to make them an example for the commonwealth of nations.'[8] What he has in view is obviously something very like Fichte's ideal state.

Rathenau also attempted to gain a hearing for these ideas by founding a 'Democratic People's League.' He sent out invitations to a number of people prominent in the intellectual and industrial world, who shared his fate of having been landed high and dry by the Revolution, and on November 16th he held a meeting to explain his aims to them: 'I appeal to that part of the nation which for the moment is included neither in the Workers' and Soldiers' Councils, nor in the self-constituted comradeship of those who have made the Revolution. Let us unite and hold ourselves ready to assist—individually, in groups, or as a whole—in the work of reconstruction, wherever our services may be required. Let us co-operate in this work freely and gladly and with all the constructive intelligence which is at our command.'[9] He did not want to form a party, for his only concern was absolute solidarity and unity. Thus the

[7] *Staat und Vaterland*, p. 48. Reprinted in *Nach der Flut.* p. 34 *ff.*
[8] *Loc. cit.* p. 37.
[9] *Reden*, p. 35.

only resolution he submitted to them was 'the demand for the speedy convocation of the National Assembly.'[10]

But Rathenau's real aims in founding the 'Democratic People's League' are to be found in the *Appeal* to the German people which he drew up for it:

1. The 'Democratic People's League' takes its stand on the German Revolution.
2. It appeals to all German men and women without distinction of religion or party, except those who openly or covertly give their services to Reaction.
3. The 'Democratic People's League' stands for a free country and a free people with the constitution of a democratic state.
4. It demands the end of privileged classes, and of the distinction between bourgeoisie and proletariat, equal opportunity for ability, and the abolition of militarism and imperialism, feudalism and bureaucracy.
5. It maintains the right of every German to both work and education. People cannot be allowed to suffer privation through no fault of their own.
6. Property, income, and inheritance should be restricted.
7. Industry is not the private concern of individuals; it concerns every one. Production must be increased by avoiding waste—of labour, of materials and of transport. Combines must be subordinated to the state. Nationalization should take place where suitable. The import and consumption of luxuries should be taxed and restricted. The standards of industrial morality must be raised. Life must be made more simple.

The Democratic People's League was short-lived, or rather it never really lived at all; for it dissolved itself after a very few days. Rathenau accounts for this failure in a private letter written shortly afterwards and still unpublished:[11] 'The Democratic People's League gave one more proof of the distaste of the middle classes for considering social problems seriously,

[10] *Loc. cit.* p. 37.
[11] It was to be included in his *Politische Briefe*, announced for publication as this volume goes to press.

and that was why it failed. It could not be got to unite on anything more definite than the colourless demand for a National
Assembly, and this had already lost much of its point, for in
the meantime all the various parties as well as the government
had made it a plank in their platform.' The *Appeal* does not
seem to have been published. And, indeed, it was not the Workers' and Soldiers' Councils, but the inertia of the middle classes
—and over and above this, of the trades union and old party
bureaucracies, which the Revolution had not affected—that
made the position of all such unprepared and unorganized
movements hopeless from the start. Hence a definite limit was
set to the work of reconstruction, or, to put it in another way,
the course of the Revolution was predetermined from start to
finish. Against the trades union and party secretariats even Karl
Liebknecht's machine-guns could do nothing. Rathenau had no
illusions in this matter. He saw that the only course that could
lead to definite results was to reform one of the old parties
and its trades union appendage from within. He had cut himself off from the Social Democratic party by his blunt repudiation of Marxism. So he turned to the 'German Democratic
Party,' which had been formed under Friedrich Naumann's
leadership out of the old Progressive People's Party and the
South German local branches of the National Liberals.[12]
Through the influence of Naumann and its strong trades union
element this party stood from the beginning for social reform;
through the influence of great intellectuals like Max Weber [13]

[12] Friedrich Naumann, a progressive Churchman, who in his youth came under
the influence of the founder of the Christian-Socialist Party, Pastor Stöcker, and
then struck out on a democratic line of his own, became a member of the Reichstag for the Radical (Freisinnige) Party, and wrote a book, *Mittel-Europa*, during
the war which advocated a great central European economic unit embracing
Germany, Austria, Poland, the Balkan Peninsula and the Turkish dominion in
Asia. His principal interests were social reform based on Christian and humani-
tarian principles, and the democratization of Germany. He died in August, 1919.

[13] Max Weber, professor at Heidelberg (1864-1920), Germany's most original
bourgeois economist. His books and essays on *The Sociology of Religion*, on
Protestant Morals and the Spirit of Capitalism (Die protestantische Ethik und

and Hugo Preuss,[14] for a predominantly intellectual outlook; and, finally, under the steady influx of diplomats and pacifists, for the policy of understanding in international affairs. Here were several points which Rathenau might hope to develop further.

He was invited by the local branch of the 'German Democratic Party' in Weiswasser (Oberlausitz), where he was chairman of the board of directors of the Vereinigte Lausitzer Glaswerke A.-G., to stand as their candidate for the National Assembly for the Reichstag constituency of Rothenburg-Hoyerswerda. He accepted the invitation. But then the Commissaries of the People, instituted by the Revolution, issued a decree that the elections were not to be held according to the old Reichstag constituencies but according to *Regierungsbezirke* (the larger, provincial units) and under a system of Proportional Representation; and thus the nomination of candidates for the district became a matter for the party organization of the *Regierungsbezirk* of Liegnitz. At the meeting of its delegates at the end of December, 1918, at which Rathenau was present, he found himself the object of strong opposition, based on anti-Semitism. He was not even allowed to speak, on the pretext that this would be unfair to the other candidates, who happened to be absent. In the end he failed to get his name placed on the list for the German federal National Assembly, and it was only through the exertions of his friends that he managed to gain the sixth place on the Prussian list, which gave him not the faintest chance of being elected.[15]

der Geist des Kapitalismus), on *The Economic Ethics of the Great World Religions* (*Die Wirtschaftsethik der Weltreligionen*), broke entirely new ground. In this, and in the way he affected German thought, his influence is comparable to that of Sir James Frazer. By the part he played during and after the Revolution in shaping German democratic ideals he became one of the founders of the German Republic.

[14] Hugo Preuss, professor in Berlin (1860-1925), the author of the new German republican Constitution, adopted at Weimar in 1919.

[15] By the German system of Proportional Representation, the voters do not

A series of similar reverses followed in rapid succession. Shortly after the Liegnitz affair he suffered a still greater mortification by being struck off the Commission for the Socialization of German industry, in obedience to the violent protests of the Independent Socialists. The tone of the letter he wrote on this occasion to the future President Ebert, then People's Commissary, shows how bitterly he felt the rebuff:

'You are doubtless aware that I was excluded from the Socialization of German Industry, in obedience to the violent and after my name had already been made public in the list of members. From all parts of the country I am being asked the reasons for this exclusion; a protest signed by fifty members of the Soldiers' Council has been handed to me. I think I have a right to know what these reasons are. . . . I doubt if there are many men on the bourgeois side who have risked their position and exposed themselves to hatred and enmity to the extent that I have done; I have openly attacked the old system, I opposed the war, and I have worked out in detail a new and complete economic system on scientific lines. . . . In the first days of the Revolution I placed myself at the disposal of the People's Government, as my conscience bade me. It has not availed itself of my services, and I am only too pleased to learn that it has no lack of more suitable talent. But if the new People's State, which I have spent my life in working for, goes out of its way to show its lack of confidence by striking me off a list of people who will inevitably have to take my own life-work into consideration, then I think that the public as well as myself have a right to know the reason why. Berlin, December 16th,

vote for one particular candidate, but for a *list* of candidates; and the party caucus allots to each of its candidates a specific number on the list. The votes polled by a list are then divided by 60,000 (or by 40,000 when the election is for the Prussian Landtag); and for every 60,000 votes polled for the party list in the constituency the party gets one member into the Reichstag. A candidate allotted number 6 would therefore be elected only if at least 360,000 votes were polled for the party list in his constituency.

1918.' (Letter 470.) The Independents upheld their veto. A few weeks later he was further exasperated by an incident that took place in the National Assembly, which had just met. In the course of the second session, on February 7th, 1919, two telegrams were handed in containing nominations for the first President of the Reich; one proposed Hindenburg, the other Rathenau. The first was greeted with laughter from the Social Democrats: the fate of the second is recorded thus in the shorthand report:

'Deputy Dr Neumann-Hofer, Secretary of the Assembly [reads out]: .
' "On behalf of many Germans abroad I propose as President of Germany the name—respected both at home and abroad by friend and foe alike—of Walther Rathenau. [Much merriment.] May he be our leader. Eugen Müller, Stockholm." [Much merriment on the Right.]' [16]

Rathenau took the 'merriment'—of which after all Hindenburg had also been the victim—more tragically than it deserved. Months later he returns to the point in his *Apology* in a tone that shows how deeply it had wounded him: 'On the day that the President of the Reich was being elected at Weimar my name was brought into a ludicrous proximity with these solemn proceedings by the arrival of a telegram—a wellmeant but highly inopportune and misguided effort on the part of some Germans abroad. It would have been easy to lay it on one side, as was done daily with so many others. However, it was read out. The Parliament of any other civilized state would have shown sufficient respect for a man of recognized intellectual standing to have passed over in silence this act of bad taste. But the First Parliament of the German Republic,

[16] *The German National Assembly* in the Year 1919. Edited by Justizrat Dr Eduard Heilfron. 2nd Session, Friday, February 7th, 1919, p. 16.

assembled in this darkest and most solemn hour and destined
to set its seal on Germany's ignominy, greeted it with roars and
shrieks of laughter. The papers talked of merriment lasting for
several minutes, and eye-witnesses related how men and
women rocked in their seats with delight at the idea. This was
their way of greeting a German whose intellectual achievement
they either did or did not know, as the case might be. I was
certainly astonished when I read it, but it did not distress me
personally. It made me think of the sardonic laughter in the
halls of Ithaca, as described by Homer' (pp. 106-107).

As a result of these incidents in Liegnitz and Weimar, Rathenau came to regard the National Assembly and indeed parliamentary government in general in a thoroughly unsympathetic
frame of mind. His disgust was brought to a head by the action of the Social Democratic Minister of National Economy,
Wissell. In the great debate on the Socialization Law, Wissell
went out of his way to stress his complete disagreement with
Rathenau, and, unintentionally no doubt, gave an entirely false
impression of Rathenau's proposals. He accused him *inter alia*
of wanting to turn German industry into a highly centralized
big business, a sort of huge A.E.G., and added: 'Rathenau's
ideal is an industrial system working under compulsion and
involving a feverish intensification of labour. We too want to
work; but only on condition that man is given what is humanly
his due.' [17]

A more complete distortion of his views it would be hard to
conceive. Rathenau was justly indignant, and in the *Zukunft*
of April 12th, 1919, he addressed an open letter to Wissell,
which displays an irritation quite unusual in him:

In justice to you I assume that you have not read my earlier
writings, in particular *The New Economy*, and that you had

[17] Shorthand reports. *Loc. cit.*, Vol. III, p. 1,490. 23rd Session, March 8th,
1919.

yourself supplied with just a few catchwords for the purpose of your argument. That is, I believe, the custom, but it is none the less an unpleasant custom. However, I felt quite inclined to forgive you your incompetence when I read how deliciously you went on to remark: 'In itself it would not be at all a bad thing for us to take over a clever man's clever idea, in so far as it is practicable.' In itself it would not be at all a bad thing! No, sir, it certainly would not be at all a bad thing! Nor would it be a bad thing if you were to favour us with a little honesty and common sense. But then that is so difficult, isn't it? It is so much more simple to dismiss a man's life-work in a few casual sentences, especially if one has not taken the trouble to find out what it is. But I will tell you what is a bad thing, and that is your empty skeleton of a law for so-called socialization. It is a matter of indifference to me, Sir, that you profess to know my writings, and then proceed to show your ignorance of them by distorting them, and that you make a pretence of socialization by turning a few sources of wealth to revenue purposes and by introducing a new bourgeois form of coal trust. But the people will not be deceived. Germany will get a new industrial system and a just one, even if not at your hands.

The dishonesty of the notorious 'As I understand it' is only equalled by the placard announcing that 'Socialization is on the march.'

With the respect due to you,

WALTHER RATHENAU

What infuriated Rathenau still more than the distortion of his ideas in a speech that was bound to carry far and wide was the misguided attempt of Wissell and his Secretary of State, Wichard von Möllendorff, to set up a new state-controlled system of industry; an attempt which he felt to be doomed to failure, both because it could not muster sufficient political support, and because neither the employers nor the men had yet acquired those new ethics which seemed to Rathenau the indispensable prerequisite for any new form of industry. He felt this clumsy and premature attempt at state control of industry to be a sort of sabotage (unintentional sabotage, of course) of the ideas which had been his life-work.

For the same reason—because the new ethics were lacking— he later on refused his assent to the more radical proposals of Kautsky, Hilferding, Kuczynski and Lederer in the Second Socialization Commission, which was convened in July, 1920, after the Kapp Putsch, under pressure from the trades unions. His point of view he set out in a guarded form in this Commission's Proposal II, to which he put his name: 'It will be our task to effect the transition to new forms of industry and to point out the paths leading from our present industrial ethics to a system based on community ethics; but at the same time care must be taken to avoid the premature formation of systems for which the driving force has not yet been developed.' (Report of the Socialization Commission, dated July 31st, 1920, p. 17.)

It was with the purpose of defending his ideas against revolutionary forces whose plans seemed to him both premature and doomed to failure that he wrote his last important book, *The New Society*, published in 1919. In it he draws a gruesome picture, or perhaps rather caricature, of this 'new society' in which the disappearance of the proletariat class is followed not, as had been hoped, by a society where every one is rich, but on the contrary 'by one where every one is very, very poor.' (*Neue Gesellschaft*, p. 10.) He tries to visualize the completely socialized Germany of the future, and finds that he is describing 'Hell' (*loc. cit.*, p. 48). But, he adds, 'this description presupposes implicitly the continuance of our present way of thought and ethical outlook. . . . Our picture simply demonstrates the

256

ISOLATION

obvious fact that happiness is not to be attained by mechanical contrivances' (*loc. cit.*, p. 51).

Does this mean that we must just fold our arms and do nothing? No. We must hasten on the change of attitude by shifting the emphasis from material to spiritual values, and thus bridge the gap between the old way and the new. Even manual and factory labour must be spiritually rejuvenated. But, one may ask, surely all this has already been discussed in great detail? And we have heard Rathenau's solution: solidarity and factory councils. True. But now he has the courage to confess that 'mechanized and mechanical work is an evil in itself, and an evil of such a kind that no amount of economic or social reorganization can remove it. Neither Karl Marx nor Lenin can get over this fact. . . . It is a mistake to suppose that craftsmanship will ever develop out of the soulless specialization which is the basis of mechanized production. . . . So long as the division of labour persists, craftsmanship is impossible and man is doomed to specialization, or at best and under the most highly mechanized state of development, to supervisory work. No one can put joy into his work if the mind and soul have no part in it. The terrible thing about the process of mechanization is that it makes labour, which occupies more than half man's working day and is his real element, in which he moves and has his being—it makes this both ugly and hateful. . . . Here lies the central problem of socialism' (*loc. cit.*, pp. 75-78).

In other words, Rathenau saw that for the majority of factory workers the way to the new attitude was blocked by an obstacle which could not be completely removed, which could indeed only be slightly dislodged even in the most favourable circumstances, and that obstacle was the 'weariness of soul' consequent upon the infinitely detailed division of labour. Solidarity, socialization, a share in the management, all required

257

something to complete them; and this something Rathenau found in the proposal for the 'equalization of labour,' which he now put forward for the first time. 'The equalization of labour aims at humanizing labour. Since it is technically impossible to humanize mechanical labour beyond a given point, the working day must be humanized by interchanging mechanical with brain work.' (*Neue Gesellschaft*, p. 78.) 'The principle of the equalization of labour is that every mechanical worker should be able to spend part of his day in some suitable form of brain work, and that every brain worker should be obliged to devote a part of his working day to physical labour. . . . To this end every young German man and woman without distinction must spend a year of training in manual labour' (*loc. cit.*, p. 80). Rathenau expands his view in a letter to Leopold Ziegler: 'The equalization of labour is not to be considered as an actual measure, but rather as a tendency. . . . For many decades the process will only be a partial one, and indeed it will only be completed when it has become superfluous; when, that is to say, the true meaning of labour has returned, and this will happen when mechanization has conquered itself.' (Letter 587.)

One may or may not have doubts as to the practicability of Rathenau's proposals,[18] but they certainly form a noteworthy climax to his theoretical labours. He acknowledges, in fact, that the soul-destroying effect of the infinitely detailed division of labour on the factory worker cannot be avoided either by the socialization of the means of production, or by a share in the management, or by any shortening of working hours at present

[18] It cannot be maintained that the 'year of training' would be impracticable in a country that had once known universal service. The equalization of labour, however, raises questions of much deeper significance, which cannot be discussed here. The professor of political economy, the industrialist, the clergyman, and even the poet would be none the worse for four hours daily at the machine; but it is not so simple in the case of the doctor, the merchant or the higher officials; and the intellectual professions which could be made available to millions of factory workers as serious occupations and not as mere recreation are at present far to seek.

258

conceivable, or even by the most highly developed feeling of solidarity; and hence that for a long period only palliatives could and should be devised. After the bright hopes which the books he wrote in his prime had held out for a liberation of the soul through a reorganization of industry on a new ethical basis, this conclusion cannot but strike one as bitterly pessimistic.

And indeed the circumstances in which he was constrained to begin the decisive struggle for his life-work justified the utmost pessimism. Germany lay prostrate. France gave open vent to her desire for our extermination, expressing it monumentally in her Prime Minister's words: 'There are twenty million Germans too many.' The continuation of the Allied blockade after the Armistice was rapidly fulfilling this wish; within six months from the Armistice it had achieved a casualty list of 700,000 children, old people and women. Not since the days of Cato's 'delenda est Carthago' had the world seen such studied ferocity. The German people, starved and dying by the hundred thousand, were reeling deliriously between blank despair, frenzied revelry and revolution. Berlin had become a nightmare, a carnival of jazz bands and rattling machine-guns. The German Government, reduced to a handful of courageous men living a precarious existence from hour to hour, were huddled together in the Wilhelmstrasse with Bolshevism and Spartacus held at arm's length. One day in January all that was left them was a few government buildings riddled by the bullets of the Spartacists. Three risings, which caused more bloodshed than the whole of the French Revolution, followed close upon one another in December, January and March; but mingling with the clatter of the machine-guns in the dark streets at night, there came floating out of bars and night clubs the strains of the latest catch or foxtrot. On the very day on which the atrocious massacre of thirty young sailors was perpetrated in broad daylight in the centre of Berlin, the streets were placarded with a poster 'Who has the prettiest legs in Berlin? Visit the Caviare-flapper dance at such and such a cabaret at 8.30 P.M.' Profiteers and their girls, the scum and riff-raff of half Europe—types preserved like flies in amber in the caricatures of George Grosz —could be seen growing fat and sleek and flaunting their new cars and ostentatious jewellery in the faces of the pale children and starving women shivering in their rags before the empty bakers' and butchers' shops. Girls and married women were selling themselves for a quartern loaf. Not only government and the state, but the very foundations of civilized life, seemed on the verge of collapse. Anti-Semitism flourished. Irresponsibility and despair were crystallizing into an attitude of mind which considered the Browning and the hand-grenade the only arguments worth using. Civil war was rapidly school-ing a section of the hot-headed youth of the country, mostly boys in their teens, to become assassins, teaching them to be brutally indifferent to human life and paving the way for that long funeral procession which began with Rosa Luxemburg, Karl Liebknecht and Leo Jogisches, and led by way of hundreds of murders perpetrated in cold blood to those of Erzberger and Walther Rathenau. And, worst of all, darken-ing every prospect of the future, there was that council behind closed doors in Paris, where the Big Three, Clemenceau, Lloyd George and Wilson, were perfecting some mysterious terror, some instrument of pitiless revenge, something still vague and shapeless, but already oppressing every heart like a lowering thunder-cloud with a sense of hopeless anxiety—an anxiety that became almost palpable when the machine-gun fire of the revolution stopped at last and a sudden deathly silence reigned in the streets.

All this must be pictured, if one wants to understand the fate that was soon to overtake Rathenau, and his own presenti-ments of this fate. But what Rathenau could not know, what nobody could know, was the rapidity with which the sound forces hidden away beneath this putrefying husk were even then building up a new Germany.

In December, 1918, Rathenau wrote two open letters, one 'To all who are not blinded by hate,' and the other to President Wilson's friend, Colonel House. 'He who visits Germany twenty years hence,' he said in the first, 'Germany which he had known as one of Earth's fairest lands, will feel his heart sinking with grief and shame. . . . The German cities will not be precisely ruins; they will be half-dead blocks of stone, still partly tenanted by wretched, careworn beings. . . . The countryside will be trodden under foot, the woods hewn down, the fields scarce showing their miserable crops; harbours, railways, canals will be in ruin and decay, and everywhere will stand the mighty buildings of the past, crumbling reminders of the age of greatness. . . . The German spirit which has sung and thought for the world will be a thing of the past, and a people still young and strong today, and created by God for life, will exist only in a state of living death.' [19]

To President Wilson's friend he wrote: 'Never since history began has so much power been entrusted to any one body of men as to Wilson, Clemenceau and Lloyd George today. Never before has the fate of a healthy and unbroken, gifted and industrious people been dependent on one single decision of a group of men. Suppose that a hundred years hence the thriving towns of Germany are deserted and in ruins, its trade and industry destroyed, the German spirit in science and art dead, and German men and women in their millions torn and driven from their homes—will the verdict of history and of God then be that this people have been treated justly, and that the three men responsible for this devastation have done justice? . . .

'Colonel, my work is done; for myself I have nothing more to hope or fear; my country has no further need of me, and I

[19] Printed in *Nach der Flut*, p. 69 ff.

do not suppose I shall long outlive its downfall. As a humble member of a people wounded to the heart, struggling simultaneously for its new-found freedom and its very existence, I appeal to you, the representative of the most progressive of all nations. Four years ago we were apparently your equals; but only apparently, for in fact we lacked that element which gives a nation its real strength: internal freedom. Today we stand on the verge of annihilation; a fate which cannot be avoided if Germany is to be crippled as those who hate us wish. For this fact must be stated clearly and insistently, so that all may understand its terrible significance, all nations and their peoples, the present generation and those to come: what we are threatened with, what the policy of hate proposes, is our annihilation, the annihilation of German life now and for evermore.'[20]

The impression which this letter made on House revived in Rathenau a small measure of hope. At the New Year of 1919 he wrote to his friend:

Once again my heartfelt thanks.

Apart from your doubly welcome greeting the New Year has brought me a piece of good news, which I will confide to you. Colonel House has let me know through an emissary—a former member of the American Embassy [Mr Dresel]—that he was deeply shocked to read my letter, and had given it to Wilson immediately on his arrival.

Affectionately,

W.

But then came the Peace, a dictate which gave expression, paragraph by paragraph, to Clemenceau's threat. The German delegation advised unanimously against signing. Rathenau had his own solution. In the *Zukunft* of May 31st he wrote an

[20] *Loc. cit.*, pp. 62-63.

article entitled *The End:* 'What is to be done? At Versailles we must do our utmost to effect some radical improvement in the Treaty. If we succeed, well and good—then sign it. But if we do not, what then? In that case neither active nor passive resistance should be attempted. In that case the negotiator, Count Brockdorff-Rantzau, must deliver to the enemy governments the duly executed decree dissolving the National Assembly, and the resignation of the President and ministers, and invite them to take over without delay the sovereign rights of the German Reich and the whole machinery of government. Hereby the responsibility for the peace, for the administration, for all Germany's actions, would fall to the enemy; and before the world, before history, and before their own peoples, they would be faced with the care of sixty millions. It would be a case without parallel, the unprecedented downfall of a nation, but at the same time a course compatible with honour and conscience. For the rest we must trust to the inalienable right of mankind—and the clearly predictable march of events.' As he says in a letter to a friend, what he expected from this step was that it would make clear to the Entente that their demands were exaggerated and could not possibly be carried out. 'The Entente governments would then be compelled to form a Condominium, which would soon realize the desirability of having a stable government in Germany that could render the country capable of discharging its obligations.' (Letter 538 of June 3rd, 1919.) It would be a waste of time to consider what would have happened if the National Assembly and the Government had followed Rathenau's advice.

The acceptance of the Peace terms involved among other things the extradition of the so-called 'war-criminals,' and it seemed possible that Rathenau's name might be included in the list. Statements to that effect appeared in the newspapers. About the middle of June he wrote to his Swedish friend Ernst Norlind: 'Some papers have published the report that the

Entente demands my extradition. Apparently a Franco-
Belgian press campaign is responsible for this. It is persistently
maintained that I occasioned the destruction of the French and
Belgian factories; that in fact a systematic *plan Rathenau* was
in existence. Now, the destructions only began in the autumn
of 1916, and I had already retired from office in April, 1915.
The *plan* is a myth. I tried to deny it in a French paper, but of
course my denial was suppressed. I know that a military court
awaits me behind closed doors. I happened to be in Paris when
the Dreyfus case was going on. However, this worry matters
little compared with the desperate state of the country. It is
more terrible than the war, and again, as in the war, the people
have no suspicion of the truth.' (Letter 553.)

The situation did indeed appear to become ever more hopeless; externally, because there was no diminution of the hysteri-
cal fear of Germany, which made Clemenceau and his followers inexorable, in spite of the annihilation of all her sources
of power; internally, because the revolutionary impulse, exhausted by its struggle with the Spartacists, was no longer
capable of that basic reformation of state and society which
Rathenau looked upon as a vital necessity for the German
people. Rathenau felt that he had been defeated in the fight for
his ideas into which he had plunged with so much weight and
vigour.

In his *Criticism of the Threefold Revolution*, published in
August, 1919, he once more stated his demands, epitomizing
them in the word 'Responsibility.' The specific propositions he
set forth were the same as those which he had propounded consistently in all his writings from the early *Physiology of Business* onwards—broadening and completing them, but never
deviating from the straight line that led to *The New Economy*
and *The New State*. We have already considered them and
need not recall them here. But Germany's helplessness, the
Peace, and the World Revolution which seemed on the way,

showed them up in a new light. The masses everywhere were clamouring for redemption. 'Neither the played-out individualism of the West, nor the abstract and doctrinaire orthodoxy of Russia, will save us from the abyss. This is where Germany can help. If her help is accepted, then it will be as if the war had never been. There will be no further question of parcelling out the world; we shall still have room to live out our destiny; we shall no longer be condemned to the bondage of the raw-materials monopolies, the boycott, and the indemnities; and the wound in the body of world industry will be healed. Co-operation instead of conflict will be the life of the peoples. . . . But if this does not happen, then Germany will become and will remain a Balkan race among Balkan races, awaiting with the others salvation from the East.' (*Kritik der dreifachen Revolution*, p. 51.)

The National Assembly realized practically none of his demands. He did not admit defeat; but he gave free rein to his bitterness and disappointment in an article which he wrote for Helmuth von Gerlach's *Welt am Montag* on the anniversary of the Revolution, November 11th, 1919. 'It was not a revolution. It was simply a collapse. The doors were burst asunder, the warders ran away, and the captive people stood in the courtyard, dazed and helpless. Had it been a revolution, the forces and ideas that it engendered would have continued to bear fruit. A real movement is only maintained by the forces it engenders. All that the people wanted was rest. . . . The first year has brought a certain measure of order; which was to be expected, for we are an orderly people. It has produced bourgeois measures, an old-fashioned republican constitution and so forth; ideas and deeds it has not produced. . . . We are what we were, and remain what we are. For ever? No. For we are now beginning to experience the pressure that will make us malleable and adaptable. . . . The next few years will give us the chance to come to grips with the problems that face us.

Then we shall see whether we are capable of something more than a mere copy of the bourgeois democracies and economic systems of the last century. I think the answer will be in the affirmative.' [21]

He did not admit defeat. About the time this article appeared he wrote to Lore Karrenbrock: 'I no longer belong to myself, I have given myself away. I have nothing left, hardly an hour of rest, scarcely sleep itself. I am merely a stranger who has come to give of himself, and I shall live only so long as there is still something to give.' (Letter 577.) And four weeks later he wrote to Ernst Norlind: 'I know for certain that in fifty years' time at the latest our country will have made a complete recovery. But I know also that for the next five years it is destined to get worse and worse.' (Letter 593.)

Rathenau now took a further step to the Left by joining the *Sozialwissenschaftlicher Verein*, which was founded by Left Democrats, Pacifists and Independents. About this time he wrote to a Swedish friend, Peter Hammer: 'I have many points of contact with the radicals, but several circumstances prevent my making this contact any closer. . . . *In Days to Come* is, I believe, the most revolutionary book that has appeared for many years. . . . *The New Economy* was the forerunner of the system of communal trading which now forms the central plank of the Majority Socialist platform as far as industrial matters are concerned. Thus I should be much less compromised than most socialists, and yet my relationship to socialism, especially to the left wing, with which I have most in common, is a very delicate one. . . . What I fear is that there is no real will to carry into effect a truly constructive policy.' (Letter 543.)

In November, 1920, something happened which profoundly influenced Rathenau's future. Ludendorff, who stuck at nothing in his efforts to escape responsibility for the loss of the war,

[21] *Welt am Montag*, November 10, 1919, No. 45.

declared before the Reichstag Committee of Enquiry: 'I regret that I am compelled to repeat a remark of Walther Rathenau's to the effect that on the day that the Kaiser and his paladins on their white chargers ride victorious through the Brandenburger Tor, history will have lost all meaning. Thus there were currents of opinion in the nation which did not subscribe to the view of the Supreme Command that we must fight to a victorious conclusion, and these currents of opinion must be taken into account.'

Rathenau immediately saw what the effect of this poisonous distortion of his words would be. In his essay, *Shicksalsspiel,* he says: 'This statement of General Ludendorff's before the Committee of Enquiry can and will be taken to mean that I helped to undermine the morale of the people, that I worked against victory, and strove to sabotage the war. I cannot allow such an imputation to be laid to my charge. I reject it, and will give my grounds for doing so. My "remark" is to be found in my essay *The Kaiser,* which appeared at the beginning of this year. Had Ludendorff taken the trouble to read this, he would have understood what it meant, namely that under Germany's leaders at the beginning of the war (the remark was made in September, 1914) we could not hope for victory.' (*Was wird werden?* p. 5.) For very many people, especially in young nationalistic circles, Ludendorff's misinterpretation stamped Rathenau as a noxious criminal on whom it would be an act of patriotism to take vengeance. From then on he was a marked man.

CHAPTER X

THE NEW FOREIGN POLICY: THE FIGHT
FOR PEACE

ON JANUARY 10th, 1920, the Peace Treaty came into
force. This brought with it as a first result the list of
so-called 'war criminals' to be surrendered to the
Allies in accordance with the terms of the treaty. Rathenau's
name was not among them.

In a letter to his friend on this occasion he writes:

Your letter was perhaps the most beautiful and moving
you have ever sent me. It made me feel all the love you had
breathed into it. I cannot answer it; I can only be grateful
for it. It came at a moment when a burden had just been lifted
from my mind, a burden which I had fully expected to have
to bear, and which I should not have shrunk from bearing.
But though it has weighed on me I cannot say I feel any freer
now that it has gone. It makes me feel all the more deeply
the burden that the others and my country have to bear: I
almost feel I would rather have shared it to the utmost limit.
But perhaps that is morbid. Up to the last moment I was almost certain I should find my name on the list; and when I
tell you some day of the exchange of notes with Belgium, which
was—and still is—being conducted on my behalf, you won't
find that surprising.

No clear line seems possible at present, so great is the general confusion of ideas on the whole subject. For on the one
hand the nation cannot be expected to surrender the victims
of its own free will. Yet on the other hand they cannot be

allowed to plunge their country into disaster. Therefore they must either give themselves up or else seek refuge in flight; the one thing they must not do is to go about here as if nothing had happened. I had made all preparations for the first alternative; but I don't ask that others should do likewise. Every effort must be made to assist those who wish to flee, but there must be no staying on here. In Greece, if a man was an innocent or unwitting victim in such a case as this, he left the country.

But now I am becoming political. Isn't that almost an answer to your question? No, it is not meant to be. Today my only answer is gratitude.

Your W.

5.2.20

The Kapp Putsch took place on March 13th.[1] Soon after this Rathenau began, at first almost imperceptibly, to regain political influence. The new government was formed on March 29th, the dictatorship having come to an ignominious end. The organized working-class, whose passive resistance had been the means of defeating the Putsch, now demanded socialization. Hence the government summoned a second Socialization Commission, of which, after the Independents had withdrawn their veto, Rathenau became a member.

More important for the future was the friendship which sprang up between him and Dr Wirth, the new Minister of Finance.[2] Their moral earnestness, the Christian conviction that

[1] A 'Putsch' is the slang German word for an attempt by a small armed force to overthrow the constitutional Government.

[2] Dr Joseph Wirth, born September 9th, 1879, in Baden. Studied mathematics and economics; became a schoolmaster at the Freiburg Realgymnasium. Entered the Baden Diet in 1913 and the Reichstag in 1914; became Finance Minister of the Federal State of Baden in 1918 and German Finance Minister in 1920 after the Kapp Putsch. Was German Chancellor (Prime Minister) from 1921 to 1923, and at present holds the post of German Minister for the Occupied Territories. Editor of the weekly *Deutsche Republik*.

269

man's soul is what really matters, was a close bond between them. And over and above this they had scientific interests in common (Wirth was a mathematician, Rathenau a physicist), both were interested in philosophy, both were lonely men and bachelors. This was what they had in common. But in their differences, too, they complemented each other. Wirth was impulsive, his mind worked in broad outlines; Rathenau, on the other hand, was distinguished by his exact knowledge of detail in all financial and economic questions. Wirth's mentality was simple and intuitive and sometimes mysterious in its workings, whereas Rathenau's was complex and ever dominated by his alert intelligence. Thus a friendship grew up between them, half political, half spiritual. In many ways this friendship resembled that between Walther Rathenau and his father, who had the same intuitive capacity for arriving at surprising decisions by obscure processes of thought. Whether Rathenau was conscious of this resemblance, I do not know; but although Wirth was by far the younger man, his attitude to him always had in it a certain element of tender considerateness—one might almost say of filial piety. The first result of this mutual appreciation was that Wirth took Rathenau to Spa with him.

By the conclusion of peace Germany was confronted with two problems which needed an immediate solution:

1. How was she, being disarmed, to regain her freedom of action, and a measure—if at first only a small measure—of self-determination in her dealings with the Allies, these being armed to the teeth? Obviously the first essential was a New German Foreign Policy, which would enable her to gain her ends without the backing of force.

2. What attitude should Germany adopt towards the stupendous material burdens arising out of the Peace Treaty, in particular her Reconstruction and Reparations obligations, so

as to prevent them from completely crushing her economic and financial life?

Up to the present day the whole of Germany's post-war policy has turned upon the solution of these two questions. Rathenau realized, virtually at once, that if there *was* an answer to them, then it could be found only by recognizing clearly their intimate connection. On the very day of the ratification of the Peace Treaty by the German National Assembly, July 16th, 1919, he wrote to Erzberger, the Minister of Finance: 'In our present desperate situation we must strive to find the central point from which the whole situation can be unravelled. This point is to be found in Belgium and North France—that is to say, in the problem of reconstruction. From this point we can—

1. Regulate our relations with France;
2. Improve the peace terms;
3. Change the character of, and effect a reduction in, the indemnity;
4. Exert influence on Germany's internal condition;
5. Restore Germany's moral strength.

It is essential that we should make the Reconstruction problem the keystone of our policy, and not treat it just as an embarrassing duty.' (Letter 551.)

On April 26th, 1920, the Allies invited the German Government to send delegates to Spa for a discussion of all questions raised by the Peace Treaty. The Conference began on July 5th. The German delegation consisted of the Chancellor, Fehrenbach,[3] the Foreign Minister, Dr Simons,[4] the ministers con-

---

[3] Constantin Fehrenbach, born January 11th, 1852, in Baden. A lawyer by profession and a leading member of the Catholic Centre Party. Member of the Reichstag from 1913 to 1918, where he made his mark by a speech against the Imperial Government in the Zabern affair. President of the German National

cerned with economic matters, General von Seeckt,[5] and a large number of experts—also Rathenau, whom Wirth had included in face of violent opposition and, lastly, as chief representative of the German industrialists, Hugo Stinnes.[6]

Stinnes was at the time the most powerful man in Germany, a sort of secret Kaiser towering above the stricken state on a pedestal of huge, if rather vague, industrial power. For the man-in-the-street, both at home and abroad, he had already become a legendary figure, a wizard, a Klingsor who alone possessed the secret of conjuring forth magic gardens from the stony ruins of German industry, a Cagliostro, an alchemist capable by some sort of sorcery of transmuting paper into gold. But even at close range he was impressive—one half, to be sure, only a big uncanny financier, but the other half a prophet, wont to say his sooth blatantly and bluntly, but yet impenetrable, and thus mysterious to friend and foe alike. He went

Assembly in Weimar in 1919. Chancellor from 1920 to 1921. Died March 3rd, 1926.

[4] Dr Walther Simons, born 1861 in Elberfeld. Studied law, became a judge, then legal adviser of the German Foreign Office. Secretary-General of the German Peace delegation at Versailles, advocated the rejection of the Versailles Treaty and resigned when it was signed. German Minister for Foreign Affairs from 1920 to 1921. Later President of the German Supreme Court. After the death of President Ebert, he became Acting President under the Constitution till the election of Field-Marshal von Hindenburg.

[5] General Hans von Seeckt, born April 4th, 1866. During the war, Chief of Staff to Field-Marshal Mackensen. Organized the great offensive against the Russians in Galicia in May, 1915, broke their front and smashed the Russian 'steam-roller' at the battle of Gorlice-Tarnow. Commander-in-Chief and reorganizer of the Reichswehr (after the Kapp Putsch) from 1920 to 1926.

[6] Hugo Stinnes, born February 12th, 1870, in Mülheim on the Ruhr, of well-to-do parents. Began life as a clerk in a small business, then worked for some time as a common labourer in a coal-pit. Went into the coal trade in 1893 and soon afterwards founded his own firm of "Hugo Stinnes." Became one of the magnates of the Coal Syndicate in Essen in 1903, went into the Reichstag in 1920 as a member of the 'Volkspartei,' acquired immense wealth by speculating on the fall of the mark and buying up industries all over Germany and Europe with the proceeds of his speculations, ultimately welding his business together into the biggest European trust, which, however, collapsed soon after his death in April, 1924.

about among German coal merchants and steel magnates, his colleagues, like a stranger; very dark, looking like a southerner, a Frenchman or an Assyrian, with a thick black beard and eyes that seemed always gazing on some inner vision, moving in what was left of Society in heavy peasant boots and clothes that hung about him as if he had just got them back from the pawnbroker's, always surrounded by a vast family, which he dragged along behind him wherever he went; a cross between a patriarch, a commercial traveller and the Flying Dutchman. Taken all in all he was, perhaps, a man possessed—possessed by the demon of big business, by an unquenchable thirst for supreme power through commercial transactions, as Hokusai was possessed by the demon of painting and drawing. For, at bottom, he was nothing but just a company promoter, with no other interest or outlook than finance. Yet, with all that, one could not call him precisely a reactionary; Stresemann was able to say of him in his obituary speech, without irony, that he was 'first and foremost a staunch Republican'—although it would probably have been nearer the truth to say that he cared as little about the Hohenzollerns as he did about the Republic. In a certain sense, he seemed friendly even to labour, being no less concerned about the 'living inventory,' the workers of his countless undertakings, about their conditions of life, their health and working capacity, than about the good condition of his machines; going to the length of promoting common workmen to leading positions in his companies, not in the interest, to be sure, of the working class (that would have been Rathenau's reason for doing so), but 'because it is a peculiar fact that the influence of the parents' wealth on the younger generation is not precisely favourable. . . . This being so, we must see to it that the blobs of fat in the great soup tureen of labour can come to the surface and take the place at present

273

WALTHER RATHENAU

occupied by the families of the rich.'⁷ In the interest of big
business, of course!

The French Premier, M Millerand, opened the Conference
with an address requesting the Germans to account for their·
failure to make the requisite coal deliveries. The Supreme
Council had decided that Germany should grant an absolute
priority for Reparations coal over all deliveries for home consumption, and should agree to a rigid control of German coal
distribution. The Allies demanded two million tons monthly,
and threatened, in the words of the invitation to the Conference, that if this was not carried out 'they would proceed to take
whatever measures were necessary to secure the fulfilment of
their demands, even if they should involve a further occupation of German territory.'

On the following day, after Dr Simons had replied, Hugo
Stinnes rose from his seat, and glaring at the Allied delegates,
began as follows: 'I make my speech standing, so that I can
look my audience straight between the eyes.'⁸ This tone he
kept up all through his address. Dr Bergmann, who was at
Spa as the representative of the German Government on the
Reparations Commission, states that 'the speech created a violent sensation and did much harm to the German cause at
Spa.'⁹ Indeed, the tension between the Germans and the Allies
became acute, and gave rise to unpleasant incidents. But it was
hardly less acute within the German delegation itself. Here,
however, it had the advantage of leading to a thorough discussion of principles, the result of which was decisive, in that it
determined the main lines of future German policy.

The two opposite points of view were represented by Stinnes
and Rathenau. Even outwardly the contrast between them was

⁷ Speech of October 29th, 1920. Quoted by Gaston Raphael, *Hugo Stinnes, der Mensch, sein Werk, sein Wirken*, p. 27.
⁸ Speech reprinted in the *Deutsche Allgemeine Zeitung* of April 10th, 1925.
⁹ Carl Bergmann, *Der Weg der Reparation*, p. 62.

274

very striking: on the one hand, Rathenau, the polished gentleman, who spoke as if from a pedestal, in wonderfully complicated periods and a highly ornamental style; and on the
other, Stinnes, clad like a common workman and averse from
fine phrases, who concealed visionary plans behind a thick
veil of 'hard facts,' an impenetrable mask of misleading common sense.[10] Stinnes demanded that the Allied ultimatum
should be rejected. What if this meant an extension of the
occupation and the Bolshevization of the rest of Germany?
Once the Allies felt the Bolshevik menace at their very doors,
they would soon come to reason and be prepared to deal justly
with Germany! His proposal really meant blackmailing the
blackmailer; in which process, however, the German blackmailer was invited first to commit suicide on the doorstep of
the French—a new and strangely mystical form of the old
Machtpolitik oddly disguised in the semblance of world revolution, though, it is true, this was the only kind of *Machtpolitik*
Germany could at that time pursue. Doubtless behind all this
Stinnes did not altogether overlook the possibility indicated by
Rathenau in his lecture on 'Democratic Development,' given in
Berlin shortly before Spa: 'We must not be deceived by those
who say to us: "Let things take their course, it will all turn out
right in the end." Among those who say this there are some
who play with the thought: if Germany is divided into three
parts, one of these, the western portion, will then regain its
prosperity and become a sort of German Belgium' (*loc. cit.*, p.
23). This 'German Belgium' was the scene of Stinnes' principal activities; and here there might actually have been a brief
spell of apparent recovery. But if the Allies had occupied the
Ruhr under the conditions which would have developed on
Stinnes' advice being taken, one can hardly doubt that Poin-

[10] I remember a visit which Rathenau paid Stinnes in Mülheim before the
war, and from which he returned disgusted by the lack of culture he had found
there.

caré would have had an infinitely better chance of achieving his aim—viz., of detaching the Rhineland from Germany and bringing it within the political and economic orbit of France. Thus what was at stake between Stinnes and Rathenau was really the whole post-war fate and history of Germany and Europe.

Rathenau vigorously attacked Stinnes' proposal. He pleaded for an answer that would at least not preclude negotiations. Negotiations would give an opportunity, as he had expressed it in his letter to Erzberger, 'to unravel the whole situation'— that is to say, to discuss and perhaps to solve not only the Coal and Reparations questions, but all the various problems raised by the Peace Treaty. To support this policy he only needed to refer to the views he had developed in his *New Era* article after the 1907 elections: 'that wars are seldom decisive—that in the game of foreign policy the protagonists have just so many counters as their economic power provides, and that a nation can win and retain just so much weight in foreign affairs as corresponds to its moral, intellectual and economic resources' (*cf. supra*, pp. 126-127).

This applied to the Allies no less than to disarmed Germany. Therefore negotiations must be the aim. Negotiations breed wishes, and these give opportunities for the expression of counter-wishes. In the course of this process the weight of intellectual and economic forces on both sides comes into play, one wheel starts another and the ascent from the depths begins. Partly to save the Ruhr, but partly also to set going the machinery of negotiation, Rathenau urged that the coal demands should be accepted and, moreover, that a definite order for the discharge of the total Reparations liability should be made forthwith.[11]

[11] Lord D'Abernon notes in his diary February 1st, 1922: 'He [Rathenau] has taken to international Conferences with passion. He wants them to go on all the

The former Colonial Secretary, Dernburg,[12] was the first to accept the point of view so brilliantly expressed and defended by Rathenau, and was of course supported by Dr Wirth, but also, which was more remarkable, by General von Seeckt and the majority of the German delegates. As Dr Wirth said in conversation with me years later: 'In this hour the Policy of Fulfilment was born.' It is remarkable that the starting-point of Rathenau's policy—'Once negotiations are possible, anything is possible'—had been Talleyrand's guiding principle at the Congress of Vienna, where he also was the representative of a country defeated, powerless, and occupied by the enemy.

The Cabinet accepted the Coal ultimatum, but declined, greatly to the injury of Germany's permanent interests, to transmit an offer for her total liability. On July 16th 'in the midst' as Bergmann reports (p. 63), 'of indescribable excitement,' a coal protocol was signed in which Germany pledged herself to deliver two million tons of coal monthly for a period of six months beginning on August 1st. As a result of this it was decided, on Mr Lloyd George's initiative, to discuss the whole question of Reparations with Germany at a new conference at Geneva.

Hugo Stinnes did not forgive Rathenau his defeat. It was Stinnes who coined the phrase in Spa about Rathenau's having the 'soul of an alien race,' Stinnes, who himself had Southern French blood in his veins and looked like a Phoenician sea captain. And Emile Buré reported in the *Eclair* that Stinnes' agents *'répandent partout des bruits calomnieux et laissent entendre notamment que monsieur Loucheur ne songe avec monsieur*

time. There cannot be too many. Let them be small in point of numbers, but long in period of time; not too many Powers to attend, but plenty of time to discuss.' (*An Ambassador of Peace*, vol. i., p. 255.)

[12] Bernhard Dernburg, born July 17th, 1865, in Darmstadt, of an old Berlin family of lawyers. Secretary of State for the Colonies 1907-1910, Member of the German National Assembly and German Minister of Finance in 1919. He it was whom Rathenau had accompanied to East Africa in 1907 and 1908.

Rathenau qu'à s'assurer la direction d'un trust européen de l'électricité.'

Rathenau opposed the whole weight of his personality to Stinnes' desire to 'Bolshevize' Germany. But relations with Soviet Russia, on the other hand, formed a logically inevitable part of his policy of negotiation: the closer the relations, the more surely and rapidly must the hoped-for results take place. Even under the Imperial Government in the summer of 1918 negotiations had taken place with the aim of transforming the one-sided Treaty of Brest-Litovsk into a basis for mutual friendly relations. The negotiations, which took place in Berlin, at first under von Kühlmann, when he was Secretary of State for Foreign Affairs, and then under his successor, von Hintze, were conducted on the Russian side by the People's Commissary, Krassin, and the Russian Ambassador, Joffe; on the German side by the head of the Eastern Department in the Foreign Office, Nadolny (now German Ambassador to Turkey), the head of the Judicial Department of the Foreign Office, Dr Kriege, by various officers representing the Supreme Command, by Dr von Prittwitz, the present German Ambassador in Washington, and myself representing the Chancellor, and, finally, by the then Member of the Reichstag, Dr Stresemann. The negotiations were prolonged by the fantastic demands of Ludendorff and his staff. It was, for instance, a long time before he could be induced to give up the idea of a Cossack republic on the Don under a German protectorate. In the end any results that had been obtained were brought to nought by Germany's collapse and the dictated Peace of Versailles.

As soon as the Peace Treaty came into force Rathenau took up the idea of an understanding with Russia. 'But,' he writes to a friend in Berlin on January 26th, 1920, 'the present government has not yet reached the standpoint which I represent— *i.e.* that we must enter into an economic relationship with Russia.' (Letter 609.) And so he took the matter into his own

278

hands, and 'in the face of considerable difficulty founded with a few friends a "Commission for the study of Russian affairs." ' (Letter 621.) On March 10th, 1920, he wrote to Professor Hoffmann, Wilhelmshaven: 'I am in complete agreement with you as to the necessity of finding some common ground between Russia and ourselves. At the present time Bolshevism is only a façade; what we are really confronted with is a rigidly oligarchic agrarian republic, which in spite of all its difficulties is, I believe, destined to last. True, it will be a long time before Russia is strong enough to grant us economic compensations. . . . It is my hope that the labours of the Commission [referred to above] will bring about the first and decisive *rapprochement* in the economic sphere, to be followed, let us hope, by a corresponding *rapprochement* in the political sphere.' (Letter 622.)

Understandings in the West and resumption of relations in the East thus became the two immediate aims of German Foreign Policy. They followed necessarily from the views Rathenau had expressed long before the war on the fundamentals of international politics. He now urged the leaders of Germany to build up a new foreign policy on these fundamentals to replace her old policy of Armaments and Power. That was the background of his speech at Spa and of the Policy of Fulfilment which it initiated; a policy which Dr Stresemann took up again and continued after Rathenau's death and after the collapse of passive resistance in the Ruhr, and constantly thereafter. The essence of this policy, which has become the common property of the vast majority of Germans, is the effort to counteract the work of Versailles and the destruction of Germany's military power by a policy of negotiation and understanding, with the aim of hastening the return of Germany to that place among the nations which corresponds to her moral, intellectual and economic resources.

WALTHER RATHENAU

It is obvious what part would be played in this scheme by the League of Nations. Rathenau could not but have welcomed it, had it become during his lifetime a meeting-place for the Foreign Ministers of all the nations as it did later when Germany and her former allies were admitted to it. He would have realized that these regular gatherings of leading statesmen at Geneva were the most effective instrument for putting into practice his policy of negotiation. But as a guarantee of peace in the event of serious conflicts between Great Powers he refused to trust it, at least in its present form of a League of Sovereign States. He made it quite clear that in his view an organization which really guaranteed world peace would differ fundamentally from the present League. It would have to be a structure held together, he explained, not only by diplomacy, but also by the everyday work and industry of the world: an international community of production and exchange organized on lines ensuring worldwide economic peace, and thereby doing away with most of the causes which lead to war. In his lecture on 'The Zenith of Capitalism' he says: 'From the point of view of foreign policy the nations are armed competitive communities, and so long as this is the case every peaceful effort on the part of individual nations to restrict the competitive method is doomed to failure. Every effort to exterminate armed warfare must be in vain, so long as obstinate commercial warfare is the main business of the nations.' (*Speeches*, p. 162.) Thus in a letter to Professor Victor Riecke, written shortly before the Armistice, he considers it 'necessary to emphasize the point that only constant creative labour can make possible true international co-operation.' (Letter 444.) As a first step towards a European industrial community he welcomed the idea of a 'European consortium' between Germany and the Western Powers, which should undertake the reconstruction of Russia. And this same thought inspired his proposal for the co-opera-

tion of German and French labour in the reconstruction of the
devastated areas of North France. The League of Nations
that he had in mind as a real guarantee of peace could be pictured as a glorified extension of this Franco-German rebuild-
ing of destroyed cottages.

When, in January or February, 1919, in order to ascertain
his views, I laid before him my plan, prepared under instructions from the then Foreign Minister, Count Rantzau, for 'a
real League of Nations' based on a bedrock of organized industry, trade and finance, but providing also for causes of conflict arising out of differences of race and civilization, he
agreed with it, though rather coldly, I thought. He also agreed
with the obvious reservation that it would take a long time to
put into practice and to perfect. At the end of 1919, however,
he wrote a letter to a correspondent (published after his death)
in which he outlined very much the same plan: 'Nothing could
be more futile,' he wrote, 'than the usual programme of an
international paradise, where the lion states lie down with the
lamb states for no other reason than that they all have democratic governments. My ideas on the subject are far more
Utopian than this programme, but at the same time far more
realistic. You will get some idea of them if you read my *New
State*. Only when the idea of the nationalist competitive state
has become discredited, and when the world has been split up
into communities on a just economic, administrative, cultural
and religious basis—communities which will differ fundamentally from the modern state—only then will it be possible to
eliminate the economic rivalry which is bound to provoke wars
and conflicts even under the most guileless democratic régimes.
This goal is certainly very far off; to reach it we must begin,
not with the others, but with ourselves. We must ourselves provide the example of the sort of state and economy that I have
described.' (Letter 602.)

Rathenau's mood on his return from Spa is reflected in the following letter to his friend:

30.9.20

The autumn flowers you sent me burn like a dark flame in my room. This is the most mysterious of all the seasons. Although for many years now it has filled me with intense fear of the approaching winter, I nevertheless feel a certain affinity with it. But a few weeks more and the endless, sunless, grey night begins.

I will gladly come to you, but I am afraid I have little to bring. The summer was an empty one, and the chill of the long rainy days is slow to leave the limbs.

I am fifty-three years old. I look backwards rather than forwards, and my work is almost done. It still keeps me going, but it is no longer a driving force. I have surmounted life's summit, and yet the peace I looked for has not come. It is not the broad valley that I see, but range upon range of mountains and the stars and horizon.

Farewell. I thank you from my heart for this and that, for everything.

Affectionately,

Your W.

Meanwhile in spite of Spa a section of the Allies persisted in its tactics of evading negotiations with Germany on questions arising out of the Peace Treaty, and continued the dictatorial methods which had so far proved so successful. It clearly shared Rathenau's view that negotiations were Germany's most dangerous weapon and the most effective instrument for her rehabilitation. The tactical situation at this time was that Germany went on trying—at first timidly and somewhat ineffectively—to open negotiations, as Rathenau had advised in Spa, while the Allies, under the influence of France, did all they could to wreck them. True, Germany was invited to the international financial conference at Brussels, which was convoked by the League of Nations for the end of 1920; but the League Council under French pressure had already decreed on August 5th that none of the questions outstanding between Germany and the Allies should be discussed at this meeting. (Bergmann, p. 66.) Ultimately this conference of responsible statesmen, arranged as far back as Spa and then consistently postponed owing to French influence, never materialized; its place was taken by a preparatory conference on Reparations between the German and the Allied experts, which began in Brussels on December 16th. It lasted till the 26th and was then postponed till January. Though no definite decisions were reached, the method of negotiation had nevertheless borne fruit. 'Allied and German delegates met in friendly intercourse both during, and in the intervals between, the regular sessions. There seemed every reason to hope that this conference of experts, free as it was from any sort of political pressure, would show at last the path that might lead to success. In the intervals of the conference each particular question was the subject of discussion between an Allied and a German representative. . . . For the first time a meeting had taken place between Allied and German representatives which left a favourable impression on all concerned and which had a universally good press.' (Bergmann, p. 72.)

But at this point the French Government, fearing that this method would lead to Germany's rapid—too rapid—recovery, entered the lists once more. On January 24th, 1921, the Supreme Council met suddenly and unexpectedly in Paris. It decided of its own accord, without giving Germany a hearing, that for the first eleven years Germany should pay from 2 to 5 milliard gold marks, and that for the next thirty-one years after that she should pay 6 milliard gold marks yearly. (This decision followed on a speech of Doumer's, the French Minister of Finance, who assessed Germany's total debt at 212 milliard gold marks [about $53,000,000,000] and demanded an annual instalment of 12 milliards.) To accept this Germany was invited to a conference in London.

Now at last the German Government did in haste and far too late what it ought to have done in Spa: it set about evolving a proposal of its own to submit to the Allies. A commission of experts was called together, to which Rathenau, among others, submitted a scheme. This was rejected; for the government prepared a scheme of its own which ran, as Rathenau wrote later, 'diametrically counter' to his. This government proposal estimated the present value of the Allied demands at 53 milliards, and then deducted 20 milliards from this sum in consideration of what Germany had already handed over. This left 33 milliards, which was scaled down to the round sum of 30 milliards (about $7,500,000,000); of this from 8 to 10 milliards were to be disposed of by means of loans, and a further 5 milliards by deliveries in kind, in the course of the next five years; customs and some excise duties were offered by way of security. With this scheme in their pockets they proceeded to the conference.

The first session of the conference took place in London on March 1st, 1921. Apart from Dr Simons and the German delegation the members were Lloyd George, Briand, the Italian and Belgian Premiers, the other Allied Ministers concerned, and a large number of Allied experts. Dr Simons spoke first.[13] 'Instead,' says Bergmann, 'of reading out the terms of the German offer, he gave a conscientious exposition of the difficulties which had attended its genesis, and then proceeded to an exhaustive criticism of the Paris decisions, which, he said, were economically impracticable. The situation at home did, in fact, preclude the German Government from putting forward any

[13] In my description of the London Conference I have followed the exceptionally clear and graphic account by Dr Bergmann, who himself played a leading part in it.

really definite proposals; but in spite of this they had decided to try and reach a solution of the Reparations problem with the least possible delay' (p. 88). Whereupon he proceeded to unfold the German counter-proposal outlined above. 'Throughout the rest of his speech Dr Simons kept returning to the 30-milliard figure. He explained that of these 30 milliards 8 should, in the first instance, be raised by international loan, and then went on, amid growing uneasiness, to discuss how he proposed to raise the remaining 22 milliards.

'This method of presenting his argument, which, so to speak, hammered the tabooed 30 milliards into the heads of his audience, and under which the total liability seemed to shrink away into ever-smaller proportions, together with the difficulty of translating so involved a speech, made a very unfavourable impression on the Allied members of the conference. Thus Dr Simons saw himself forced to break off in the middle, and proceeded to read out the formulated proposals, at which point Lloyd George declared with considerable acerbity that this was unnecessary. . . . The excitement in the Allied camp was astonishing. . . . People talked in all seriousness of a German challenge, and there was an immediate and universal cry for sanctions' (p. 89).

In the second session, on March 3rd, Lloyd George described the German proposals as a clear defying of the Treaty of Versailles. . . . It would be merely a waste of time to go into them. It only remained for the Allies to say that in view of the repeated breaches of the Treaty of Versailles on the part of the German Government punitive measures would now have to be resorted to. Unless Germany accepted the Paris Decisions by March 7th the Allies would proceed to sanctions, including the occupation of Düsseldorf, Duisburg and Ruhrort. On March 4th, 5th and 6th private negotiations took place between Dr Simons, Dr Bergmann, Briand, Loucheur, Lloyd George and Lord D'Abernon at Lord Curzon's private house, and attempts were made to pour oil on the troubled waters; but they did not lead to any practical result. The last session, at which Lloyd George announced the sanctions, was held on March 7th; and on March 8th Düsseldorf, Duisburg and Ruhrort were occupied. Owing to the clumsy behaviour of the German Government and Press and the adroitness of a certain section of the Allies, which preferred anything to negotiations, the policy of negotiation had been sabotaged once more.

At this point the Reparations Commission was entrusted with the task of calculating the German liability for Reparations, which, in accordance with the Treaty of Versailles, had to be determined by May 1st. The Commission concluded their labours on April 27th, and decided on a total figure of 132 milliard gold marks. The Supreme Council met again in London, drew up a scheme of its own, and then summoned the Reparations Commission to London from Paris, in order that it might communicate the completed scheme to Germany as its own work. This was done on May 5th, and was accompanied by an ultimatum from the Allied Governments which threatened the occupation of the Ruhr if the whole scheme was not accepted unconditionally within six days by the German Government.

The consternation in Germany was intense. Many declared that under no circumstances should one sign an I.O.U. for the utterly impossible sum of 132 milliards. Even the Government took this line, for which, as Bergmann shows conclusively, there was no justification. 'For on closer investigation it became clear that the scheme by no means involved the payment of 132 milliards. In contrast to the stipulations of the Treaty of Versailles the total debt was not to be definitely funded. That is to say, the really important point was not the nominal total sum, but the amount of the annuity. This was made up of a fixed instalment of 2 milliards and a sum which varied in accordance with the amount of Germany's exports.

At that time this was between 4 and 5 milliards a year, from which 26 per cent. had to be deducted. This worked out at something over a milliard, so that the annuity would amount altogether to a round 3 milliards. That corresponded to 5 per cent. interest and 1 per cent. towards a sinking fund on a capital of 50 milliard gold marks.

'Thus the London ultimatum was no worse than the recent German offer to the United States. This consisted of a promise to pay 50 milliards present value and in addition to make deliveries in kind on a basis of apparent increasing prosperity. Hence there was no logical justification for rejecting the ultimatum—quite apart from the fact that every effort had to be made to avoid the occupation of the Ruhr. It was certainly not easy to see where Germany was going to get the money from; one just had to rely on the hope that Germany's really earnest exertions in the matter of Reparations would in time produce a better understanding of her economic necessities in the minds of her opponents. This argument was decisive. The Reichstag declared for acceptance by a small majority, and a new government under Dr Wirth's leadership accepted the ultimatum, as the Allies had stipulated, without condition or reserve.' (Bergmann, pp. 104-105.)

The new Chancellor, Wirth, begged Rathenau, in whose patriotism and expert knowledge he had unlimited confidence, to take over the Ministry of Reconstruction. And now at last Rathenau had conquered; at last he was free to put his ideas into practice. At the same time this meant that he was exposed to greater personal danger than before. His mother implored him to refuse, and at the last moment he seems himself to have hesitated—seems, for inwardly everything moved him to accept. The negotiations were very protracted. On May 25th he writes to Gerhart Hauptmann: 'Unfortunately I have not yet earned your congratulations and confidence, for the negotiations

of the last ten days have failed to convince me that I can really
be of use to my country in the present extremely complex
political situation. I have not yet made my decision. My inner
barometer stands far to the left of "variable," near the point
which is designated "rain and snow" or, politically speaking,
"refusal." ' (Letter 711.) And on the 27th he writes to his
mother: 'Since you went away I have been as busy and worried
as ever, and have had to take part in still further discussions.
Finally, after a long conference on Sunday evening at the Chancellor's between him, Rosen (who had been given the Foreign
Office in the interval) and myself, I *refused;* but I could not
avoid an appointment to lunch with Rosen, which was of course
taken to mean that the last word had not yet been said. In the
meantime the news had got into the papers, though, as you
know, for twelve days nothing whatsoever had been allowed
to leak through; and now to my astonishment it turned out that
a really large number of people, even in the heavy industries,
had wanted me to take the post—no doubt partly out of *Schadenfreude,* but partly too for serious reasons. I have made no
effort to deny the thing in the papers; I am assuming that the
rumours will evaporate of their own accord, and hope that the
matter will be finally decided within the next few days, and
then at last there will be an end of all these discussions.'
(Letter 715.)

But then he made his decision. He accepted. And within
twenty-four hours he had severed his connection with industry,
given up his post as president of the A.E.G. and all his directorships, and entered the government. On June 1st he wrote to his
mother at Carlsbad: 'I can't tell you in a letter of all that has
happened in the last few days. Things have followed each
other in bewildering succession. I was appointed on Sunday;
yesterday I took over the office; I have taken part in two cabinet
meetings; tomorrow I shall probably speak in the Reichstag.

I am very glad you have been spared all this excitement. The final decision was a very hard one.' (Letter 716.) And three days later he writes to President Julius Frey: 'It was the most difficult decision I have ever had to make. . . . And now I am confronted with an endless range of questions and problems, some visible, some not yet visible. In the face of this great complex the individual is as good as helpless. Man after man will have to jump into the ditch before it can be crossed; but, equally, it will never be crossed, unless somebody takes the plunge.' And he writes in the same sense to Privy Councillor Witting: 'I consider my task to consist in smoothing the way for my successors. The first two or three people can only point out the road; the fourth will build it. But a start must be made somewhere.' (Letter 724.)

The tone of these remarks is more cheerful than their content, but it is the tone which counts and which corresponds to the real state of his feelings. True, the decision was difficult for him, when he approached it from the intellectual point of view; but his patriotism, together with the instinct which really dominated the whole of his complex personality, his longing for activity and power, made it a foregone conclusion. That, however, was merely his personal concern; what interests us equally is the political effect his decision had. Did his entry into the government bring about any real change? It must be remembered that his policy of negotiation and understanding had already been accepted at Spa by the government of the day, and that, since then, it had been followed in principle. Was, then, the game really worth the candle? And here one is up against the problem of what part personality plays in history. Does it exert a decisive influence on the direction and course of events, or does it merely stir a little eddy, past which the stream of history flows at majestic and predestined pace? In the present case I believe one is bound to admit that Rathenau's entry into the government did make a fundamental difference to the position of Germany. The difference was that the Policy of Fulfilment, which had indeed been adopted at Spa, but since then had been conducted in a half-hearted manner and with a dreary lack of imagination, now had behind it the driving power of both will and ideas. The Allies felt for the first time that it was in the hands of a man who really counted, a man of firm will and fertile mind; and for the Germans this policy assumed at last, now that it had become active and intelligent, a really tangible form—also, to be sure, a vulnerable form, for henceforth it offered its opponents the target of positive proposals and a man behind them.

Rathenau lost no time. Only a few days after taking office he arranged a meeting with Loucheur at Wiesbaden, where he started negotiations for Germany's participation in the reconstruction of the devastated areas of Northern France by direct deliveries in kind to those who had suffered. On the evening of his departure for Wiesbaden he wrote to his friend:

It is better as it is. Do you really believe that I wanted to drag you into this vortex, when I scarce know myself whether I shall be able to stand it?

These snow-white carnations and the wonderful letter that accompanied them are sufficient proof to me that you are at my side in this hour of my fate.

You don't know at what a moment your letter has reached me, and what strength it has given me. It is half-past eight on Saturday evening, and this very night I have to set out on a course beset with difficulties, taking nothing with me but your words and your affection. I shall not be able to see you again tomorrow, but I hope I shall within the next few days. I dare say you will find me more tired and disappointed than last time, but yet nearer freedom.

An hour ago, in the thick of my work and surrounded by

people, I was quite alone. Now, when I want to submerge myself in my solitary cares I feel your hand and breath upon me. Can you really doubt where true life is to be found?

In deepest gratitude and affection,

W.

In his first speech to the Reichstag on June 2nd Rathenau had said: 'I have entered a Cabinet of Fulfilment. We must discover some means of linking ourselves up with the world again.' The best way of building a bridge over the abyss that had opened about Germany seemed to him to be the reconstruction of the devastated areas of Northern France. Why? Because here the French and German nations could accomplish a great work in common. Because it was a necessary work; 'for this wound in the body of Europe persists, and not until it has closed shall we have peace on earth again.' (Reichstag speech of June 2nd, 1921.) Because by means of so tremendous an achievement Germany would be able to prove her goodwill (which was questioned) and her unbroken capacity for work. And, finally, because it was essential in the interests of German currency that the payments in gold should be replaced by deliveries in kind and by work for the Allies. The payment of the first milliard gold marks on August 31st had already sent up the dollar from 60 to 100 marks (the normal rate is, and was before the war, a little over 4 marks to the dollar). Further payments in gold on the same scale opened out the certain prospect of a collapse of the mark.

On the basis of Rathenau's negotiations with Loucheur the 'Wiesbaden Agreement' was signed on October 6th and 7th. This agreement set up a German corporation of a private character whose business it was to take over control (to the exclusion of both governments) of the deliveries to the French war victims. Deliveries in kind took the place of part of the gold payments, and direct relationships between French customers

291

and German producers the place of the old roundabout method through the two governments. The French war victims were to receive deliveries in kind up to the value of 7 milliard gold marks within a period of four and a half years; the German producers to be compensated by the German government in German currency. If the scheme proved practicable, it would greatly accelerate not only reconstruction, but also trade in general between the two countries; it would improve relations and create the atmosphere for further negotiations and understandings, and it might preserve the mark from a further collapse. If, on the other hand, it proved impracticable, owing to France's being unable or unwilling to absorb so great a quantity of foreign goods, then this experiment would demonstrate the fact that the amount of Germany's war indemnity was circumscribed not only by Germany's capacity to pay, but also by the Allies' capacity to receive. Rathenau doubtless expected that the Wiesbaden Agreement would enable him to kill both birds with one stone, in that a considerable fraction of the deliveries in kind arranged for would be absorbed by France, and would thus further both reconstruction and trade in general; but that a still larger proportion would be refused by France, and thus she would have to recognize the impracticability of Allied demands.

In practice the Agreement proved almost wholly unworkable. It came to grief on the very comprehensible resistance of the French industrialists, who at that time found the devastated areas their most profitable market. In 1922, instead of the threatened milliards, France demanded and received deliveries in kind to the value of only 19 million gold marks! This indeed showed the impracticability not only of the Wiesbaden Agreement, but of the London scheme as well, since it did not lie in Germany's power to furnish the money payments imposed; while on the other hand, as was now evident, these could not be replaced by payments in kind, as the Allies were not in a position to accept goods on the suggested scale without severe injury to their own trade and industries (*cf.* Bergmann, p. 216).

Nevertheless, Rathenau was greeted with a storm of opposition in Germany, on the ground that the deliveries in kind promised in the Agreement actually exceeded what was due to France from the London ultimatum. Von Rheinbaben, a 'Volkspartei' Member of the Reichstag, says in his book *Von Versailles zur Freiheit* that 'in retrospect one cannot but express amazement at this storm; indeed, it was largely a matter of party politics' (*loc. cit.*, p. 47). In reality the opposition was fanned by certain industrialists who, as Rathenau's assistant, H. F. Simon, says, 'strove against being paid for Reparations deliveries with the declining mark instead of with reliable securities.' (H. F. Simon, *Reparation und Wiederaufbau*, p. 128.) But it was a misfortune for both countries, for Germany as well as for France, that so little came of the Agreement; it would have averted several disasters: amongst others the Ruhr invasion, the collapse of the mark and the franc, and the ruin of the French and German middle classes.

On October 20th, 1921, a fortnight after the signing of the Wiesbaden Agreement, the League of Nations Council assigned the most valuable portion of Upper Silesia to Poland on the strength of a highly questionable interpretation of the Treaty of Versailles. As a protest the Democratic Party withdrew their ministers from the Cabinet. Thus against his wish and without any visible advantage to Germany Rathenau had to retire.

According to the London scheme of payments further instalments of gold were due from Germany on January 15th and February 15th. It had already become clear by the autumn that there was no hope of producing the full sum. The attempt to raise a loan of a milliard gold marks ($250,000,000) in London met with no success. The Governor of the Bank of England replied to the request of the German Government that in view of Germany's far-reaching obligations under the London scheme of payments it would be impossible to raise 'either a long-term German loan or a short-term bank credit.' (Bergmann, p. 133.) Whereupon, on December 14th, 1921, the Chancellor notified the Reparations Commission that there could be no question of Germany's being able to produce the payments due on January 15th and February 15th: at the very utmost between 150 and 200 millions would be available. Hence Germany would be compelled to ask for a moratorium. To this the Reparations Commission replied very curtly that the contents of the Chancellor's note had surprised them, and that they could not take into consideration the proposal for a moratorium so long as no detailed reasons for it were given. In their embarrassment the German Government asked Rathenau to go to London to try to bring Lloyd George and the City financiers to some understanding of Germany's position.

Whether Rathenau's journey was politically advisable as far as its immediate aim, the moratorium, was concerned may seem doubtful. Bergmann criticizes it; in his view Rathenau overlooked the fact that 'negotiations with one of the Allied Powers would only occasion all the more violent protests from the others, and would thus prove definitely harmful to German interests.' (Bergmann, p. 134.) That is certainly true if one has in mind only the moratorium. And it is also true that German post-war policy has been only too apt to run after the will-o'-the-wisp of being able to play off England against France in an acute crisis. This was, in Rathenau's time, partly due to the personality of the British Ambassador in Berlin, Lord D'Abernon, who had no French counterpart of the same calibre, or with anything like the same knowledge of the world, resource, initiative and imagination; and partly also to a confused idea of the fundamentals of Anglo-French relations. In every acute crisis France had behind her her geographical position, the greatest army and air force in the world, and, in addition, English public opinion, which was still in the grip of war feeling; whereas England's sole weapons against France were the pressure of the English money market on French currency and of English demands in the matter of war debts on French finances—both of which were slow in action and thus useless to compel a quick decision. In the struggle over the Ruhr England availed herself of this pressure, because her own interests were threatened and public opinion had swung round against France; and in this instance it did prove effective and contributed materially to the frustration of Poincaré's Rhine policy, because the struggle was long drawn out and gave the City time to prepare the attack.[14]

But a moratorium for Germany in December, 1922, was of no vital interest to England. Moreover, if it was going to receive the assent of France at all, then it had to do so within the shortest possible time. Hence Rathenau himself can scarcely have hoped for success in trying to extort it from France under pressure from England. But he thought that the opportunity of enlightening English statesmen and financiers at first hand as to Germany's real situation and intentions might enable him to make a breach in the wall of hatred and distrust that encircled Germany; and this opportunity he seized, even though he was conscious, presumably, of the considerations that Bergmann mentions.

For the first aim of Rathenau's foreign policy was necessarily a persistent effort to break through this befogging atmosphere of hatred and suspicion, and thus open the way for negotiations on a business basis, from which, as he had ex-

[14] The last shred of doubt about Poincaré's intention to confront England with a situation which would have threatened its most vital economic and political interests was dispelled by the publication by an English journalist in the *Manchester Guardian* of a 'Secret note of May 28th, 1922, from the French Senator Dariac to Poincaré,' on the ways and means of detaching the Rhineland and Ruhr from Germany and annexing them to France. In this light France's financial support of the Separatist movement took on a new and sinister meaning in English eyes.

plained at Spa, he felt the recovery of Germany, by virtue of her natural position and importance, would inevitably follow. He recognized that the only weapon left to Germany after her collapse was the industry and intelligence of the German people, and from this he drew the logical conclusion by undertaking to build up a policy which should depend on these alone. To this plan of campaign he was ready to sacrifice tactical successes even in the case of important and tangible advantages, because he knew that they were bound to come his way again once his chief goal was within reach. How truly he aimed and with what skill he laid his plans has been abundantly proved by subsequent events. Every step taken towards the improvement of Germany's position has been along the road that Rathenau marked out, the road which has diminished, step by step, the hatred and distrust of Germany's opponents, and thus created an atmosphere in which purely business conversations at last became possible.

But this policy of Rathenau's stood in open conflict with the policy of Poincaré, who for his part was anxious to utilize to the full all remaining signs of war feeling, in order to secure by their aid those aims in which he had been thwarted at Versailles by President Wilson—namely, a paramount influence for France in the Rhineland and the destruction of German unity. Possibly M Poincaré was not the author of this plan himself, but being embarrassed and doubtful about the right course for France to follow, merely adopted it from the head of the political department of the French Foreign Office, the former French Ambassador in Petersburg, M Maurice Paléologue. Also it would be both unjust and inaccurate to call this the 'French' plan, without further qualification, for ever since Versailles it had been opposed by large and influential circles in France, who had as their spokesmen not merely pacifists and socialists, but also men like Loucheur, Briand, François-Poncet and Professor Haguenin, the distinguished representative on the Committee of Guarantee in Berlin. Nevertheless, French official policy remained firmly bound to this conception until after the collapse of the Ruhr adventure, and hence did all it could, whether openly or secretly, to sabotage Rathenau's endeavours to the end of his life. It finally met its doom at Locarno, defeated only by the greater political weight of Rathenau's pacifist conception, which Stresemann took over and carried on.

Rathenau's conversations with Mr Lloyd George and the City financiers led to a promise from the former that he would support a reduction of the German payments in gold for 1922 to 500 million marks. And it also led to a scheme for the rehabilitation of Russia by means of a so-called Consortium, in which both Germany and Russia and the Western Powers should be represented; and further to plans for the cancellation of inter-allied war debts in Europe, and for the drawing up of a great peace pact, in relation to the Rhine frontier, between England, Belgium and France, with a view to the eventual inclusion of Germany—the first appearance of the Locarno idea. (H. F. Simon, p. 119.)

In connection with Rathenau's visit Anglo-French conversations took place at Chequers on December 18th, 1921, where it was decided to hold a conference at Cannes, which should in its turn lead on to a pan-European economic congress. The five principal Allied Powers immediately agreed to both these conferences; the economic conference was to be held at Genoa in the following spring.

In fulfilment of this agreement, the Supreme Council met Cannes in the first half of January. On Lloyd George's initiative Germany was invited to come to Cannes as a guest and take part in the discussions on Reparations. 'A small German delegation,' Bergmann relates (p. 146 ff.), 'with Dr Rathenau at its head, arrived at Cannes on January 11th, 1922.

Dr Rathenau and I were summoned forthwith to a confidential discussion at the Villa des Broussailles in the neighbourhood of Cannes, where we met M Loucheur and Sir Robert Horne. They both impressed on us the seriousness of the position. The political situation in France was a very delicate one. If the Cabinet were to meet Germany halfway in the spirit of the London conversations it would be exposed to very grave danger. But the atmosphere at Cannes was favourable to Germany, if only we could make up our minds to immediate acceptance. There seemed a possibility of granting a moratorium for one year. The cash payments for 1922 were, it is true, to be reduced not to 500, but only to 720 million gold marks. Moreover, we should be committed to deliveries in kind to the value of 1,450 million gold marks, of which 950 million were to go to France. Any delay on our part in accepting these terms was dangerous; the French Cabinet might fall tomorrow.

'Immediately after this,' continues Bergmann, 'the Germans were summoned to the Reparations Commission, which had likewise been called to Cannes by the Supreme Council. Here Rathenau took the opportunity to expatiate in a long speech on Germany's position and on her capacity to pay. In the course of this speech a member of the Reparations Commission pushed a note over to me, on which stood the words: "Accept quickly, the conditions are 720 million gold marks and 1,450 million in deliveries in kind."

'But Dr Rathenau did not feel justified in acting on these repeated hints. He preferred not to make an agreement with the Reparations Commission, who, like him, were at Cannes merely in the position of guests, but to wait upon the decision of the Supreme Council, hoping at the same time to get the cash payments for 1922 reduced to the 500-million figure. On the following day, January 12th, a very fully attended session of the Supreme Council took place, at which Dr Rathenau delivered an important speech lasting more than an hour. Dr

Rathenau was still in the middle of his speech when the news suddenly came that Briand's Cabinet had fallen.'

The news of Briand's resignation occasioned an interval of half an hour. Lloyd George made it clear at once that now the support of the French Government had been withdrawn, a new situation had arisen and the Supreme Council was no longer competent to take decisions. However, he invited Rathenau to proceed with his address. This Rathenau did, emphasizing once more in conclusion Germany's willingness not only 'to go to the limits of her capacity,' but also 'to help together with the Western Powers and Russia in the reconstruction of Eastern and Central Europe.'

On the same evening Rathenau had an hour's interview with Lloyd George, on the latter's invitation, at the Villa Valletta. Lloyd George took the situation more seriously than he had done at midday, and explained the impossibility of continuing the deliberations of the Supreme Council. The Conference at Genoa, on the other hand, would still take place. And then he turned to Sir Robert Horne and commissioned him to get the Italian Prime Minister, Bonomi, to invite Germany to Genoa.

As a result of the breakdown of the meeting of the Supreme Council the Reparations Commission again became the proper authority to deal with the German moratorium. On January 13th it conceded a postponement of the current cash payments due on January 15th and February 15th; during this respite, however, Germany was to pay 31 million gold marks every ten days.

Bergmann makes it quite clear that he did not approve of Rathenau's behaviour at Cannes in not accepting the offer of the Reparations Commission at once, but insisting instead on first making his great speech before the Supreme Council. In practice not much harm was done; for on March 22nd the Reparations Commission fixed Germany's obligations at precisely the same figures as the offer which Rathenau had passed

over: 720 million gold marks and 1,450 million in deliveries
in kind for 1922. (Bergmann, p. 153.) And any harm done
was more than made good by Rathenau's success in convincing
a section of the Allies of the German Cabinet's honest desire
for fulfilment, and by his own increased prestige, which in
its turn redounded to Germany's credit. For the first time since
the war a German statesman had forced the world to take him
seriously and to glimpse behind the picture of Germany distorted by war and post-war propaganda another Germany, industrious, honest, peaceful, and ready to fulfil her obligations.
In the first round of the duel between Poincaré and Rathenau,
Poincaré had certainly won, by turning out Briand and breaking up the Cannes Conference; but Rathenau had succeeded in
putting German policy on the path that led to her reinstate-
ment as a Great Power at Genoa, to the interment at Locarno
of Poincaré's Rhine policy, and to Poincaré's own conversion
to Rathenau's policy of understanding at Carcassonne.[15]

A few days after Rathenau's return Dr Rosen, the German
Foreign Minister, resigned. He was an authority on Persian
poetry, a shrewd diplomat of the old school, and one of the
few who had shown courage as civilians during the war; but
he was no longer able to stand the strain of repeated encounters
with the Allied Military Commissions.[16] Stinnes, on being
asked to suggest a successor, proposed von Rosenberg, the German Minister in Vienna.[17] Wirth, however, turned to Rathenau,

[15] In his famous speech there on April 1st, 1928.

[16] Dr Rosen began his career as a dragoman to the German Embassy in Constantinople, held a large number of diplomatic posts, including Morocco at the
time when the Kaiser made his sensational landing at Tangiers, then Persia, and
later The Hague during the war. Published a number of admirable German
translations of Persian poets.

[17] Von Rosenberg, born December 12th, 1874. One of the German delegates
to the Peace Conference with the Soviet at Brest-Litovsk, in 1917-1918. Be-
came Minister to Austria after the war and Minister of Foreign Affairs after
Rathenau was assassinated, remaining at the Foreign Office all through the
Ruhr conflict. Resigned when the Cuno Cabinet fell and Dr Stresemann became
Chancellor and Minister of Foreign Affairs.

who seemed the most suitable, because he was the originator of the policy of fulfilment, because of his personal relations with Lloyd George, Loucheur and other leading Allied statesmen, and finally, because of the European prestige he had won at Cannes. Once again Rathenau hesitated; again his mother implored him to refuse. Yet finally he accepted, as he had accepted his first ministerial post, with a clear recognition of the personal danger involved, but driven irresistibly by the same motives which had proved decisive the time before. He tried to hide his decision from his mother for as long as possible. She learnt of it, as Etta Federn-Kohlhaas has related, from the newspapers: 'Rathenau lunched as usual with his mother; they sat opposite one another, toying about with their food, until finally his mother asked him: "Walther, why have you done this to me?" And he replied: "I really had to, mama, because they couldn't find any one else" ' (*loc. cit.*, p. 233).

On the evening before this he had written to his friend:

31.1.1922

It is late at night, and I am thinking of you with a heavy heart. You will have heard from F. of the decision I had to make this evening. I stand before this task in deep and earnest doubt. What can a single individual do in the face of this torpid world, with enemies at his back, and conscious of his own limitations and weaknesses? I will do the best I can, and if that is not enough, then I know you at least will not forsake me like the others.

Your W.

The way in which Rathenau had been appointed suddenly and secretly overnight against the wish of influential industrial circles aroused deep resentment. The industrial magnates hated him, his nationalist and anti-Semitic enemies overwhelmed him with insulting and threatening letters, and even some of his

301

closest political friends thought him the wrong man for the post. The anxieties of the situation told on him. He aged noticeably in these weeks before Genoa. The courage and novelty of his foreign policy was understood only by a dwindling minority in Germany, of whom, it is true, the Chancellor, Dr Wirth, was one. Nevertheless, he set to work to remodel German foreign policy in accordance with his ideas. 'It is a question,' he said to me, 'of giving a new turn to the whole machinery of the Foreign Office, and that is a truly superhuman task. After German foreign policy has been completely passive for eight years, we have got to get it under way again little by little; every day we must thrust another iron into the fire.'

The most formidable obstacle he had to contend with was, as he said, 'the antagonism which every attempt at a reasonable foreign policy calls forth in German opinion.' Poincaré, who had succeeded Briand as French Premier, did all he could to magnify this obstacle by exasperating German public opinion through a continuous series of calculated insults and new demands; that was part of his plan of operations. General Nollet, the head of the Inter-Allied Military Commissions, who had so far always gloried in being 'a pacifist,' now had to reform his ways and employ even harsher methods than hitherto. 'The effects of Poincaré's policy,' said Rathenau in a speech in the Reichstag at the end of March, 'were first made manifest in the hail of notes which the Inter-Allied Military Commissions began showering down on our heads. I have calculated that in the course of some two months we have had to reply to a hundred of these notes. You can see for yourselves that the work of the office is virtually paralyzed, when the officials have to spend all their days and nights in answering this stuff.' (*Speeches*, p. 378.)

At the same time Poincaré entered into relations with Stinnes, presumably in the hope of being able to turn to account the antagonism between him and Rathenau. He even sought to

WALTHER RATHENAU'S MOTHER

establish relations with Radek—to him the arch-fiend himself
—in order to prevent a *rapprochement* between Russia and
Germany. Towards French adherents of the policy of understanding he maintained a mysterious silence, or else behaved as
though he were pursuing this particular policy merely out of
fear, and would be quite willing to change it for another if
the danger were removed. One of these French opponents of
Poincaré's policy of bullying Germany, who held high office,
said to me with tragi-comic exasperation, after visiting him
shortly before Genoa: 'Poincaré knows that force is not going
to get him anywhere, but he is *un monstre de lâcheté*.' Meanwhile the French people had grown more and more accustomed, under artificial stimulus, to the idea of using force
against Germany, and this fact was utilized in its turn to exacer-
bate the state of public opinion in Germany. On March 21st
the Reparations Commission replied to the German request
for a moratorium in a note whose tone and content were deliberately insulting. The Wirth-Rathenau Cabinet gave a negative reply, and things came to such a pitch that even Rathenau
began to lose his nerve. His Reichstag speech on the subject of
the note shows his barely concealed exasperation and disappointment.[18]

On the evening before his departure for Genoa he wrote
to his friend, who was ill:

I am writing this late at night, dead tired by these last days'
work and distressed by your letter. Do you mean to say you

[18] Lord D'Abernon sets down in his diary: 'Berlin, March 14, 1922, Rathenau
came to luncheon today in a state of some nervous excitement. He said he was
driven wild by the perpetual notes of the French Embassy regarding this and
that supposed default of the German Government. . . . He would send me the
number of the French notes he had received. I should see that life was impossible under these conditions, as the whole time of the Foreign Office was taken
up answering more or less futile accusations' (p. 279). I may add that Rathenau
spoke to me at the time almost exactly as he did to Lord D'Abernon, showing
a degree of exasperation and nervous tension quite unusual in him.

really believed I was not suffering with you just because I tried
to distract you from your suffering for those few minutes!
Perhaps the reason I wasn't successful was because I myself
was, and still am, suffering. This period which you call the
highest of my life is certainly the most difficult; it is simply
a farewell, for I know that what I have to undertake, whether
I will or not, means the breaking of a life. For he who bows
beneath this burden even for an instant is crushed to atoms. I
shall return only to be overwhelmed in the abyss. . . .

At such a time, before and during such a journey as this,
my thoughts have always turned in calm and peace to you, and
from time to time I have written you a few lines in token and
greeting. Now I do this once more, and no less tenderly, though
with heavier heart than usual.

I felt your suffering too deeply—and not only the visible
suffering. I know and understand that this time it was out of
your power to ease my path. You would have done it if you
could; and perhaps I should do more to try and ease this hour,
which is not a farewell, for you. May you feel that I think of
you this night in love and troth.

W.

These were the auspices under which the Genoa Conference
met. Italy, where after a short period of chaos the last liberal
and constitutional governments before the dictatorship had
firmly re-established order, and which had been the first of the
combatant nations to rid itself of war feeling, was anxious,
both in its position of host and for reasons of prestige, to avoid
a breakdown at all costs. But Poincaré had dealt the Conference
its death-blow before it ever started by threatening that France
would refuse to take part unless he was assured that the Reparations question would not be raised in any form; a condition to

which Lloyd George had eventually agreed at his meeting with
Poincaré at Boulogne on February 25th. In spite of this, Poin-
aré regarded Lloyd George and Loucheur and their doings
with the utmost suspicion, as though all they did and planned
was a conspiracy to subvert his Rhine policy, the foundations
of which their schemes did indeed threaten. Consequently he
did not attend the Conference in person. For if things should
not turn out to his liking in spite of Boulogne, it would be
easier, he felt, to wreck it from afar by a telegram, acting as
sort of *deus ex machina;* he sent in his stead his Minister of
Justice, M Barthou, with a delegation which he left in the dark
about his real intentions, and whose activity he thus seriously
crippled.

Lloyd George, on the other hand, felt that the success of the
Conference was a vital necessity for his own prestige as well as
for British currency and trade. Besides, he thoroughly disap-
proved of Poincaré's ambitions on the Rhine, and was bent on
appearing as the sponsor of the rehabilitation of Russia. This
was to be effected by a sort of pan-European receivership or
consortium,' such as he had outlined to Rathenau in London
before Cannes.[19] He was all the more anxious for some such
accession of prestige, as things were going badly for him in
the East, where the Greeks, whom he was supporting against
Kemal Pasha, were getting beaten, and he had fallen out with
the French, who had taken up the cause of the Turks. His
chief difficulty, however, was that an important section of
English public opinion blindly supported Poincaré, being unaware of his real intentions. Hence one of Lloyd George's

' Mr Winston Churchill, in a letter to Lord Curzon written during the
Genoa Conference (April 26th, 1922), says: 'The great objective of the
Prime Minister's policy has been Moscow, to make Great Britain the nation in
closest possible relations with the Bolshevists, and to be their protectors and
sponsors before Europe.' (Quoted by him in *The World Crisis: The Aftermath,*
315.)

principal aims at Genoa was to force Poincaré to show his hand and thus to gain freedom of action to dissolve the Entente if he thought fit.

Thus from the very beginning the Conference was influenced and moulded by the fact of the deep and unbridgeable gulf between the official French and English policies, a gulf which paralleled, rather than coincided with, the antagonism between the policies of Rathenau and Poincaré.

The two other leading figures, Germany and Russia, had to play their parts in the setting of this antagonism. The Russians wanted three things not easily compatible: to get a loan for their government, to lessen the external pressure on their country, and to use Genoa as a platform for their world-revolutionary propaganda. Germany, on the other hand, was in Genoa to protect the Rhine frontier from the encroachments of Poincaré, and to win back her rightful place at the side of the other Great Powers; at the same time she wanted a thorough cleansing of the European atmosphere and the economic rehabilitation of Europe, including Russia, as the pre-condition for her own economic and political recovery. For Rathenau, moreover, the Genoa Conference provided the first serious test of whether and how his new foreign policy would fit into the network of European relations and prove a protection against the ambitions of Poincaré.

Thus the cards were dealt; the game could begin. The Conference opened on April 10th. Such a gathering had not been seen since Bismarck called the Congress of Berlin. Under the chairmanship of Signor Facta, the last constitutional Prime Minister of Italy, all the leading statesmen of Europe had assembled together, nominally in order to heal the wounds of world trade—but, in fact, to end the war. The Central Powers, the Allies, Russians, Neutrals, all were there; only Poincaré, like the witch in 'The Sleeping Beauty,' had chosen to abstain. The most important bankers and industrialists, the most influential trades-union leaders, the ablest journalists from every quarter of the globe were in attendance, either as experts or observers; Wall Street and Fleet Street, Downing Street and the Wilhelmstrasse had poured their officials, financiers, leader-writers, busybodies into the deep gully of the Via Garibaldi, frowned on by the towering palaces of Genoa. It was an Œcumenical Council, comparable to those the mediaeval Church used to summon for the salvation of Christendom. And, as in the Middle Ages, a terror overhung the gathering that failure might portend catastrophe to European civilization.

The very first session revealed the rift between the British and French points of view and the isolation of the French. The function was staged in a dim crypt-like mediaeval hall near the harbour, which, notwithstanding the brilliant southern sunshine, had to be lit by artificial light; and at first, being surrounded with much pomp and circumstance, secular and religious, and a rich display of flowers and greenhouse shrubs, it somewhat resembled a funeral service. The three Prime Ministers in ceremonial black, Signor Facta, Mr Lloyd George and Dr Wirth, and Poincaré's representative, M Barthou, opened the proceedings by reading out set speeches prepared for them by their secretariats and stuffed with the ordinary platitudes. These the audience received with perfunctory applause while it sat waiting for some sensational event to occur. And indeed, no sooner had M Barthou, the last of the allied statesmen, read his speech, than Chicherin, the Soviet Commissary for foreign affairs, rose from his seat in front of a prelate gorgeously robed in scarlet, and set himself to the task of enlivening the rather sepulchral proceedings with a brilliantly entertaining political comedy. Chicherin also read his speech, and as his French accent is a very individual one, his audience took some time to find out that he was not speaking Russian. But soon isolated words became intelligible and then whole sentences. He was

307

proclaiming, one understood, Russia's earnest desire to co-
operate in the rehabilitation of the world. He hoped that Genoa
might be only the first of a whole series of European economic
conferences. He expected that not only European assemblies,
but some day a universal congress, in which all the nations of
the earth would take part, would be necessary to complete the
task which his distinguished colleagues were tackling at Genoa.
And then, in a sentence which he pronounced distinctly and
with surprisingly little accent, he launched the word *disarmament*: Russia, he said, was ready to disband the Red Army as
soon as the other nations disarmed. The Russian Government,
he added, wished this to be understood as a solemn pledge.

It had been rumoured for some time that Lloyd George was
egging on the Russians to raise the question of disarmament
at Genoa. A week before, a high British official, a personal
friend of Lloyd George, had told me that the latter expected
much from some such move. Nevertheless, Chicherin's announcement came as a surprise and made part of the audience
shiver; it seemed quite possible that his bomb would wreck the
Conference. He, however, having finished the French version
of his speech and appearing quite unmoved by the agitation of
his audience, proceeded to read his document a second time in
English: giving particular emphasis again to the passage about
disarmament. International commonplaces and amenities were
immediately cast to the winds. No sooner had the Russian Commissary ceased reading than M Barthou sprang to his feet; with
well-feigned excitement and with the artificial indignation and
rhetoric of an old stager of the Paris Bar he proceeded to lodge
a protest—a protest, he said, against any discussion of disarmament in Genoa 'in his own name, in the name of the French
delegation, in the name of France!' But his pathos fell flat; the
greater part of the assembly remained visibly unconcerned.
And hardly had he finished when Chicherin was on his legs
again, replying in very intelligible French and with evident

relish that the Russian Government had been moved to make its pledge to disarm under certain conditions by a speech of M Briand's in Washington, in which he had described the Red Army as the chief obstacle to French disarmament; it had therefore flattered itself that it would be performing a service for France, to say nothing of mankind in general, if it removed the obstacle mentioned by M Briand by means of a binding declaration here and now. But, of course, the Russian delegation would bow to the decision of the Conference, should it desire to exclude disarmament.

There was a little subdued tittering and some applause, and then Lloyd George rose to speak. Although he was known to be in sympathy with the Russian proposal, he now proceeded with remarkable unconcern to drop it and pour the oil of humour on the troubled waters, stating, however, that in his view the Conference would be a failure unless it led to disarmament. Everybody knew, he added, that the League of Nations was at present occupied with the disarmament problem, and he felt sure M Barthou would be the last person to place any obstacle in the League of Nations' path. But in the circumstances he begged M Chicherin to leave disarmament aside for the moment, in order not to sink the already top-heavy vessel of the Genoa Conference. For if this vessel were to founder, M Chicherin might well be one of those lost in the wreck.[20]

Lloyd George's words completed the discomfiture of the French; but they were spoken so softly, with such artistic detachment, that the speaker might have been seated by his fireside chatting pleasantly with two old friends and patting them both on the back. A storm of applause rang through the hall; delegates, experts, journalists, spectators, rose to their feet and clapped for minutes on end; the French alone remained seated

[20] It is curious to note that of all the Foreign Ministers assembled at Genoa the only one who has not been murdered or lost office up to date is M Chicherin.

in painfully conspicuous isolation, hopelessly outmanoeuvred and exposed. After a moment, however, M Barthou, who was now evidently in a genuine rage, sprang up and tried to speak again; but the President of the Conference, Signor Facta, interrupted him, then sharply called him to order, and while he continued beating the air with his arms, finally almost forcibly made him sit down. Thus the first day of Genoa ended with the marked isolation of the French and a triumph for Lloyd George, who henceforth became the centre and, as it were, the benevolent despot of the Conference.

On the following day the French measured forces again with the British on a question which concerned both the Germans and the Russians. Sub-commissions were being formed. The five 'inviting Powers'—*i.e.* the four Great Powers and Belgium—claimed their right to a seat and vote in *every* sub-commission. Great Britain, supported by Italy, proposed to extend the same right to Germany and Russia. This was opposed by France, who wished to put them on the same footing as the smaller states, who had to submit to election for each commission, instead of being members as a matter of course. When it was put to the vote, France proved to be almost alone in her attitude, even the Poles joining the British and Italians. Barthou, however, did not admit defeat. On the following day he made yet another attempt, on Poincaré's telegraphic instructions, to carry the French point of view, by basing it on the German Government's negative answer of April 10th to the note of the Reparations Commission of March 21st; only once more to be rebuffed. In common fairness, however, it must be admitted that Poincaré's resistance was logical from his point of view, for the decision was of great, in fact, of fundamental, importance: it reinstated Germany and Russia as *de facto* Great Powers in the Concert of Europe, and created a precedent, as was pointed out at the time, for making both countries, when they joined the League of Nations, permanent

members of its Council. It was, perhaps, the most valuable
moral gain that Germany brought back with her from Genoa,
a gain due in great measure, without doubt, to the international
prestige won by Wirth and Rathenau.

In spite of Poincaré and his brutally open hostility to Germany, Rathenau did not give up the hope of entering into
closer relations with France. On the very first day of the Conference he commissioned me to arrange a meeting as soon as
possible between Dr Bergmann and M Seydoux, the head of
the department of trade in the French Foreign Office. Rathenau
himself wanted to keep as much as possible in the background
at first. Seydoux belonged to the not inconsiderable number of
Frenchmen in high position who were working behind the Poin-
caristic façade for an understanding with Germany; and despite severe physical suffering he worked with great tenacity
and contributed many good suggestions towards this end. In
this way Rathenau hoped to find a means of getting the
reparations question discussed at Genoa in spite of the Boulogne agreement—not within the official limits of the Conference, but parallel with it; and Seydoux did not prove averse.
Bergmann says in his book (p. 159): 'An unimpeachable opportunity presented itself. On April 4th, 1922, the Reparations Commission had decided to call together a Committee of
experts to determine the conditions under which the German
Government might raise loans abroad, whose proceeds should
be applied to the partial redemption of the German Reparations liability.' Bergmann seized the opportunity provided for
him, and the first conversation took place on April 12th. The
plan he put before Seydoux was to raise a loan of four milliard
gold marks, with which to pay off four Reparation annuities
straight away, so that in the four years' respite which this gave
Germany a really final solution of the Reparations problem
might be reached. This scheme met with the approval of Seydoux and other influential Frenchmen in Genoa, with the

reservation, it is true, that they could not answer for Poincaré's attitude in the matter. Philippe Millet, the editor of the *Petit Parisien*, who was anxious to promote a pact on this basis between Germany, France and England, and was apprised of the scheme, held, and held rightly, that these conversations between Bergmann and Seydoux were more important than all the official Conference negotiations put together; because they did succeed in coming to real grips with the problem of the rehabilitation of Europe, which the Conference itself could only discuss theoretically in consequence of the Boulogne agreement. They were proceeding favourably, when the Treaty of Rapallo put an end to them.

From the very first the Rapallo Treaty has been shrouded in legend. People have tried to read into it a Russo-German military alliance, and the fact that it was signed at Genoa has been interpreted as a deliberate challenge to the Allies. Both views are false. Neither on paper nor in conversation did its contents go beyond the innocuous and immediately published text. That Rathenau of all people, Rathenau who put no faith whatever in armaments, should have concluded a secret military convention was a peculiarly futile, in fact ridiculous, suggestion. The treaty was nothing more than it professed to be: a *peace treaty*, the first treaty since the war which aimed at re-establishing a real state of peace between two peoples mutually estranged by the war. Perhaps for this very reason it was bound to look suspicious to people still dominated by war feeling. For the rest, it may or may not have been wise to sign it at Genoa, but its conclusion was certainly not prompted by any wish to bang the fist on the table; it was an almost inevitable result of circumstances for which the major responsibility lay with the Allies.

Some readjustment of Russo-German relations was already long overdue. Since Versailles, which had annulled the Treaty of Brest-Litovsk, there had been no regular relations between the two countries, and this readjustment, as we have shown formed one of the main items in Rathenau's programme. Under his instructions Baron von Maltzan, the head of the Eastern department of the Foreign Office,[21] had already entered on preliminary negotiations with the Russians in Berlin. A treaty had been drawn up, and would have been signed, had it not been for Rathenau's scruples about presenting the Allies just before Genoa with a *fait accompli* which might have awakened their suspicions. Also he was influenced by his discussions with Lloyd George on the subject of a pan-European 'Consortium,' which was to take in hand the problem of the relations between Russia and the rest of Europe, and so set going a pan-European relief scheme for Russia.

When Rathenau came to Genoa he was extremely anxious to co-operate with Lloyd George and the Allies in working out a scheme for the rehabilitation of Russia and to effect the readjustment of Russo-German relations within the framework of this scheme. The first shock to his faith in Lloyd George's desire to co-operate with Germany loyally and on an equal footing came at the first session of the so-called 'Political Sub-Commission' on April 11th, when the British handed in a memorandum to serve as a basis for the negotiations with Russia. Now Article 6 of this memorandum was found expressly to confirm Russia's right to war compensation from Germany on the ground of *Article 116 of the Versailles Treaty*, while two further articles of the memorandum precluded any German claim against Russia.[22] This proposal meant the increase of

---

[21] Baron Ago von Maltzan, afterwards Secretary of State for Foreign Affairs under Dr Stresemann during the Ruhr conflict, and subsequently German Ambassador to the United States. Killed in a flying accident on September 23rd, 1927.

[22] By Article 116 of the Peace Treaty 'Germany accepts definitely the abrogation of the Brest-Litovsk Treaties and of all other treaties, conventions and agreements entered into by her with the Maximalist Government in Russia.' From this it followed that Russia, who by these treaties had renounced her rights to compensation for war damages or Reparations from Germany, automatically got them back; and Article 6 of the British Memorandum expressly interpreted Article 116 in this sense.

German Reparations by an unknown quantity and was bound to seem to the Germans very much like the spider's invitation to the fly; no responsible German statesman could possibly have entertained it. The Russians themselves were taken aback. They cautiously replied that this was the first they had heard of the memorandum; that it had been compiled by the interested Allied Powers without their knowledge or participation; and that thus they were not in a position to express an opinion on it forthwith and must request that the meeting be adjourned till Thursday, the 13th. This motion for adjournment was seconded by the Powers responsible for the memorandum and accepted by all.

On the same evening (April 11th) Maltzan, in conversation with the head of the Russian Department of the British Foreign Office, Mr Gregory,[23] pointed out that the German position with regard to the British memorandum was rendered very difficult by Article 6 and two other articles of the British Memorandum,[24] and explained to him why this was so. Gregory expressed great surprise, said that he had not attached this significance to the article himself, but had to admit Maltzan's contention that it was justified by the text. It was obvious that Germany could not be asked to commit suicide.

On Wednesday, April 12th, Gregory invited Maltzan and the German Foreign Office expert for British affairs, Herr Dufour-Féronce, to tea at the Hotel Miramare. There the Germans met Mr E. F. Wise,[25] the head of a department of the British Board of Trade, who was supposed to be Lloyd George's confidant and did most of the negotiating between the British

[23] Mr John Duncan Gregory, born 1878. Assistant Under-secretary of State, Foreign Office, 1925-8.
[24] Article 6 of the Memorandum and Articles 11 and 15 of Annex 2 of the Memorandum in conjunction with Article 116 of the Peace Treaty.
[25] Mr Edward Frank Wise, C.B., born 1885. British representative on the Permanent Committee of the Inter-Allied Supreme Economic Council during the war, economic adviser to the All-Russian Central Union of Co-operative Societies (Centrosoyons).

and the Russians. Maltzan again stressed the fact that the inclusion of Article 116 of the Versailles Treaty in the British memorandum forced Germany to proceed with the utmost caution. He had, he said, pointed out to Lord D'Abernon in Berlin what disastrous effects this article of the Peace Treaty might have on Germany if the Russians chose to make use of it. He now hinted that its inclusion in the memorandum might force Germany to renew her private conversations with the Russians here in Genoa. The British tried to dismiss the whole affair as trivial. They would communicate with the Germans again as soon as possible; and anyhow these would have an opportunity of giving formal expression to their objections in the forthcoming discussions in the sub-commission.

It being obviously absurd to expect the friendly co-operation of Germany in a scheme which might double her Reparations debt, it must seem doubtful whether Lloyd George had grasped the significance of the British Memorandum any better than Gregory, or whether he had even read it; but Barthou certainly had, and he saw his opportunity. If it was intended not to co-operate with Germany, but to coerce her into paying Reparations to Russia, it was clearly necessary first to persuade the Russians to claim them. They were by no means eager to do this, because whatever they got from Germany would merely accrue to France as compensation for her pre-war loans to Russia, and because Reparations might prove a stumbling-block in Russia's way to a general understanding with Germany, from whom she was promised economic assistance which would not be tapped by France. Barthou, being still sore about the inclusion of Germany in the official sub-commissions, and his policy being one of coercion, suggested to Lloyd George that *private conversations* should be arranged between the Allies and the Russians without the participation of the Germans at Lloyd George's private quarters, the Villa de Albertis. His aim in suggesting this was, of course, in the first place to secure in German Reparations to Russia a source from which France might derive compensation for her pre-war loans to Russia; but also, incidentally, to bring Russia into line with Poincaré's policy of coercion against Germany. And from the Poincaré-Barthou point of view the 'private conversations' had the further advantage of being a trap for Lloyd George by which he might be ensnared into wrecking with his own hands the Conference which he had forced on Poincaré. Lloyd George, who rather surprisingly overlooked the trap and may have thought it desirable to apply some soothing balm to Barthou's wounds, complied with the suggestion to his own undoing.

On Thursday, April 13th, the day originally fixed for the discussion of the memorandum in the sub-commission, the first 'private discussion' of the London Memorandum with the Russians (but, of course, without the Germans) took place at the Villa de Albertis; the session of the sub-commission fixed for that morning was first postponed till the afternoon and then adjourned *sine die*. The Germans were thus deprived of the opportunity Gregory had held out to Maltzan of bringing forward their objections in the sub-commission. Rathenau, alarmed by the turn things were taking, begged Lloyd George for an interview, twice by letter and once by telephone, but all three requests were refused.[26]

On Friday, April 14th, it was persistently rumoured that the French were using Article 116 and the German Reparations

[26] 'Lord D'Abernon gives as the reason for these refusals Lloyd George's wounded vanity at the fact that in a speech in the Reichstag, Rathenau had spoken of 'Lloyd George's declining star.' (D'Abernon, p. 309.) However Lloyd George may have resented these or other words of Rathenau at the time, in a message to the German Government after Rathenau's death he paid him a tribute which certainly does not sound like a merely conventional expression of sympathy: 'I have learned with deep regret of Dr Rathenau's death, and I wish to express my sorrow at the abominable crime which has deprived the German people of one of its most distinguished representatives. The whole world must honour those who incur the risk of public hatred, as he did, from devotion to their country's good. Please convey my profound sympathy to his family.'

burdens arising out of it as a pawn to bargain with the Russians. If Russia were to acknowledge the pre-war debts, her claims on Germany arising out of Article 116 of the Peace Treaty would serve as securities, and effect would be given to these securities by deducting a certain amount from all goods exported from Germany into Russia. Late in the evening, at 11 p.m., the Commendatore Gianini appeared unexpectedly at Dr Wirth's on behalf of Signor Schanzer. He had come, he said, to inform the Chancellor that the conversations between the 'inviting Powers' and the Russians were progressing favourably. The 'inviting Powers' were convinced that the German Government would, as he expressed it, lend their approval to the matter. When Gianini began to enter into details the Chancellor begged him to accompany him to Rathenau's rooms, where they continued the conversation for an hour with Rathenau, Maltzan, and another official of the German Foreign Office, von Simson. Gianini explained that in the course of the discussions on Thursday and Friday between the Russians and the 'inviting Powers' at Lloyd George's villa it had been agreed that Russia's *war* debt should be balanced against her claims on the Entente in connection with the Denikin, Koltchak and Yudenitch ventures, but that on the other hand Russian *pre-war* debts should stand, and that bonds should be issued in respect of them, about the redemption, interest and duration of which agreement would certainly be reached. At this Rathenau asked whether this proposal was to be taken by itself or in connection with the London Memorandum (and Article 116 of the Peace Treaty), to which Gianini replied: 'In connection with the London Memorandum, of course.' Whereupon Rathenau thanked Gianini most courteously for his visit, but explained that in the circumstances Germany could not be expected to take any interest in the proceedings. When Gianini expressed surprise at this, Rathenau replied: 'The agreement with Russia has been made without consulting us. You have arranged a nice dinner-party to which we have not been invited, and now you ask us how we like the menu.' He repeated this remark several times, to which Gianini's only reply was: *'C'était seulement préparé pour nous.'* Rathenau said that so long as the liabilities from Article 116 remained we could not express agreement with the memorandum. Gianini gave no sort of indication that there was any possibility of the memorandum's being altered. At which Rathenau gave him to understand that we should then have to look round for other means of obtaining security. To this Gianini said: 'I am not authorized to make any other sort of statement. I was commissioned solely to inform the German delegation of what I have already said.'

From this conversation the German delegation deduced:

1. That the negotiations between the Western Powers and Russia were nearly concluded,

2. That the impending understanding would do nothing to remove the serious disadvantages in which the London Memorandum involved Germany on three separate points, and

3. That the information conveyed by Gianini amounted to an invitation to Germany to assent to an agreement on which she could have no further influence.

On Saturday, April 15th, Maltzan met Joffe and Rakovsky at 10 o'clock in the Palazzo Reale, as had been previously arranged. He discussed with them the events of the last few days, and obtained an exact account of the negotiations at Lloyd George's villa. They mentioned that in spite of certain difficulties these secret negotiations were proceeding favourably Apparently it was the aim of the 'inviting Powers' to come to an understanding with the Russians before appearing again before the sub-commission. Maltzan cautiously sounded the Russians about the possible resumption of the Berlin discussions, and pointed out that if the negotiations at Lloyd George's villa were to lead to a separate understanding, Germany would hardly be in a position to lend Russia economic support a

318

hitherto. He held out hopes, however, of renewed support on the basis of the negotiations in progress between the Russians and German industrialists, but asked in return that Germany should be allowed to share in the most-favoured-nation terms which the Allies had secured for themselves in the negotiations at Lloyd George's villa, and that the Russians should grant Germany guarantees against the liabilities that might result from Article 116. Joffe and Rakovsky emphasized the fact that despite the separate negotiations with Lloyd George they laid the greatest store on co-operation with Germany, and that the best way to attain the guarantees desired by Maltzan was to sign the Russo-German treaty which had been prepared in Berlin.

While this discussion was taking place quite openly on the veranda of the Palazzo Reale, Herr Dufour was waiting outside for Maltzan to accompany him to the Hotel Miramare in order to enlighten the British about the German *démarche* with the Russians. As they were not in, letters were left for Wise and Gregory, saying that Maltzan was particularly anxious to see them. Wise came to the Hotel Eden about 4.30, and had a two hours' conversation with Maltzan in the garden of the hotel. Afterwards Maltzan introduced Wise to Dr Hilferding (the present German Minister of Finance, who took part in the Genoa Conference as a financial adviser of the German delegation) and asked him to tea. He explained everything to Wise once more and informed him of the previous day's conversation with Signor Gianini, as a result of which the German delegation had lost all hope of the London Memorandum's being altered in accordance with their wishes. He made it perfectly clear that Rathenau had told Gianini that we would now have to make our own arrangements. He also told him quite openly that he had approached the Russians that very day on the basis of the Russo-German Berlin conversations in order to secure most-favoured-nation terms and some guarantee from them with respect to Article 116. The German delegation, he said, had intended to voice their objections officially in one of the sessions of the sub-commission, but were prevented from doing so by the fact that the latter now sat in Lloyd George's private villa, to which apparently Germany was denied access. To this Wise replied: 'The question has been brought before the Prime Minister, but you know . . . !' and he shrugged his shoulders, as if to hint at the fruitlessness of his endeavours. He expressed no surprise at Maltzan's move with the Russians, and honestly admitted the difficulty of the German position. On Maltzan's explicitly asking him, he confirmed the fact that the negotiations with the Russians were being continued and were apparently going on well.

After Wise's departure about 6.30 it was reported on all sides that an understanding had been reached in the course of the evening between the 'inviting Powers' and the Russians. The following seemed to the German delegation especially significant:

(a) In the official communications of the Italian chief of the Press to the foreign journalists it was admitted that for some days separate discussions had been taking place between the 'inviting Powers' and Russia at Lloyd George's villa, and that they appeared to have led to a provisional understanding that very evening.

(b) The correspondent of the *Vossische Zeitung*, Herr Reiner, informed Rathenau and the Chancellor that he had good grounds for believing that 'this evening' the Russians had come to an agreement with the Allies.

(c) On the occasion of a dinner given by one of the German experts, Dr Hagen,[27] on this same evening, the Chancellor was

[27] Louis Hagen, banker and head of the firm of A. Levy in Cologne. One of the chief industrial magnates of the Rhineland, exerting great economic and political influence there.

nformed on the strength of an authentic remark by the Czecho-
Slovak Foreign Minister, Dr Benes, that agreement between
he Russians and the Allies had at last been reached.

(*d*) This was confirmed by one of the guests, the Dutch
banker van Vlissingen, from neutral sources.

When he heard this, Herr Hermes, the German Finance
Minister,[28] expressed to von Simson and Maltzan his deep
concern and disappointment at the conclusion of the agreement,
which meant that Germany was now completely cut off com-
mercially and politically on the east as well as on the west, and
he besought Maltzan on the ground of his good relations with
the Russians to try and arrange something with them before it
was too late; we must avoid being cut off on the east, he said,
all costs.

The German delegates went back to their quarters in very
low spirits. Maltzan, Rathenau and Hagen, and, for some of
the time, Wirth, sat together mournfully in the hotel lounge.
About 11 p.m. Wise rang up Maltzan to ask for exact par-
ticulars of the offending articles of the British Memorandum.
When Maltzan mentioned Article 260 of the Versailles Treaty
well as Article 116, Wise replied that in his view this former
article did not come into question, as the rights it conferred
the Entente had expired. But not even now did he give
Maltzan any sort of assurance that Article 116 would not be
used against Germany. Maltzan informed the others of what
had passed.

Later, when all had retired for the night, at 1.15 a.m. on
Easter Sunday, April 16th, Joffe rang up Maltzan to say that
the Russians were ready to renew negotiations with the German delegation, and would be grateful if they would meet

[28] Dr Andreas Hermes, member of the Reichstag, chairman of the 'Vereinigung
Deutscher Bauernvereine' (Association of German peasant unions) and Vice-
President of the International Commission on Agriculture in Paris. Born July
16, 1878, at Cologne.

them in Rapallo for this purpose at 11 o'clock that (Sunday) morning. The truth was that the private negotiations between the Russians and the Allies had come to a deadlock; and Joffe and Chicherin were in a hurry to resume negotiations with the Germans, because they feared that the Allies might now come to terms with the Germans over Article 116 and that they would thus find themselves left out in the cold and faced with a united front of Allies and Germans. There can be no doubt that they were right, and that Wise's call was the forerunner of the attempt Lloyd George made next day to get into touch again with the Germans.

Maltzan had apparently been informed of the deadlock, but had not informed Rathenau, probably thinking that the hitch might be only temporary. In this opinion he was now confirmed by Joffe, who, when Maltzan questioned him about the state of the negotiations, evasively replied that though no definite agreement with the Allies had yet been concluded, one was expected, and that negotiations were to be resumed on Easter Monday or Tuesday. Whereupon Maltzan, feeling justified in not mentioning the deadlock, woke Rathenau and informed him of Joffe's invitation only. 'It was then,' Maltzan told Lord D'Abernon later, 'about 2.30 a.m. Rathenau was pacing up and down his room in mauve pyjamas, with haggard looks and eyes starting out of his head. When Maltzan came in, he said: "I suppose you bring me the death warrant?" Maltzan replied: "No; news of quite a different character." When told of Joffe's telephone call and invitation, Rathenau said: "Now that I realize the true situation, I will go to Lloyd George and tell him the whole position, and come to terms with him." Maltzan replied: "That would be quite dishonourable. If you do that, I will at once resign my post and retire into private life. It would be behaving monstrously to Chicherin, and I can be no party to such action." Eventually, Rathenau was converted to the Maltzan point of view.' (D'Abernon, p

321.) They then both called the Chancellor, and after he had been informed of the situation the three, the Chancellor in his night-dress, Maltzan in a black silk dressing-gown and Rathenau in his mauve pyjamas, took the momentous decision that Rathenau and Maltzan should go to Rapallo next morning and, if they came to an agreement with the Russians, sign the treaty.

Maltzan was instructed to inform Wise of this by telephone. early in the morning.

At 7.30 a.m. on Sunday, therefore, Maltzan rang up Wise, out was told that he was still asleep. When Maltzan asked that he should be awakened, he was told that Wise himself would elephone to him as soon as he got up. As no call had come hrough by 9.30, Maltzan again rang up Wise between 9.30 and 10, and was told that 'the gentlemen were out.' [29] Whereupon Rathenau, Simson, Gaus (the legal adviser of the German Foreign Office) and Maltzan proceeded to Rapallo, which hey reached about 12. Rathenau discussed the situation with Chicherin, and proposed that they should re-examine the text of the treaty, with the special object of making it perfectly clear that Germany would be granted the same treatment as the other states in case of compensation for damages due to socialization. The Germans then lunched alone at the Hotel Central. After lunch Gaus and Maltzan met Litvinoff, as arranged, to discuss with him the text of the treaty and the increased German demand for security against damages due to socialization; while Rathenau went to visit Baron von Mumm, the former German Ambassador to Japan, who lived some miles away near Portofino.

Hardly had Rathenau left, when Maltzan was informed by telephone from Genoa that Lloyd George had just rung up to say that he would like to speak to the Chancellor and Dr

[29] It is to be presumed that Wise, greatly embarrassed, was waiting for instructions from Lloyd George.

Rathenau at once. Evidently, he, too, wished for the immediate resumption of negotiations with the Germans, now that
the 'private conversations' with the Russians had come to a
deadlock. Chicherin's and Joffe's suspicion that this would be
his next move was thus justified; but they had forestalled him
by ringing up in the small hours of the morning. It proved
impossible now to get into touch with Rathenau because Baron
von Mumm's residence had no telephone. When Rathenau
returned to Rapallo, Maltzan, who was very much upset,
thinking that Rathenau might change his mind and decide to
see Lloyd George before signing the treaty, rather tremulously
informed him of the call. Rathenau paced up and down the
room once or twice, then turned to Maltzan and said: '*Le vin
est tiré, il faut le boire,*' stepped into his car and drove off, with
Maltzan still pale with emotion on the front seat, to sign the
treaty. At 6.30 he and Chicherin set their names to the draft
prepared by Maltzan and Gaus.

Thus was enacted the last scene of what was indeed a comedy
of errors and intrigue. How things would have developed if
Barthou had not suggested 'private conversations,' if Lloyd
George had got up earlier on Easter Sunday, or if Rathenau
had been informed of all that was going on, it is, of course,
impossible to say with certainty. But even if Rathenau had been
to see Lloyd George early on Easter morning, it does not seem
very likely that the French, with their huge pre-war claims
against Russia, and with Poincaré looking out for allies in his
policy of coercion against Germany, would have agreed to any
treaty cancelling Germany's liability, based on Article 116 of
the Peace Treaty, to pay Reparations to Russia. And if they
had not, it is difficult to believe that Lloyd George would really
have dared or had the power to break up the Entente by signing a separate treaty with Germany and Russia. French policy
being what it was at the time, Lloyd George's policy was fated
to be wrecked, if on nothing else, then on Article 116; and

sooner or later, after a great deal of useless parleying and protracted intriguing between the French and English, Russian and German delegations, Germany and Russia would anyhow have had to resort to a separate treaty, and most likely to a separate treaty at Genoa. For once the question of Article 116 had been raised and a general agreement on it had finally proved impossible, Germany could not have been content to put off settling it till later; and Russia was permanently eager to seize any opportunity of running a wedge into what she considered the united front of Capitalism. Rapallo was therefore but a short-cut to something that was probably inevitable. As to the charge of bad faith brought against Rathenau, it will not bear examination. He made several attempts to see Lloyd George personally, in order to explain to him the dilemma in which he was placed. Besides this he gave Signor Gianini clearly to understand on Good Friday that in certain circumstances he would be compelled to take separate action. And Wise, who was supposed to be Lloyd George's specialist on Russian affairs, was warned repeatedly in the same sense by Maltzan. Wise himself is said to have remarked, when he heard of the treaty, 'I am not at all surprised.' [80]

[80] Lord D'Abernon (p. 298 ff.) prints some 'German Notes on the Events leading up to the signing of the German-Russian Treaty' which give a chronicle of the Russo-German negotiations almost identical with the above. I should like to state, however, that Lord D'Abernon had no knowledge of my book when he wrote his Memoirs; neither had I any opportunity of using his, as it was published several months after mine. I am not aware of who wrote Lord D'Abernon's 'Notes'; but internal evidence points to Maltzan, and I can testify to their accuracy. On one point, however, I venture to differ from Lord D'Abernon. Personal vanity, to which he attributes 'a considerable part' in the signing of the Russo-German pact at Genoa (p. 308), did not, I think, contribute anything to the final result so far as Rathenau was concerned. Rathenau knew for certain that the signing of the treaty would be offensive to President Ebert, whose constitutional rights it infringed, as there was no time to ask his consent; and that it would be far from popular not only in Government and some circles, but also in his own delegation at Genoa, who were much more anxious for an agreement with France and England than with Russia. If proof were needed that Rathenau was not out for a personal triumph, it could be found in a long confidential letter which he wrote to President Ebert on Good

WALTHER RATHENAU

After Rathenau's return to Genoa from Rapallo, in the evening, Sir Basil Blackett (Director of Finance of the British
Treasury) called, and Rathenau informed him immediately
of the Russo-German agreement. Sir Basil received the news
calmly and seemed in no way surprised.

Late that evening Rathenau wrote to his friend:

16.4.1922

Warmest greetings. Today, Easter Sunday, I have been in
Rapallo and signed something there.

W.

And a fortnight later:

(Genoa) 28.4.1922

Your trust and confidence has done me good; it came just
at the right moment. This feeling of being confronted by a taut
and rigid world ready to pounce on the first sign of weakness—
it is like something physical, and wears down the nerves. And
what difficulties in one's own camp: F. . . . has been a real
help to me and I'm sorry that he's going. He will tell you all
the news.

I am convinced that we have acted as we should. Of course,
it was bound to cause trouble, and the storm is not yet over.
Even Nature refuses to be kind. I am looking down on a huge
green garden full of half-blossoming red and white chestnut
trees with a line of mountains beyond, and everything is draped
with grey rain-laden wisps of cloud. The damp cold goes right
through one's limbs to the very tips of one's fingers.

That you let H. . . . come, just now, when he is doing
everything in his power to discredit my work, doesn't put me
out, but I strive to find some clear and genuine feeling, which

Friday, and which the President received on Easter Sunday, the very day of the
signing of the treaty; in this letter Rathenau does not even mention the possibility
of a separate agreement with Russia, a circumstance which particularly angered
the President. The real motives and circumstances which led to the signing of
the treaty I have endeavoured to explain above.

326

can explain your doing this. I should like to feel you were somewhere where the sun was really shining and spring not chary of her favours. This winter clings to everything like the war, and is still capable of evil. But summer will come at last and make you well again.

While I have been writing this letter, not a single person has come in—a marvel! And so in the midst of this cold and conflict I have had a whole quarter of an hour with you alone.

Affectionately yours,

W.

Early on Monday, April 17th, Maltzan informed Wise by letter of the conclusion of the treaty, enclosing the only available copy of it which he possessed. Wise acknowledged the receipt of this letter between 8 and 9 p.m.[31] Later it was reported that an American who dined with Lloyd George on Sunday had got the distinct impression that the Prime Minister had been fully aware of the Russo-German negotiations.

But for a day or two it certainly looked as though the treaty would break up the Conference. Feeling in the Allied delegations ran high and ranged from anger to panic. With some, in the first flush of excitement, it assumed grotesque forms. M Barthou issued a note in which he accused Dr Wirth of '*allégations mensongères.*' The French delegation ostentatiously packed their trunks in the Hotel Savoy. In Paris people got ready to go back to the trenches. A luncheon party which I hap-

---

[31] In a letter quoted by Lord D'Abernon (p. 310) Wise states that 'on the Monday morning after the treaty was signed he received personally a note from Baron Maltzan enclosing what was in fact an incomplete copy of the treaty— the signatory clause and date had been torn off—in which it was indicated, not that the treaty had been signed, but that it was under consideration.' Of course, nobody could doubt Mr Wise's good faith; but perhaps his memory is at fault, as there could have been no motive for Maltzan to mislead him on Easter Monday, when the whole of Genoa was in a turmoil of excitement over the signature of the treaty, and Rathenau himself had informed Sir Basil Blackett on the night before of the facts. Perhaps Mr Wise has kept Maltzan's letter and could publish it.

pened to be giving on Monday with one of the permanent officials from the German Foreign Office was partly wrecked at the last moment because the French delegates we had invited were strictly forbidden to attend by Barthou. Poincaré suspected that Germany had sought and found Russian military support against his Rhine plans.

Lloyd George at first raged picturesquely, but not very convincingly, demanded the unconditional withdrawal of the treaty, which was refused with equal energy by both Germany and Russia, and then suddenly on April 19th granted the interview which Rathenau had so long sought in vain. In the meanwhile he may have found the rumours of a Russo-German military convention at the back of the treaty not altogether unwelcome; the suspicion that such an agreement perhaps existed might act as a check on Poincaré's ambitions on the Rhine, which Lloyd George was bent on frustrating. At any rate the interview between him, Wirth and Rathenau went off without any dramatic incidents and the Germans found it quite satisfactory. When Maltzan, who was in attendance, pointed out that he had warned Mr Wise of what was going on, Lloyd George replied: 'But who is Mr Wise? [32] Why did you not come to *me*?' To which Maltzan replied very appositely: 'You wouldn't receive Dr Rathenau whom you did know, so how could I expect you to receive me whom you did not know?' Lloyd George gave Wirth and Rathenau the choice of relinquishing either the treaty or else their participation in the negotiations with Russia in the sub-commission. The Chancellor and Rathenau referred the matter to the German delegation, who were divided in their views. However, the Italian Foreign Minister, Signor Schanzer, intervened; and as the result of his interview with Rathenau on the morning of the 20th

[32] Lord D'Abernon says that 'the German delegation did not realize the purely rhetorical character of this question, being unaware that, in the Welsh vernacular, imprecations and expletives frequently assume an interrogative form' (p. 322).

it was agreed that in their reply to the protest of the Allies, the Germans, after clearly emphasizing their point of view and rebutting the charge of disloyalty brought against the Chancellor by Barthou, should voluntarily renounce taking part in the negotiations with the Russians in the sub-commission when the memorandum of the Allies was under consideration. But whenever other questions, particularly those touching on the economic rehabilitation of Russia, came up for discussion the Germans were to resume both their seats and their vote.

Immediately after Signor Schanzer and Rathenau had come to terms, and even before the written German reply had been despatched, Lloyd George summoned all the journalists in great haste to the mediaeval hall of the Palazzo San Giorgio, the scene of his triumph on the first day of the Conference, and there and then declared that all was forgotten and forgiven and the treaty incident closed. He was so boyish and playful and appeared to find such pleasure in giving the proceedings the popular and democratic appearance of a variety entertainment, moving up and down behind a table and answering any written question handed up to him like a music-hall medium, that one could not help feeling he must have some secret source of enjoyment; presumably he was thinking of Poincaré, whom he had outwitted and forestalled by the lightning rapidity with which he was clearing up the mess. And, in fact, a few days later, Maltzan, who had at first been cut dead by some of the English delegates, was seen dancing at the Hotel Miramare with Miss Megan Lloyd George.

Meanwhile the 'gentleman in Paris,' as Lloyd George had dubbed Poincaré, was belabouring his representative in Genoa with telegrams at the rate of one about every twenty minutes urging him to take forceful action; and when this merely resulted in the unfortunate Barthou's lodging a belated and vain protest against Germany's only partial exclusion from the sub-commission, he hastened to deliver an inflammatory speech of unparalleled violence at Bar-le-Duc on April 24th. He said that if France could not get her principles accepted he would withdraw his delegation from the Conference. He accused Germany and Russia of concealing a military convention behind the outwardly innocuous paragraphs of the Rapallo Treaty, said that the treaty constituted a direct menace to France, and threatened that if Germany did not fulfil the obligations laid upon her by the decision of the Reparations Commission of April 10th 'France would take measures to force her, *even if she had to do so alone, as she was entitled to by the Versailles Treaty*': thus revealing his ambitions on the Rhine.

The effect of this speech on the Conference was hardly less sensational than had been that of the Russo-German treaty. Battle was now joined openly between Poincaré and Lloyd George, who forced Barthou to transmit to his chief an invitation to come to San Remo so that they might discuss orally the sanctions Poincaré was contemplating. At the same time he announced his intention of submitting the question of whether an individual Allied power could resort to sanctions of its own accord to the signatories of the Versailles Treaty; and allowed it to leak out into the newspapers that he was thinking of revising his attitude to the Entente and would certainly do so if he had to choose between the Entente and Peace. Partisans and journalists on both sides joined in the fray. Mr Garvin, who was in Genoa, wrote a vigorous article in the *Observer* entitled: *France* versus *Europe: a failure in Genoa means War!* The French, on the other hand, maintained that Lloyd George wanted to force the French delegation to withdraw and break up the Conference in order to expose to the world France's moral isolation. Even the ever-peaceful and Anglophile Philippe Millet, the correspondent of the *Petit Parisien*, was stung to the remark: Europe will only get peace '*quand elle aura vomi Lloyd George.*' Finally Barthou, utterly bewildered

THE FIGHT FOR PEACE

and overwhelmed by a deluge of despatches, announced his
intention of going to Paris himself to speak with his chief.

The effect of this conflict on the position of the German
delegation was remarkable. Rathenau had been convinced from
the start that the English could accomplish nothing in the
face of French opposition; and so, when the storm broke, he
kept deliberately in the background. But both sides now began
to try to win the good graces of the German delegation. A
permanent link between the French and German delegations
had been arranged for in Berlin before the Conference met
through the person of Professor Hesnard, one of the members
of the French delegation; but although I saw him daily, in
fulfilment of this agreement, the results of our interviews were
nil, because from the very first Barthou, doubtless on Poincaré's instructions, refused to meet Rathenau or Wirth privately. Now suddenly Barthou himself, only a week after he
had publicly accused the Chancellor of 'lying allegations,' asked
Professor Hesnard to arrange an interview. When I trans-
mitted the invitation to Rathenau, he replied that he and the
Chancellor would not object to meeting Barthou socially, but
that a purely business discussion was no longer desirable, because it would not now get them any further. The interview,
therefore, did not take place. Nor is it likely that it would have
done anything to alter the attitude of Poincaré, who was
firmly set on his separatist Rhine policy;[33] and it might have
seemed suspicious to the British delegation. For as a result of
the Rapallo Treaty, the Germans were gradually drawn into
the position of confidential intermediaries between the British
and the Russians.

But even if there ever had been a chance of success, it was
too late now to rescue the Conference or to save Europe from

[33] Senator Dariac was just then busy preparing his secret report to M Poincaré on the ways and means of separating the Rhineland from Germany which
the *Manchester Guardian* disclosed some years later.

331

the disastrous consequences of failure. Things had come to the point at which Poincaré was at last offered the opportunity he had sought of stabbing the Conference in the back. In the course of their negotiations with the Russians the Allies had decided to hand them a new memorandum embodying their conditions for re-establishing diplomatic and economic relations with Russia. In Cannes, in January, all the Allies had signed a binding agreement embodying the principles which were to govern their negotiations with Russia at Genoa. By Article 1 of this agreement they recognized that 'nations cannot claim the right to dictate to each other the principles upon which they may organize their property rights, their industry and their government. Every country must be entitled to choose for itself the system it favours in this respect.' By Article 2, however, it was laid down that 'it would be possible to give economic assistance to a country only if the foreigners who supplied the necessary capital were sure that their possessions and rights would be respected and the rights accruing to them out of their undertakings were assured them.' From these principles it followed necessarily that the Soviet Government could not be denied the right of confiscating alien property, if it undertook to compensate the owners. This right was therefore acknowledged by Article 6 of the new memorandum; which further proposed that in case the former owner and the Soviet Government disagreed about the amount he could claim as compensation, the sum should be fixed by an International Tribunal. As the Belgians had signed the Cannes agreement, they could not with any show of reason refuse their assent to this article. But when it came up for discussion on May 1st in the Inter-allied sub-commission, the Belgian Prime Minister, M Jaspar, unexpectedly declared that he could not agree to this article, and therefore would refuse to sign the memorandum. Whereupon Lloyd George remarked: 'Well then, the Belgians had better withdraw.' M Barthou, who had already given his consent to the article in question, intervened, saying, 'in a voice quivering with emotion': 'I respectfully implore Mr Lloyd George not to inflict this humiliation on little Belgium,' whereupon M Jaspar all of a tremble stood up and said: 'No one can humiliate Belgium, not even England!' and Mr Lloyd George retorted: 'Who ever thought of humiliating anybody? At an election, when one is beaten, one is not humiliated. . . . Well, we are here to cast our votes.'

M Jean de Pierrefeu, a French journalist in close touch with the French delegation at Genoa, from whom I have borrowed the details of this melodrama,[34] suggests that M Jaspar's opposition was concerted behind poor M Barthou's back with Poincaré, who had lost all patience with the 'weakness' and lack of success of his representative. Whether this surprising suggestion is true or not, at any rate Poincaré seized the opportunity offered him by M Jaspar. He summoned Barthou to come to Paris immediately; and in the meantime entrusted the French delegation to the care of the French Ambassador in Rome, M Barrère, who had all along taken a view closely akin to Poincaré's. The first thing that Barrère did on Poincaré's instructions was to declare that the French could not uphold the consent Barthou had given to the memorandum in their name unless the Belgians also agreed to it. That was the stab in the back which could be trusted to kill the Conference; for it extinguished all hope of a general agreement with Russia in Genoa. This was on May 2nd.

Lloyd George was now fighting with his back to the wall. He decided that the memorandum must be handed to the Russians then and there, without the signature of the Belgians and with the French signature invalidated by the declaration of M Barrère. And then, on May 4th, at his request a long con-

[34] Jean de Pierrefeu, *La Saison diplomatique*, p. 169 ff. I have given M de Pierrefeu's version, but accounts still more highly coloured were freely circulated in Genoa at the time.

versation took place in the morning between him, the German Chancellor and Rathenau at the Villa de Albertis. All the current questions, including the memorandum, were discussed, but nothing definite was agreed on between the three statesmen. Lloyd George, however, expressed the wish that these conversations should be continued. It was on the evening before that Miss Megan Lloyd George had danced with Maltzan at the Miramare. The long private interview between Lloyd George and the German Ministers created uneasiness in the French delegation, and was, of course, intended to do so and to serve as a danger-signal. In the afternoon the French chief of the Press asked me to dine with him. In the course of dinner he said that Poincaré had by no means given up the idea of military sanctions; that he was more than a match for Lloyd George, and that nobody could say with certainty which of the two would win in the end. A friendly warning which sounded very much like a threat.

From the very first Rumour had played a considerable part in the doings of the Conference. Its hub was the 'Casa della Stampa' which the Italian Government had established in a stiff eighteenth-century palazzo in the Piazza della Zecca and lavishly fitted up with every device for collecting and broadcasting news—a very beehive, in and out of which buzzed hundreds of journalists and busybodies gossiping and intriguing scandalmongering and endeavouring to spy on each other's information. The atmosphere issuing from this hotbed of half truths and suspicions settled down on Genoa like a fog and thickened as the Conference and the various quarrels between delegations proceeded. It was partly responsible for the signing of the Rapallo Treaty, by the suspicions it fostered about the 'private conversations' at the Villa de Albertis. And, of course, each delegation tried to make use of it for its own purposes. On May 5th a number of English journalists began spreading the news that the rupture of the Entente was in minent; that Lloyd George did not really want to part from France, but that British opinion might very soon force him to do so; that his growing intimacy with Wirth and Rathenau must be looked upon as a grave symptom, and that unless Poincaré mended his ways and the French delegation put its signature to the Russian Memorandum the break might become inevitable.

On Saturday, May 6th, towards midday, Barthou returned from Paris and immediately went to see M Jaspar; in the evening he visited Lloyd George. M de Pierrefeu records, on what authority he does not state, that Lloyd George's face 'wore an expression of deep melancholy,' but that he was calm, although when he spoke his voice betrayed bitter disillusionment. When Barthou told him of the resolve of the French Government to support M Jaspar, he said: 'I congratulate you, M Barthou, you who have always been helpful here at Genoa, in not bearing on your shoulders the weight of this heavy responsibility.' M de Pierrefeu affirms that these were Lloyd George's very words. We may well believe it; for Lloyd George can hardly have missed the touch of subtle and rather cruel irony that lay in stressing the helpfulness of M Barthou, who had been helpful principally in exposing the isolation of France. Were the melancholy, the stoicism and the disillusionment of Lloyd George only half sincere and just a piece of consummate acting, as the French journalist suggests? At any rate, Lloyd George, lion-hearted in defeat and convinced that he was conducting a great offensive for the restoration of prosperity to England and of peace to Europe, would not yet admit to himself that he was beaten. So next day, Sunday the 7th, he summoned M Philippe Millet, the correspondent, whose newspaper, the *Petit Parisien*, commanded the widest circulation in France, and inspired him to write an article which was, in fact, a desperate appeal over the head of Poincaré to the French people. He told the French journalist that Englishmen were sick of the Entente and that, unless something un-

335

expected happened, its end was at hand. So far as the British Empire was concerned, after dissolving its partnership with France, it would for a time withdraw from Europe; but later on it might quite possibly conclude arrangements with certain other Continental Powers. The significance of the conversations with Rathenau and Wirth was more than hinted at. Lloyd George evidently hoped that his threat to end the Entente would create a wave of panic in France and that Poincaré would either be swept away or have to give in over the memorandum.

But then something happened. Millet, greatly alarmed, warned the correspondent of the *Echo de Paris*, 'Pertinax' (M Géraud), with the object of inducing him to stay the violent campaign he was conducting against Lloyd George in his newspaper. Instead, Pertinax, who had already been informed more or less exactly of the grave words that Lloyd George was rumoured to have spoken to Barthou, forthwith saw Mr Wickham Steed,[35] the *Times* correspondent and delegate of Lord Northcliffe (whose personal vendetta against Lloyd George had become a factor in European politics and whose papers were doing their utmost to counter the policy of the British Government and support Poincaré). Mr Wickham Steed immediately despatched a report of the conversation between Lloyd George and Barthou to the *Times*. Thus on Monday morning, May 8th, Paris woke up to read in the *Petit Parisien* the article inspired by Lloyd George, and London to learn with a shock that Lloyd George had officially informed M Barthou that 'England and France had reached a parting of the ways.' The reaction to the *Times* despatch was such as Mr Wickham Steed had expected. Notwithstanding a great deal of bickering and discontent, British opinion was not ready to support a rup-

[35] Henry Wickham Steed, born 1871. Studied in France and Germany, where he was a pupil of the philosopher Paulsen in Berlin. *Times* correspondent at Berlin in 1896, Rome 1897-1902, Vienna 1902-13; foreign editor 1914-19 and editor 1919-22. Editor of *The Review of Reviews*.

ture with France. There were questions in the House of Commons and the beginnings of a Stock Exchange panic in the City, telegrams began pouring in at Genoa asking for explanations, and Lloyd George, hard pressed by his Government, suddenly put in an appearance at the headquarters of the British journalists late at night, and indignantly denied Mr Steed's allegations. But, worse still, he had to implore Barthou to issue a denial. After prolonged negotiations Barthou, late in the evening, complied. The denial was a reprieve for Lloyd George and his Government; but the Conference was, for all practical purposes, dead.[36]

For a short time, while its testament was being drawn up by the technical sub-commissions, it lingered on, saved from its death-bed mainly by Lloyd George's hope that in spite of all something might turn up, and by the desperate need of the Russians for a loan. In these circumstances, whatever was left of it of course centered around negotiations between Lloyd George and the Russians. The Germans continued lending their assistance. Dr Wirth impressed on Chicherin and Litvinoff Lloyd George's request that they should go and see him before they answered the memorandum.[37] Rathenau discussed privately with Lloyd George the size of a Russian loan that might possibly be floated in England, and I had long conversations every day with Mr Wise on the same subject. When the Russians failed to understand certain financial details of the memorandum, Lloyd George asked that a German expert (Dr

[36] It is a pity that Mr Wickham Steed, in the two or three rather jejune pages which he allows Genoa in his Memoirs, has not thought fit to give a more detailed account of this incident, which ultimately had a far-reaching influence, not only on Lloyd George's and his own fortunes, but also on post-war European history. (Wickham Steed, *Through Thirty Years*, p. 383 ff.)
[37] All along the French had bitterly resented Lloyd George's attitude of being above paying visits, or even receiving them when they displeased him. While Barthou had to move about visiting delegates, Lloyd George just 'sent for' his colleagues when he wished to speak to them, 'like a Sovereign,' as a disgusted Frenchman said at the time.

Hilferding) should explain their significance to them.[38] All the time Hilferding and Maltzan acted as willing intermediaries with the Russians. Rathenau, although more sceptical, remained particularly anxious for an understanding, because he clung to his aim of fitting the Rapallo Treaty into something more European, a treaty between all the Western Powers and Russia, or at least one between Great Britain and Russia.

Having realized at last that the sums they needed were not to be extracted from the Allies except on terms which they could not grant, the Russians handed in their answer on May 11th. After criticizing the Allied memorandum with an acid irony that was unmistakably Chicherin's and commenting bitterly on the indisputable fact that the Allies in Genoa 'had spoken to Russia the language of a victor to the vanquished, although Russia was not vanquished,' they pointed out that the financial questions pending between the Allies and Russia needed a more thorough investigation, and proposed that this task should be entrusted to a mixed committee of experts on whose date and place of meeting Russia and the Allies should agree. The memorandum being the only subject left for discussion at Genoa, the Russian answer amounted to a motion for the adjournment of the Conference. Of course, the French and Belgians were delighted; and even Lloyd George found the proposal acceptable, because it allowed him to place the blame for the failure of the Conference on the Russians. All parties there-

[38] Dr Rudolf Hilferding, born 1877, in Vienna, joined the Social Democratic party and wrote *Das Finanzkapital*, which has become a standard work of Marxian economics. Editor of the Berlin *Vorwärts* 1906-1915. Was an army doctor with the Austrian army on the Italian front from 1915 to 1918. In 1918 returned to Berlin and edited the organ of the 'Independent' Social Democrats, the *Freiheit*. Was one of those principally instrumental in detaching the 'Independents' from the Spartacists (Communists), and in bringing about their reunion with the old Social Democratic party. Entered the Reichstag and became German Minister of Finance (for the first time) in the Stresemann Cabinet which stopped passive resistance in the Ruhr in 1923; prepared the rehabilitation of the mark, which was later carried through by Dr Luther and Dr Schacht. Minister of Finance in the present German Cabinet since 1928.

ore agreed to hold a meeting of Allied and Russian experts at
The Hague in June to discuss the memorandum. And then the
Conference was buried with becoming pomp in a last grand
ceremonial plenary session held in the same sombre mediaeval
all which had seen its opening.

Limelight and laurels there had been, in triumph and de-
eat, more than enough for Lloyd George; but British opinion
ad abandoned him in the crisis, and his prestige, both at home
ad abroad, had suffered severely. The problems which he had
heart, that of Reparations and that of the restoration of
osperity to Europe, were as far from a solution as ever; while
s attempt to bridge the gulf between Russia and the Western
wers had failed disastrously. The achievements of the Con-
rence, apart from a few excellent technical reports, seemed
ore than disappointing.

And yet, on looking backwards, one cannot help seeing that
noa marked the turning of the tide in post-war history. To
gin with, Poincaré, who appeared as the victor, had really
ined the foundations of his policy of coercing and disrupting
rmany, both by forcing the Russians to side with his victim
d by taking up a position which called the attention of the
rld to his aims and ambitions. For little as Russia's support
y have weighed materially, psychologically it was one of
se 'imponderables,' as Bismarck called them, which some-
es play a decisive part in history; and the disclosure of
incaré's plans for establishing French influence on a perma-
t basis in the Rhineland ended, in spite of war memories,
undermining English acquiescence in French policy. Ger-
ny, on the other hand, had regained her status as a Great
ver. Besides this she was bringing home, in the teeth of
nch opposition, her treaty with Russia; and Rathenau had
pared the ground for a further advance on the path of
otiation and understanding by establishing relations of mu-
l confidence with some at least of the Allied statesmen.

339

After Genoa, Germany was no longer an outcast. In the terrible years which were still in store for her, her new position helped decisively to bring about the collapse of the French ambitions on the Rhine. Had Russia been drawn back into a ring with the Allies against Germany, as Poincaré plotted, and had not British politicians begun to trust her more than they did France, the Separatist movement in the Rhineland in 1923-24 might possibly have been successful and the disruption of Germany have become, for a time at least, one of those political *faits accomplis* which it requires both years and a genius to reverse. It was the intellectual force and steadiness of Rathenau which convinced some of Germany's former enemies that his 'policy of fulfilment' was honest, thus averting these dangers and preparing the way for Germany's slow rise from the abyss.

To him and his character the Conference, as its ultimate sign of life, paid a spontaneous tribute, when it responded to his last words at the last plenary session with an ovation similar to that which had greeted Lloyd George's performance at the opening session. In the peroration of his speech he had said: 'The history of Italy is more ancient than that of most European nations. More than one great world movement has originated in this soil. Once more, and, let us hope, not in vain, the peoples of the earth have lifted up their eyes and their hearts to Italy out of the depths of that feeling which has been expressed for all time in Petrarch's words: *Io vò gridando: Pace, Pace, Pace!* (I go calling: Peace, Peace, Peace!).' Again, the sophisticated audience of elder statesmen and diplomats was swept off its feet. But what gripped it now, more than the words, was the man. While Lloyd George's speech had been applauded for its dexterity, its wit, its nimbleness, its charm, in short for being of the same stuff as perfect comedy, here was tragedy speaking. And indeed the words were even more pathetic than they seemed; they were Rathenau's swan song, and the verse from Petrarch summed up in a symbol his life-work.

CHAPTER XI

THERE IS NO DEATH

᷈ROM the moment that he became Foreign Minister the
police began warning Rathenau almost daily of plots
against his life. When I entered his office in the Wil-
strasse for the first time after his appointment, and greeted
with the usual 'Good-morning, how do you do?' he replied,
ng a pistol out of his trouser pocket: 'This is how I do!
gs have got to such a pitch that I cannot go about without
little instrument.'

enoa gave him a breathing space. The perfect order main-
d by the Facta Government all over Italy and the care
was taken to protect every single delegate to the Confer-
gave him back that feeling of security which he had so
missed. We wandered for hours, alone and apparently
arded, through the streets of Genoa. He knew every nook
cranny (as a young man he had superintended the build-
f the electric trams there), and nothing pleased him better
to point out some vestige of the Middle Ages or Renais-
not mentioned in Baedeker. His last letter from Genoa to
riend reflects that halcyon calm akin to happiness which
times comes to those doomed, a short breathing space
re their death.

17.5.22 *Sunday night*

What is the meaning of this? You write me a letter full of
and sorrow and send me all manner of bitter-sweet things
h are much too good to perish on my writing-table between
tations and daydreams.[1]

his evidently alludes to a project of publishing in some form or other at
a part of this correspondence. Unfortunately his friend's letters were all
after Rathenau's death.

Why trouble to ponder over it all? When we look back over these years, hasn't everything that happened and had to happen been for the best?

I often think, and it is my greatest comfort: What a wretched sort of life is that which merely runs its even course untroubled! The wonderful thing is that all true sorrow is beautiful. Only the stupidly awry and the arbitrarily distorted is ugly. In our life everything has been Law; thus were the facts, and thus their predestined course. Nothing has been in vain, nothing can now be thought away or given up.

And if you honestly reflect you will find that even what seemed to be Chance was really Necessity. And is Chance going to have his own way now? My life has run too far along its course for that to be possible.

Now at last I am free of my fellow-men. Not in the sense that I could ever be indifferent to them. On the contrary, the freer I am the nearer and dearer—despite all—they are to me; and I joyfully recognize that I exist for them, not they for me.

The one person who exists for me, freely and consciously, without need of support, help or even thanks, and who shares completely my inmost life—that person is you, and I thank you for it.

Certainly there is not much more that I can do. The flame burns low. But you know it is my destiny to be ready to lift from others the burden that oppresses them and to remain myself without desire. Whatever I still keep back or guard in secret, that is yours.

Affectionately,
W.

After his return to Berlin at the end of May there were increasing signs that his life was in real danger. From all sides warnings poured in. Dr Wirth writes to me about one of them which was particularly impressive: 'In those dark days of German history, at a time when we were deeply anxious about the preservation of the unity of our country, and when disruption and civil war seemed at hand, a Catholic priest came to see me at the Chancellery and informed me simply and soberly in a few sentences, but with great earnestness, that Rathenau's life was in danger. I could not question him; the interview took place in absolute privacy between the Catholic priest and my-self. I immediately understood how serious was the warning, and myself passed on the information to my officials. Then Rathenau himself was called in. I implored him with all my might to give up his resistance to increased police protection for his person. In his well-known manner, with which many of his friends were familiar, he stubbornly refused. Thereupon I informed him of what had happened, and asked him whether he did not see that the step taken by the Catholic priest was a very serious affair. My words impressed Rathenau deeply. He stood motionless and pale for about two minutes. None of us dared break the silence or speak a single word. Rathenau seemed to be gazing on some distant land. He was visibly struggling with his own feelings. Suddenly his face and his eyes took on an expression of infinite benevolence and gentle-ness. With a calm such as I had never witnessed in him, al-hough I had gauged the measure of his self-control in many a discussion on difficult political and personal questions, he stepped up to me, and putting both his hands on my shoulders said: "Dear friend, it is nothing. Who would do me any harm?" Our conversation, however, was not at an end. After I had once more laid stress on the seriousness of the information and on the absolute necessity for police protection, he left the room with an expression of incomprehensible security on his face. Unfortunately, Rathenau, as I heard later on, once more expressly protested against special protection.'

Unfortunately; for there could no longer be any doubt that

343

the agitation against him, which had now been going on for
years, was beginning at last to bear dangerous fruit. Political
murder had at that time become one of the commonplaces of
German public life to a degree hardly credible. In his pamphlet *Four Years of Political Murder*, Herr Gumbel [2] gives
the names and exact circumstances of the assassination of more
than three hundred republicans and radicals, who (quite apart
from those killed in actual civil war or street fighting) were
murdered in cold blood by Nationalists between 1918 and 1922.
The 'Feme' murder trials have since disclosed that in the
'Black' Reichswehr and similar organizations assassination had
been elevated into a regular system, and that the assassins belonging to them performed their job as a mere matter of routine.[3] With public morality at this low ebb and murder practised
as a fine art by a horde of fanatics, and almost honoured as a
legitimate form of political activity by a quite considerable
fraction of the German people, the Nationalists, far from feeling that they were in common decency bound to moderate their
agitation against Rathenau, strained every nerve to extend and
intensify it. The responsibility for this reckless campaign rested
with their leader, the former Imperial Vice-Chancellor, Karl
Helfferich, an ex-professor who had attained to high office
thanks to the war, and in whom, after he fell from power,
statistics and chicanery had whetted one another into dagger-

[2] Lecturer on statistics at the University of Heidelberg. The title of the
pamphlet is *Vier Jahre politischer Mord*, published by Verlag der Neuen Gesellschaft, Berlin—Fichtenau, 1922.

[3] The 'Black' (or illegal) Reichswehr was organized secretly, nominally to
defend the eastern provinces of Prussia against a Polish invasion during the
Ruhr occupation; practically it was an armed force at the disposal of the Nationalists, who wanted to overthrow the Republic. After the Ruhr was evacuated,
it was disbanded. An appalling number of illegal executions of members of
the Black Reichswehr by their comrades for 'treason' was revealed later on,
when those who were responsible for them were tried and condemned for murder. The illegal executions were called 'Feme' murders, after the name of the
German mediaeval secret tribunals, which disposed of those condemned by them
in a similar illegal and secret manner.

like instruments of deadly precision.[4] His pamphlets and invectives were in great measure responsible for the assassination of Erzberger.[5] Since Erzberger's death he had concentrated on Rathenau. The Nationalists, who were armed, at a time when all but a few big industrialists and landowners were destitute, with an immense party fund whose sources have never been disclosed, made a regular system of denouncing Rathenau. Day by day speeches in the Reichstag and the various Diets, leading articles, vast popular meetings, pilloried him as the Jew responsible for the depths of shame to which Germany had been brought and for the ruin of the German middle classes. In the imagination of millions of impoverished and famished Germans, Rathenau became a sort of arch-traitor, in league with the Jews, the Bolshevists, and the Entente to give the

[4] Karl Theodor Helfferich, born July 22nd, 1872, in Neustadt in the Palatinate. Studied law and economics, specially statistics, of which he became Professor in Berlin in 1901. Was commissioned by the Deutsche Bank to look after its interests in Anatolia in 1906, where he remained till 1908. Became Secretary of State of the Treasury in 1915, was promoted Minister of the Interior in 1916, and retained this post and the Vice-Chancellorship from 1916 till the Revolution. In the meanwhile he had been for a short time Ambassador to Russia, after the assassination of Count Mirbach in Moscow. Became a member of the Reichstag in 1920. Was killed in a railway accident near Bellinzona on April 23rd, 1924.

[5] Mathias Erzberger, member of the Reichstag and one of the leaders of the Centre (Catholic) party in the Reichstag. Born September 20th, 1879. Began life as an elementary school teacher. First contributed articles to the Catholic Press in 1896. Entered the Reichstag at the age of twenty-four in 1903, and became a sort of parliamentary secretary to Prince Franz Arenberg, one of the most influential Catholic leaders, who was at the same time an intimate friend of the Chancellor, Prince Bülow, and thus formed an important link between the Chancellor and one of the Government parties. It was in drudging for Prince Arenberg that Erzberger, then quite a young man, first won his spurs. Nevertheless, he violently opposed the Government colonial policy, and brought about the dissolution of the Reichstag on this question in 1906. At the beginning of the war he took up an imperialist attitude; but later on, in 1917, got a Peace resolution passed by the Reichstag. Became Imperial Secretary of State in October, 1918, negotiated the Armistice with Foch, and became Minister of Finance after the Revolution. The Nationalists held him responsible for the terms of the Armistice and the humiliation of Germany, and he was assassinated by two Nationalist fanatics on August 26th, 1921, while walking with a friend in a wood near Griesbach in Baden.

death-blow to Germany. We get an idea of the depths of hate
which this agitation produced, when we hear that the members
of the Upper Silesian *Selbstschutz* [6] when tramping the roads
were wont to sing a song of which the chorus went:

'God damn Walther Rathenau.
Shoot him down, the dirty Jew.'

The police urged Rathenau to take the necessary precautions.
At first he acquiesced. Later, however, he refused uncom-
promisingly; for he believed in Fate, and he did not really
believe in Death. In *The Mechanism of the Mind* he asks:
'Is it possible to conceive mortality?' and answers: 'It is only
when we contemplate the part instead of the whole that we
become aware of death. The ancients compared the end of a
man's life to the fall of the leaf; the leaf dies, but the tree
goes on living. If the tree falls in its turn, the wood will still
go on, and if the wood should die, then the earth, which feeds
and warms and absorbs its creatures, will still sprout green and
fresh. And if the planet itself grows cold, there will be a thousand other planets to rejoice in the rays of yet other suns.
Nothing organic can die. Everything is perpetually being reborn, and to the God who watches from afar the centuries
reveal ever the same picture and the same life.

'In the whole visible world we know nothing mortal. For
what is mortal could not be born. True, everything that strives
towards a goal, everything that frets and struggles, consumes
itself away; and thus a materially organic world is only conceivable on the assumption of the eternal change of substance,
from the mechanism of the body to the mechanism of the
atom. But this change is no more like dying than the growth
of the individual plant, which would be impossible without
change of substance. The conception of dying arises from false

[6] A semi-military organization formed in Upper Silesia in 1920-21 to protect
the country against the ruthless terrorism of bands of Polish Nationalists.

observation, through the eye being fixed on the part instead of the whole. Nothing real in the world is mortal. We may still, if we wish, use the word "death" as a metaphor for the power that sets limits to the phenomena in the world of appearances; but this power we must salute as a glorious spirit, as the warden of life, the lord of transfiguration, and the witness to the truth' (p. 177). Goethe has expressed the same view in one of his most profound poems:

> 'Denn alle Kraft dringt vorwärts in die Weite,
> Zu leben und zu wirken hier und dort;
> Dagegen engt und hemmt von jeder Seite
> Der Strom der Welt und reisst uns mit sich fort:
> In diesem innern Sturm und äussern Streiten
> Vernimmt der Geist ein schwer verstanden Wort:
> Von der Gewalt, die alle Wesen bindet,
> Befreit der Mensch sich, der sich überwindet.'

In April, a seventeen-year-old schoolboy, Hans Stubenrauch, confided to a certain student, one Günther, his intention of murdering Rathenau. This Stubenrauch was the son of a general, and despite his years already a member of the *Bund der Aufrechten;* [7] he was vain and precocious, but still half a child. Günther had been previously convicted for desertion, and was, as the medical evidence at his trial showed, a pathological liar and braggart.[8] Stubenrauch gave as the grounds for his decision the passage in Rathenau's pamphlet *Der Kaiser,* interpreting it as Ludendorff had done: 'That day will never come on which the Kaiser will ride victorious through the Brandenburger Tor. On that day history would have lost all meaning.' According to Günther's evidence at the trial, this passage was what decided

[7] 'League of the Upright,' one of those small semi-secret Monarchist associations, numbers of which shot up like mushrooms overnight immediately after the Revolution.
[8] His own co-conspirators attempted to poison him during the trial, suspecting him of having betrayed them.

Stubenrauch, for it 'was taken to be a proof that Rathenau had not wished for victory.'

After Rathenau's return from Genoa to Berlin at the end of May, Günther put Stubenrauch into touch with an ex-naval officer named Kern, a fair-haired, blue-eyed young man of twenty-five, the very type, Nordic and blond, tragic to relate, which Rathenau trusted most completely. Kern came to Berlin with a friend, Fischer, who was also twenty-five and fair-haired. Both were members of the Organization Consul, a terrorist society which had been formed out of the Ehrhardt Brigade after the Kapp Putsch.[9] Kern saw Stubenrauch, but found him too young, and unsuitable in other respects also. Nevertheless he enlisted his services along with Fischer's, and then got into contact with Ernst Werner Techow, the Berlin agent of the Organization Consul. Techow was only twenty-one, the son of a deceased Berlin magistrate, and a grandson of one of the heroes of the Revolution of 1848. He was somewhat decadent, a 'rather effeminate boy,' according to his uncle's evidence, and, as one of the other conspirators, Tillessen, explained at the trial, was taken on by Kern merely as a 'handy tool, who would do as he was told and ask no questions.' Techow brought along with him his sixteen-year-old brother Gerd, who had joined the Organization Consul at the age of fifteen.

And so the conspiracy came into being: the typical conspiracy,

[9] Captain Ehrhardt, an officer of the Imperial Navy, after the Revolution received the command of a brigade of the Reichswehr, and in March, 1920, with the help of this brigade and the connivance of former high imperial officials and generals, attempted to upset the Republican Government of President Ebert and to set up in its place a dictatorship under a certain Kapp. This was what was called the 'Kapp Putsch.' It collapsed ignominiously within a few days, because not only the trades unions, but also practically all the acting officials of the different Government offices declared a general strike. After this, Ehrhardt, who had been dismissed from the service, formed the Organization Consul, which was responsible for the murder of Erzberger and a number of other Republicans. It was officially dissolved after the assassination of Rathenau, though doubts were entertained whether it did not go on existing as a secret society.

as it has existed in all the troubled ages of history, just such
a one as Otway pictures in his *Venice Preserved*. Kern, its
leader, handsome, narrow-minded, easily deceived, rash, obstinate, the born fanatic, fanned by Nationalist agitation into a
fervour of hatred against Jews and the Republic; apart from
this, not devoid of charm, a young Hotspur, who exercised a
mysterious and irresistible attraction on men younger than himself. In these years after the war, when the older generation
had lost all its authority, such gatherings of small groups of
boys and youths about some one only a little older than themselves were by no means uncommon. Bruno Lemke, the editor
of the *Freideutsche Jugend* (Free German Youth), shortly
after Rathenau's assassination wrote an essay on *The Ethics of
the German Youth Movement*, in which he says of the personal relationships in the Youth groups and secret societies:
'One finds here a very delicate, but at the same time rather
noble, appreciation of the relationship between two men. . . .
The friendships between different members of the group frequently reach a degree of intimacy that can easily be mistaken
for eroticism.' (*Vossische Zeitung*, October 15th, 1922.)
Kern became the centre and the moving spirit of the little
group of conspirators; the others he made into his willing
tools. Much light is thrown on the nature of this personal
ascendancy by two remarks made in the course of the trial of
the assassins before the Supreme Court of Justice. Firstly, Ernst
Werner Techow's replies to the President of the Court's question as to why he had given Kern his word of honour on the
preceding evening to join in the crime, although he professed
to disapprove of it:

Kern held out his hand and said: "Come on." I *had* to do it
whether I wanted to or not. Kern would have shot me down;
it was a question of life or death.'
PRESIDENT: 'So you were afraid of him?'

Techow (*sobbing*): 'Yes. Kern said to me: "If you refuse I'll shoot you." '[10]

And secondly, the ex-naval officer Tillessen's answer to the question why he had not informed the police of the projected murder when he was anxious, so he said, to prevent it: 'As I was very fond of Kern, I don't think the idea ever occurred to me.' We get some idea of the moral qualities of this group of conspirators from the fact that one of them—his name is neither here nor there—put the police on the murderers' tracks (after the crime, it is true) in return for cash.

On June 18th Günther, Gerd Techow, Kern, and Fischer met at the house of Frau Techow (the Techows' widowed mother) and worked out the plan according to which Rathenau's murder did actually take place—*i.e.* they decided to pursue his car in a car of their own and shoot from car to car. On June 20th they met again in the Steglitzer Ratskeller (Town Hall Cellar Restaurant) and elaborated their plans.[11] Kern, however, began to have doubts as to whether one could be sure of one's mark with an ordinary revolver in shooting from one car to the other in rapid transit. And in order to clear up this point, Günther, Ernst Werner Techow, Fischer, and Kern met next day at the Lützow-Platz, whence they proceeded in a big six-seater car (they had borrowed it for the murder from one Küchenmeister, an engineer) to the Grünewald, where they had some shooting practice. As a result of this Kern came to the conclusion that an ordinary revolver could not be depended on for their purpose, and that what they needed

[10] After the murder, when Kern and Fischer were surrounded by police in an old tower near Kösen in Thuringia, Kern first shot Fischer and then himself. Ernst Werner Techow fled to a place owned by his uncle, a big landed proprietor near Berlin, and implored him to hide and save him; but his uncle gave him up to the police.

[11] Steglitz is a suburb of Berlin.

was an automatic pistol. So he set off with Techow and Fischer
to Schwerin in Mecklenburg to fetch one, which he had left in
the keeping of a certain Ilsemann, an ex-naval cadet and member of the Ehrhardt Brigade. Having got this, the three returned to Berlin. How these impecunious young men managed
to get the money for all this remains a mystery to this day, in
spite of 'searching enquiries' at the trial.

The conspirators spent the evening before the event—*i.e.* the
evening of June 23rd—together. They drank considerable
quantities of beer, cognac, and wine, and went once more over
the reasons why Rathenau had to be put out of the way. Kern
told Ernst Werner Techow that Rathenau was a supporter of
the surreptitious type of Bolshevism—that is to say, a Bolshevism which sought to gain its ends without a Terror; he had
signed the Rapallo Treaty and, so Kern said, married off his
sister to Radek.[12] He had got the Foreign Office by sending
a twenty-four-hour ultimatum to President Ebert. Moreover
he wanted to bring Germany under the influence of the Jews;
he had made a secret agreement with the Entente which would
be to the advantage of the latter; and finally, his policy of
fulfilment was treachery to Germany.

While the conspiracy was maturing, about June 20th or 21st,
Rathenau took a surprising but very characteristic step. In this
desperate situation he trusted to the power of his intellect, if
only he could get a quiet hearing, and asked Helfferich and his
chief lieutenant Dr Hergt[13] to dine with him alone in strict
privacy at his home in the Grünewald, with the purpose of
going over the whole ground of their differences and lifting
them out of the heated atmosphere of public meetings into the

[12] This was, of course, nonsense. Rathenau's only sister was the wife of the
Berlin banker Andreae.
[13] Oskar Hergt, born on October 22nd, 1869. Prussian Minister of Finance
from 1917 to 1918. One of the founders of the Nationalist Party. German
Minister of Justice in the Marx Cabinet from 1927 to 1928.

cooler regions of a business discussion.[14] Helfferich and Hergt accepted, the dinner took place, and the conversation lasted into the small hours of the morning. Of course, the two Nationalist leaders could not agree with Rathenau; that would have been a miracle. But they promised him that, while thinking his methods quite wrong and continuing strenuously to oppose them, yet they would do so in a manner that would not hamper him unduly in conducting Germany's foreign policy. The discussion was lively but quite friendly, and at parting the two Nationalists and Rathenau agreed that they would renew the experiment shortly.

Nevertheless, on the afternoon of June 23rd—the day on which the conspirators met to perfect their arrangements for the murder—Helfferich delivered in the Reichstag an onslaught on Rathenau in which he once more launched against him the charge of utterly ruining Germany and the German people in subservience to the Entente, the very charge which Kern was to use a few hours later in the Steglitzer Ratskeller to convince the other conspirators that the assassination of Rathenau was justified and necessary.

Helfferich's speech was an answer to a speech of Rathenau's replying to questions put to him in the Reichstag by Dr Stresemann and Dr Marx, the leader of the Centre Party and future Chancellor. He had told Stresemann, who had questioned him on the subject of a supposed Anglo-French scheme for the 'neutralization' of the Rhineland: 'In the name of the Government of the Reich I have to state that in no circumstances whatever will it consent to surrender the Rhineland in whole or in part—that Rhineland which has so often during the period of occupation testified its firm determination to remain part of the Fatherland.' In answering Dr Marx, who had ques-

[14] Helfferich, when a young man, had been befriended by Rathenau's father and mother, and it seems that Walther Rathenau and Helfferich had never quite broken off their personal relations.

tioned him on conditions in the Saar, he said: 'On June 16th, 1919, our former enemies expressed their complete confidence that the inhabitants of the Saar area would have no reason to look upon the new administration as being less concerned with their interests than with those of Berlin or Munich. If anything has been contradicted by the actual facts, it is this sentence! It is true that the Government Commission actually sits in the Saar area itself, but as a matter of fact the gulf between it and the population is greater than if it were stationed in another continent. The picture of conditions in the Saar Basin which I have taken the liberty of disclosing to you in the preceding remarks is not a pleasant one. But as Germans we can point with pride to the fact that in these difficult years of alien domination, of which only a few have passed as yet, the population of the Saar area have held together as never before, in order to preserve that which they regard as their most precious possession, their German nationality and culture.'

To this Helfferich replied on the 23rd: 'I know that God has given the diplomat the gift of speech (after Talleyrand's well-known remark) in order to hide his thoughts. But there are moments when even a Foreign Minister should refrain from using this gift. The day before yesterday was such a moment. Therefore, I can find no justification—there is no personal animus in what I say—for what I can only call the more than calculated style of the Minister's exposition of the state of affairs—this state of affairs which positively cries out to Heaven for redress. The Minister introduced the last part of his exposition with the words: "The picture which I have taken the liberty of disclosing to you is not a pleasant one. . . ." "I have taken the liberty," forsooth! . . . By God, the lemonade is flat! Is it not the case that in the present state of things in the Saar the population cannot help feeling both deserted and betrayed when once more the Government refers to them

353

in such feeble terms as these? . . . I repeat: is there not a
danger that these feeble words, betraying, as they do, hardly
the faintest trace of indignation, will give the inhabitants of
the Saar area the impression that they were uttered more out
of regard for French susceptibilities than from any real sympathy with their own sufferings? And then, right honourable
gentlemen, when Herr Dr Rathenau holds out as solitary comfort, so to speak, the hope of a better understanding of the position on the part of the League Council, surely they have nothing left, with the precedent of the Upper Silesian decision before them, but absolute despair. Indeed, must not the whole
world, as well as the Saar area, have the feeling that here we
have a Government which is willing to entrust all and everything to the League Council? To sum up, the policy of fulfilment has brought in its train the appalling depreciation of German currency, it has utterly crushed the middle classes, it has
brought poverty and misery on countless families, it has driven
countless people to suicide and despair, it has sent abroad large
and valuable portions of our national capital, and it has shaken
our industrial and social order to its very foundations!' (De-
bates of the Reichstag. Shorthand report, p. 1988 *ff*. Berlin,
1922.) Whether the assassins had or had not read Helfferich's
speech, which was indeed published in an evening paper, does
not much matter, as Helfferich merely repeated what was being
said up and down the country day and night by his adherents.
Instead of pouring oil on the troubled waters of Nationalist
agitation, as Rathenau was entitled to expect after their confidential pact, he once more stirred them up to their very
depths. The words of his peroration could have been used by
Kern himself to persuade his still hesitating companions.

That same evening Rathenau was the guest of the American
Ambassador, Mr Houghton, at a dinner at the American Em-
bassy in honour of Colonel Logan, who was the semi-official
American observer on the Reparations Commission. Rathenau

arrived late, and was obviously upset by Helfferich's attack. During dinner the conversation turned on certain Reparations coal deliveries, and Rathenau suggested, half ironically, that the Ambassador should invite Hugo Stinnes to take part in the discussion. The Ambassador agreed, and Rathenau sent a telephone message to Stinnes, who replied that he would come as soon as he had finished his own dinner. He arrived about ten o'clock, and after a purely technical discussion of the coal question began to attack Rathenau's policy in general. This developed into a lively political debate, which went on till long past midnight, and which was continued, after they had left the Embassy, at the Esplanade Hotel till almost four o'clock in the morning. The Ambassador got the impression from this discussion that the two were not so far apart, politically speaking, as was commonly supposed.[15]

Next morning, June 24th, Rathenau was a few minutes late in leaving his house in the Grünewald for the Foreign Office. He usually arrived between ten and eleven, but this morning it was nearly eleven before he set out in his old and rather slow open car.[16] The conspirators had decided to lie in wait for him at the corner of the Wallotstrasse, where the Königsallee makes a double turn and where the cars would therefore have to slow down. It had been decided that Ernst Werner Techow should drive the car, that Kern was to fire with the automatic pistol, and that Fischer was to throw a hand grenade into Rathenau's car. At this particular spot in the Königsallee some labourers were working on a new building, and one Krischbin, a mason, gave to the *Vossische Zeitung* immediately after the time a very vivid account of what happened:

[15] I owe this account of Rathenau's last evening to some notes of Mr Houghton, which he has kindly placed at my disposal.
[16] Dr Weismann, the Commissary of State for Public Order and chief of the Prussian police, told me a few hours after the murder that he had warned Rathenau the day before that if he persisted in driving to his office from his residence on the outskirts of Berlin in a slow open car, no police in the world could guarantee his safety.

'About 10.45 two cars came down the Königsallee from the direction of Hundekehle. The first one, the slower of the two, kept more or less to the middle of the road and had one gentleman in the back seat. One could see exactly what he was like, as the car was quite open and the hood was not up. The second, which was equally open, was a high-powered six-seated touring-car, dark field-grey in colour, and contained two gentlemen in long, brand-new leather coats with caps to match which covered all but their actual faces. One could see that neither of them had beards, and they didn't wear goggles. The Königsallee is always crowded with cars, so that one naturally doesn't notice every car that passes. But we all noticed this one because of the smart leather things the occupants were wearing. The large car overtook the smaller one, which had slowed down almost on the tram lines in order to take the double bend, on the right —*i.e.* the inner side, and made its swerve right out to the left, almost on to our side of the street. When the large car was about half a length past it, the single occupant of the other car looked over to the right to see if there was going to be a collision, and at that moment one of the gentlemen in the smart leather coats [Kern] leant forward, pulled out a long pistol, the butt of which he rested in his armpit, and opened fire on the gentleman in the other car. There was no need for him to aim even, it was such close range. I saw him, so to speak, straight in the face. It was a healthy, open face, the sort of face we call an officer's face. I took cover, because the shots might easily have got us too. They rang out in quick succession like a machine gun. When he had finished shooting, the other man [Fischer] stood up, swung his weapon—it was a hand grenade—and threw it into the other car, which he drove right up alongside. The gentleman had already sunk down into his seat and lay on his side. At this point the chauffeur stopped the car, just by the Erdenerstrasse, where there was a dustheap and shouted out, "Help, help!". Then the big car sprang for

356

ward with the engine full on and tore away down the Wallotstrasse. Meanwhile the other car had come to rest by the pave-
ment. At the same moment there was a bang and the hand
grenade exploded. The impact raised the gentleman in the
back some way off his seat, and even the car gave a slight jerk
forward. We all ran to the spot, and found nine cartridge cases
and the fuse of the hand grenade lying on the road. Bits of
the woodwork had splintered off. Then the chauffeur started
up again, a young girl got into the car and supported the gentleman, who was unconscious if not already dead, and the car
dashed off the way it had come along the Königsallee back to
the police station, which is some thirty metres further on at the
end of the Königsallee towards Hundekehle.' (*Vossische
Zeitung*, Sunday, June 25th, 1922.)

The young girl who so bravely sprang into the car was a
nurse, Helene Kaiser. She said at the trial: 'Rathenau, who was
bleeding hard, was still alive and looked up at me. But he
seemed to be already unconscious.' The chauffeur drove the
dying man straight back to his house from the police station,
where he was carried into his study and laid down on the floor.
When his servant tried to make him comfortable, he opened
his eyes once more. But the doctor, who arrived immediately
afterwards, was too late to do anything but certify death. The
body had been hit in five places; the spine and lower jaw were
smashed to pieces. Next day, Sunday, June 25th, he lay on the
same spot in an open coffin, his head bent back slightly to the
right; he wore a very peaceful expression, and yet there was
immeasurable tragedy in the deeply furrowed, dead, wounded
face. A handkerchief covered the lower broken part; only the
short grey crumpled moustache was visible.

Meanwhile by noon on the day of the murder the news had
spread, and the workers began swarming from the factories
and shops to form countless processions. These soon merged
into one and moved solemnly and irresistibly through the

streets of the middle- and upper-class West. Four deep they marched in their hundred thousands, beneath their mourning banners, the red of Socialism and the black-red-gold of the Republic, in one endless disciplined procession, passing like a portent silently along the great thoroughfares lined by immense crowds, wave after wave, from the early afternoon till late into the June sunset. The Nationalists had speculated on a rising which they hoped would have to be suppressed by force, and thus prepare public opinion for a dictatorship; the silent display of their power was the answer of the workers. It gave the German people a striking and unforgettable vision of the real forces governing its political constitution and of what had up to then been but an abstract conception, the birth of the German Republic.

The Reichstag met at three o'clock. Helfferich's appearance was greeted with shouts of 'Murderer! Murderer! Out with the murderers!' The tumult subsided only when Helfferich had disappeared. Later in the day Wirth spoke. 'Ever since we first began to serve this new state under the flag of the Republic, millions have been spent in pouring a deadly poison into the body of our people. From Königsberg to Constance the campaign of murder has menaced this country of ours, to whose service we have devoted all our powers of body and mind. In return we are told that what we are doing is a crime against the German people, and that we deserve to be brought to justice [cries of 'No, Helfferich, Helfferich!' from the Left]; and then people are surprised when mere deluded boys resort to murder.' Next day, which was Sunday, there was a special session of the Reichstag. Wirth did not intend to speak. But when he entered the House it was almost empty, most of the members being in the lobbies discussing the situation. He turned to me and whispered that as there seemed to be nothing in particular going on he would seize the opportunity of saying a few words in memory of our poor friend Walther Rathenau. As soon as he began speaking members flocked in, and then he launched his indictment against the Nationalists. 'When a statesman of the rank of Dr Helfferich speaks here as he did, what must be the effect on the brains of youths who have combined in secret or semi-secret Chauvinist, Nationalist, anti-Semitic and Monarchist organizations? It is evident that the result is a sort of "Feme". . . . The real enemies of our country are those who instill this poison into our people. We know where we have to seek them. *The Enemy stands on the Right!*' he exclaimed, pointing at the empty benches of the Nationalists, only a few of whom had dared retain their seats, sitting there ill at ease and pale as death, while three-quarters of the House rose and faced them. The effect was tremendous.

Rathenau's funeral took place on Tuesday, June 27th. The coffin lay in state in the Reichstag, draped under an enormous Republican flag where the Speaker's chair usually stands. Foreign Office attachés kept guard. In the Kaiser's box sat Rathenau's mother, deadly pale and as if turned to stone, never moving her eyes from the coffin beneath. President Ebert delivered the funeral oration. 'The atrocious crime has struck not only at Rathenau the man,' he said, 'but at the whole German people.'

Not since the assassination of Abraham Lincoln has the death of a statesman so shaken a whole nation. The trades unions had decreed a general holiday throughout the Reich from midday Tuesday to early Wednesday morning. Stupendous processions, such as Germany had never witnessed, marched in order under the Republican flag through all the cities of the land. Over a million took part in Berlin, a hundred and fifty thousand in Munich and Chemnitz, a hundred thousand in Hamburg, Breslau, Elberfeld, Essen. Never before had a German citizen been so honoured. The response which had been denied to

Rathenau's life and thought was now accorded to his death.

And rightly. For through its effects the human tragedy became a national tragedy. At the very moment that Poincaré was preparing to strike a death-blow at German unity his most serious obstacle was suddenly removed; that is to say, the measure of confidence and trust which Rathenau as the director of Germany's foreign policy had won for himself and his country. One blow cleared the way for a renewal of the prejudices which had made possible the Treaty of Versailles and the London Ultimatum. Poincaré had to thank those responsible for the assassination of Rathenau when he found himself at liberty to occupy the Ruhr without encountering any serious opposition from French or British opinion. For in Rathenau the symbol of the policy of understanding had gone from the scene, and in its stead German Nationalism, red-handed, loomed large before the world, and could be plausibly represented as justifying any measure of foreign intervention to safeguard the peace of Europe. Thus the bullets which killed Rathenau came very close to destroying Bismarck's life-work, German unity. It was only the German people itself, its stubborn will to live, its patience and thrift, which after a period of frightful suffering averted the danger and reconquered the position that had been lost through Rathenau's assassination.

But the last word on the human side of the tragedy was spoken by Rathenau's mother. At first her only thought was revenge. Her one desire was to write and tell Helfferich *he* was the murderer of her son, and then to die herself. But afterwards she thought better of it, as her son would have done, and wrote the following letter to the mother of the one survivor of the murderers, Ernst Werner Techow:

In grief unspeakable I give you my hand, you, of all women the most pitiable. Say to your son that in the name and spirit of him he has murdered, I forgive, even as God may forgive, if before an earthly judge he make a full and frank confession of his guilt and before a heavenly one repent. Had he known my son, the noblest man earth bore, he had rather turned the weapon on himself than on him. May these words give peace to your soul.

MATHILDE RATHENAU.

APPENDIX

APPENDIX

POINCARÉ has raised objections to the amount I have given of his Rhine policy in my *Life of Walther Rathenau*, and thereby initiated a correspondence which I reprint here for the light it throws on his political methods. Especially illuminating in this connection is his secretary's letter (No. III), in which—after carefully disclaiming responsibility for the first letter of the series, which might therefore, for all he writes, be a forgery—the French premier (with all respect for his political eminence, be it said) takes upon himself the part of Pontius Pilate in this great historical crisis. I am unable to see however that this correspondence has done anything to invalidate my account of his policy, which was in its essential aims the traditional one of Richelieu, Louis XIV, and Napoleon.

The first letter of the series appeared in the Pacifist weekly *Menschheit* for July 22nd, 1928, signed by the former Rhineland Separatist leader, J. F. Matthes (No. I):

In the interests of Franco-German friendship and historical accuracy I should be grateful if you would publish the following letter of M Poincaré's.

J. F. MATTHES

RÉSIDENCE DU CONSEIL   RÉPUBLIQUE FRANÇAISE
      CABINET   *July 10th,* 1928
DEAR SIR,
In your letter of June 26th of this year you very kindly drew my attention to Count Harry Kessler's book, entitled *Walther Rathenau, his Life and Work.*
In one passage of this work Herr Kessler states that it was the aim the French Government at the time of the Occupation of the Ruhr annex the Rhineland to France. This statement is entirely without

foundation; the French Government has never aimed at annexing the Rhineland.

I remain, etc.,

(*Signed*) POINCARÉ

In reply to this I wrote to M Poincaré (No. II):

BAD HOMBURG V.D. HÖHE

July 24th, 1928

MONSIEUR LE PRÉSIDENT,

In Professor Foerster's *Menschheit* for July 22nd, I find a translation of a letter which purports to have been addressed by you to the former Separatist leader J. F. Matthes in connection with my biography of Walther Rathenau. You must permit me to state that M Matthes has abused your good faith. Nowhere in my book did I say that it had been your intention to *annex* the Rhineland; on the contrary, I agree entirely with your statement that the annexation of the Rhineland in the political and juridical sense of the word has never in the post-war period been one of the aims of the French Government. But what I did say, and must still maintain, was that your policy aimed at separating the Rhineland from the Reich by creating an 'autonomous' Rhine state, which, politically speaking, would have belonged neither to the Reich nor indeed to France, but which, occupied for an indefinite period by mainly French troops, and attached to France by powerful economic ties (devised and set out in detail by Senator Dariac in his report of May 28th, 1922), would have passed inevitably under the preponderating influence of France. In effect it was not at all a question of 'annexation' but of 'association' (*Angliederung*) of the Rhineland with France, a relationship analogous to that existing between France and Tunisia, England and Egypt, and the United States and Cuba.

I do not see, Monsieur le Président, what other significance you yourself can attach to the facilities afforded by the French Occupation authorities to the Separatist Movement—a movement which aimed quite openly at establishing an autonomous Rhine state under the guarantee and protection of France.

Yours, etc.,

(*Signed*) COUNT KESSLER

366

APPENDIX

M Poincaré replied to this through his secretary as follows (No. III):

PRÉSIDENCE DU CONSEIL

PARIS
July 30th, 1928

SIR,

The President has received your letter of July 24th relating to the translation of a letter which purports to have been addressed to M Matthes in connection with your biography of Walther Rathenau. M Poincaré instructs me to inform you that it has never been the wish of the French Government, so far as he was concerned, to foster (*favoriser*) a Separatist Movement; at the same time, he holds that it was not his business to forbid the spontaneous demonstrations of a section of the population. As for the report of the deputy Dariac, it never professed to be anything but an expression of personal opinion.

.Yours, etc.,

(*Signed*)   GUIGNON

I replied to M Poincaré through my secretary as follows (No. IV):

BERLIN
August 30th, 1928

SIR,

Count Kessler, who is on holiday, has instructed me to thank you for your secretary's letter of July 30th, which unfortunately reached him, through your courier, only after several weeks' delay. He has noted your statement that the French Government, so far as you are concerned, has never fostered the Separatist Movement in the Rhineland, but simply desired to allow a spontaneous rising of the population to take its course. Count Kessler does not wish to cast doubts upon the honest belief—however mistaken—of the then French Government in the existence of a spontaneous movement in the Rhineland, but he is convinced that the lasting friendly co-operation of the French and German peoples is only possible if both peoples are ready to acknowledge actual facts without fear of destroying their mutual good relations. Thus he feels that it can do no harm to draw your attention to circumstances which played a decisive part in the Separatist Movement, but which may possibly have escaped your memory. So with all respect for your high authority and subsequent efforts towards friendlier relations between the two peoples, he has no hesitation in recalling certain facts which can be attested either by French official documents or by countless people in the Rhineland itself: that according to his Report

367

of April 16th, 1923, to the French High Commissioner in Coblenz, M Tirard (Document 42 LW/23), the French district delegate in Wiesbaden, the Marquis de Lillers, had been officially entrusted since May, 1921, with the task of fostering relations with Herr Dorten, the head of the Separatists; that according to this same Report, 'the High Commissioner had gone to the utmost limits to make Dorten's task as easy as possible,' and to this end had supplied him with considerable sums of money, so that the High Commissioner had actually felt justified in reproaching Dorten with his insufficiently energetic leadership of the Separatist Movement; and, further, that the French railway authorities conveyed Separatists to Separatist meetings by special trains; that the French Occupation authorities permitted the Separatists to carry arms and even to carry out military manoeuvres, both of which were, of course, forbidden to the loyal section of the population under threat of the severest penalties; that in the chief towns of the Rhineland, such as Düsseldorf, Bonn, Treves, Mainz, Wiesbaden, and even in Coblenz, the headquarters of the French High Commissioner—in his presence and, so to speak, under his very eyes—everything was done by the French civil and military Occupation authorities to ensure the success of the Putsches, which the proclamation of the 'Rhenish Republic' aimed at bringing about: first, by disarming the German police shortly before the Putsch was to take place; secondly, by military and police protection of the Separatists during the Putsch; and, thirdly, by the immediate recognition after the Putsch of the new revolutionary so-called 'Rhenish' Government on the part of the French civil and military authorities in the Rhineland, in contrast to the usual attitude of reserve adopted towards all new revolutionary governments, and also by the proclamation of the state of siege in many places.

These facts, which were of enormous assistance to the Separatist in carrying out their plans, are well established and universally recognized, and, as said before, can be attested by countless eye-witnesses in the Rhineland.

Count Kessler is very ready to admit that the occupation of part of an alien state almost inevitably leads the authorities of the occupying Power, even against the will of their Government, to foster separatist movements in the occupied territories. But as one has never heard of any action being taken against the French authorities in the Rhineland who would appear to have so flagrantly violated the intentions and instructions of the French Government and in particular its supreme head, Count Kessler feels that it is difficult to absolve the then French

Government from the moral responsibility for the attitude of these authorities. On the other hand, Count Kessler believes that all who, like himself, have striven from the first for a Franco-German understanding will hear with satisfaction that, whatever may have been the aims of French policy in the years 1922-1924, today undertakings such as these (which would have constituted, had they been successful, an invincible obstacle to Franco-German reconciliation and a permanent menace to the peace of the world) would find no support with the French Government as it exists under your leadership today.

Yours, etc.,

(*Signed*) FRITZ GUSECK
Secretary

This letter remained unanswered. It therefore suffices to say that the Report of the Marquis de Lillers, quoted above in No. IV, was first printed in the London *Observer* of June 24th, 1923, and that the reputed authorship of the then French district delegate in Wiesbaden, the Marquis de Lillers, has never received either official or semi-official denial. Further, that the document is reprinted without abridgment in *Loslösungsbestreungen am Rhein 1918-1924*, a book based on official documents by Professor Max Springer of Heidelberg, where it can easily be examined and where it helps, along with a mass of other relevant material, to throw a vivid light on the quite unequivocal character of French policy on the Rhine at that time.

INDEX

1904. 'Weakness, Fear and Purpose' *(Zukunft)*, 25, 55, 57.
1907. 'Unwritten Works,' 60, 62, 114.
1908. Reflections *(Reflexionen,* reprinted from *Zukunft),* 131-2.
'The New Era' *(Hannoverscher Courier),* 121, 139, 208, 276.
'England's Present Position' (Memorandum to Bülow), 126.
1909. Article in the *Neue Freie Presse,* 117.
1911. 'The State and the Jews,' 27-8, 127, 138, 226.
'Politics, Humour and Disarmament' *(Neue Freie Presse),* 139, 167.
1912. 'England and Ourselves: A Philippic' *(Neue Freie Presse),* 142-3.
'Political Selection' *(Neue Freie Presse),* 143.
'Festal Song for the Centenary of 1813' *(Zukunft),* 144.
1913. 'The Sacrifice to the Eumenides' *(Neue Freie Presse),* 155-7.
'German Dangers and New Aims' *(Neue Freie Presse),* 158.
1914. 'On the Situation' *(Berliner Tageblatt),* 169.
1915. 'The Organization of Germany's Raw Materials' (Address to the Deutsche Gesellschaft), 171-2.
1917. 'Safeguards' *(Frankfurter Zeitung),* 233.
1918. 'A Black Day' *(Vossische Zeitung),* 245.
'Staat und Vaterland,' 247-8.
Open Letter 'To all who are not blinded by hate,' 261.
Open Letter to Colonel House, 261-2.
1919. 'The End' *(Zukunft),* 262-3.
Article in *Welt am Montag,* 265-6.
'Schicksalsspiel' (The Game of Fate) *(Berliner Tageblatt),* 232, 267.
1920. Lecture on 'Democratic Development,' 275.
Lecture on 'The Zenith of Capitalism,' 280.

NOTE. Most of these were reprinted in the *Collected Works* (5 volumes) or in one of the collections *Zeitliches, Nach der Flut, Was wird Werden?,* and *Speeches.*

INDEX

Abeken, Mme [Widow of Heinrich Abeken, one of the collaborators of Bismarck. A well-known Berlin society leader in Bismarck's time. Born 1829, died April, 1919], 45-6
Adam, the brothers, 68
A.E.G., 13-14, 15, 43, 58, 117-9, 131, 173, 229, 246, 254, 288
Agadir crisis, 137-41
Algeçiras, 121
Allied Military Commissions, 300, 302
Andrassy, Count, 231
Apponyi, Count, 231
Arenberg, Prince, 345 n.
Arnim, Bettina von, [Born April 4th, 1785, at Frankfurt. Daughter of Goethe's friend Maximiliane Laroche and sister of the romanticist poet Clemens Brentano. Was intimately acquainted with Goethe, and after his death published her correspondence with him (*Goethe's Briefwechsel mit einem Kinde*). A very romantic and eccentric personality and the center of a literary and artistic circle in Berlin in the forties and fifties. Died January 20th, 1859], 6, 46
Aschkenasi, Rabbi, 116
Asquith, H. H., 163, 164 n.
Augusta, Empress, 48

Baal-shem-tov, 82
Ballin, Albert, 120
Balzac, 240
Barrère, 333
Barrès, Maurice, 88 n.
Barthou, Louis, 305, 307 ff., 327 ff.
Basserman, 125, 138, 230-1
Baudissin, Count, 45-6
Bauer, Otto, 218
Beneš, Dr, 321
Bergmann, Dr Carl, 274, 277, 283, 284-6, 293-5, 297-300, 311-2
Bergson, Henri, 62
Bernhard, Georg [Editor of the Berlin

Vossische Zeitung, one of the leading democratic newspapers, and since 1928 a member of the Reichstag], 231
Bethmann-Hollweg, Theodor von, 49, 137-9, 164, 222-3
Bismarck, 8, 48, 306, 339, 360
Blackett, Sir Basil, 326, 327 n.
Blanche Trocard, 30 ff., 64
Bodenhausen, Eberhard von, 120
Boehme, Jacob, 86
Bolshevism, 200, 241, 259, 275, 278
Bonomi, 299
Boothby, Robert, 215
Boulogne agreement, 305, 311, 312
Brest-Litovsk Treaty, 278, 312
Breviarium Mysticum, 74 ff.
Briand, Aristide, 284-5, 296, 299, 300, 302, 309
Britain's Industrial Future, 180 n., 207
Brockdorff-Rantzau, Count [Born May 29th, 1869, in Schleswig. German minister to Denmark during the war, and the first Republican Foreign Minister after the Revolution. Led the German delegation at Versailles, but refused to sign the Versailles Treaty, and retired when the National Assembly in Weimar decided to accept the Allied ultimatum. Ambassador to Russia 1922. Died 1928], 212, 263, 281
Brunner, Professor Constantin, 66
Brussels Conference, 283
Buber, Dr Martin, 82
Buddha, 86
Bülow, Prince, 49, 122, 125-6, 137, 140, 170, 345 n.
Bülow, Princess, 48
Bund der Aufrechten, 347
Buré, Emile, 277
Business, large scale (*see also* rationalization), 14-17, 39-42, 119-21, 192-3

Caillaux, Mme, 162
Cambon, Jules, 137

373

INDEX

ure of the new rich. His best-known drawings have been collected in a book, *Das Gesicht der herrschenden Klasse*], 260
Guignon, 367
Guild socialism, 209, 216-20
Guilleaume, F. von, 119, 120
Gumbel, Dr E. J., 344
Günther, Wilhelm, 347-51
Guseck, Fritz, 369

Hagen, Dr, 120, 320, 321
Haguenin, Professor, 296
Haldane, Lord, 141-2, 154-5
Hammer, Peter, 266
Hansabund, 134
Harden, Maximilian (*see also Zukunft*) [The most celebrated political pamphleteer of his period. Began publishing a violently pro-Bismarckian and anti-governmental weekly, *Die Zukunft*, in 1892, and kept it up till after the Revolution. Frequently attacked the Kaiser, and was several times imprisoned for *lèse-majesté*. Was a friend and patron of the whole post-Bismarckian generation of young German poets, writers, and artists. A number of his best essays on contemporary politicians and writers have been republished under the title *Köpfe*. Died October 30th, 1927], 36, 52, 53, 55, 66, 123, 127, 144-5, 146, 148
Harrach, Countess, 48
Hassidism, 82, 84-6   [287
Hauptmann, Gerhart, 30, 53, 148, 165,
Haussmann, Conrad, 170, 175
Hegel, 142
Heine, Dr Wolfgang, 230
Helfferich, Karl, 344, 345, 351-5, 358-9, 360
Helmholtz, Professor, 22
Henckel-Donnersmarck, Prince Guido, 117, 120, 231
Henckel-Donnersmarck, Princess, 48
Herder, J. G., 88
Hergt, Dr Oscar, 351, 352
Hermes, Dr Andreas, 321
Hesnard, Professor, 331
Hilferding, Rudolf, 218-9, 256, 319, 337-8
Hindenburg, Field-Marshal von, 232, 246, 253
Hindenburg, Herbert von, 44

Hindenburg, Frau von, 48, 51, 169
Hintze, von, 278
Hirsch, Julius, 206
Hobson, S. G., 218 *n.*
Hoetzsch, Professor Otto, 231
Hoffmann, Professor, 279
Hofmann, Professor, 22
Hofmannsthal, Hugo von [Poet, dramatist, and essayist. Born February 1st, 1874, died July 16th, 1929. Wrote, when still a boy, some of the most perfect lyrical poems in the German language, and later on a number of librettos for Richard Strauss—amongst others the *Rosenkavalier* and *The Legend of Joseph* in collaboration with the author of this book], 25, 53
Horne, Sir Robert, 298, 299
Houghton, A. B., 354, 355 and *n.*
House, Colonel, 261-2
Hugenberg, Alfred, 231
Humboldt, 8

Ibsen, Henrik, 30
Ilsemann, 351
Inheritance, 110, 185-6, 188

Jaspar, 332-5
Joffe, 278, 318-9, 321-4
Jogisches, Leo, 260

Kaiser, Helene, 357
Kaiser, the (William II), 27 *n.*, 43, 46, 49 *ff.*, 122 *ff.*, 141-2, 164, 166-7, 208, 231, 247, 267
Kalckreuth, Countess, 45
Kapp Putsch, 256, 269, 348
Karrenbrock, Lore, 65, 266
Kautsky, Karl, 219, 256
Kemal Pasha, 305
Kern, Erwin, 348-51, 352, 354, 355-6
Keynes, J. M., 207
Kiderlen-Wächter, 137
Klingenberg, Professor, 173
Klöckner, 120
Kluck, General, 231
Koeth, Lieutenant-Colonel, 175
Koltchak, 317
Krassin, Leonid, 278
Kriege, Dr, 278
Krischbin, 355-6
Kropotkin, 182
Krupp (the elder), 8, 41
Krupp von Bohlen, 120
Küchenmeister, 350

375

INDEX

377

Roche, Jules, 163
Rodin, Auguste, 163
Rosen, Dr, 288, 300
Rosenberg, von, 300
Ruhr, 276, 279, 286, 293, 295, 297, 338 *n.*, 360
Ruskin, John, 217
Russell, Bertrand, 217, 218 *n.*
Russia (*see also* Bolshevism), 112, 123, 162, 169, 278-9, 280, 297, 299, 303, 305 *ff.*

Saar, 353-4
Sanctions, 285-6
Saenger, Professor, 24
Salomonsohn, Dr A., 120
Salter, Sir J. Arthur, 177-8, 234
Sarajevo, 163
Schacht, Dr, 338 *n.*
Schanzer, 317, 328-9
Scheuch, Heinrich [General. Born June 21st, 1864, at Schlettstadt in Alsace. Became Prussian War Minister in October, 1918. Retired after the Revolution], 171-2, 246
Schleinitz, Frau von, 48
Schwabach, Paul von, 120
Schwaner, Wilhelm, 66, 226, 228, 230, 234
Seeckt, General von, 272, 277
Selbstschutz, 346
Separatism. *See* Rhineland.
Seydoux, 311-2
Sheraton, Thomas, 68
Siemens, Werner, 16
Silesius, Angelus, 86
Simmel, Georg [Professor of Philosophy and Sociology in Berlin and afterwards in Strassburg. Born in Berlin March 1st, 1858. Died September 27th, 1918. His most important book was a *Philosophie des Geldes* (*Philosophy of Money*)], 26
Simon, H. F., 293, 297
Simons, Dr, 212, 271, 272, 274, 284-5
Simson, von, 317, 321, 323
Solidarity, 111-3, 183, 192
Sombart, Werner [Professor of Economics in Berlin. Born January 19th, 1863. His most important book is *Der Moderne Kapitalismus*, which he began publishing in 1902 and has since continued in a number of volumes], 92
Sonntag, Henriette, 45-6

Spa Conference, 270-1, 284
Spartacist rising, 241, 259, 264
Spinoza, 83-8, 113
Springer, Professor Max, 369
Steed, Wickham, 336 and *n.*
Stein, Charlotte von, 150
Stein, Professor Ludwig, 230
Steiner, Rudolf, 165
Stendhal, 18, 44, 240
Stinnes, Hugo, 120, 231, 272-6, 300, 302, 355
Stöcker, 250
Strauss, Richard, 163
Stravinski, Igor, 163
Stresemann, Dr, 125, 231, 273, 278, 279, 297, 300 *n.*, 352
Stubenrauch, Hans, 347-8
Südekum, Dr, 230, 247
Sudermann, Hermann, 30
Sukhomlinoff, General, 162

Talleyrand, 138, 277, 353
Techow, Ernst Werner, 348-51, 355, 360-1
Techow, Frau, 350, 360
Techow, Gerd, 348
Tieck, Ludwig, 45, 46
Tillessen, Karl, 348, 350
Tirard, 368
Tirpitz, Admiral von, 141
Tittoni, 140
Tolstoi, 116, 137
Tsar, the (Nicholas II), 222

Unruh, Fritz von, 165, 242

Van de Velde, Professor Henry, 53
Van Gogh, Vincent, 68
Van Vlissingen, 321
Varnhagen, Karl August, 45
Varnhagen, Rahel, 45
Vauvenargues, 34
Versailles Treaty, 260, 261, 262, 268 *ff.*, 278, 279, 285, 296, 312-3
Vildrac, Charles, 31
Vollmöller, Dr Karl, 230
Voss, 45

Wagner, Richard, 48
Weber, Professor Max, 250
Wedekind, Frank, 53, 57
Wedgwood, Josiah, 68
Weismann, Dr, 355 *n.*

Westarp, Count, 231
Wiesbaden Agreement, 291-3
Wilde, Oscar, 30, 34, 217
Wildenbruch, Ernst von, 45
William II. *See* Kaiser
Wilson, President, 223, 242, 246, 260-3, 296
Winterfeldts, 164
Wirth, Dr Josef, 269, 270, 272, 277, 287, 300, 302-3, 307, 311, 317, 320 *ff.*, 327 *ff.*, 342-3, 358
Wise, E. F., 314, 319 *ff.*, 337
Wissell, Rudolph [One of the leaders of the German social-democratic party in the Reichstag. Born March

18th, 1869, in Göttingen. Secretary of State of the German Minister of Economics from February to July, 1919. Minister of Labour in the present German Cabinet], 254-5
Witting, 289
Wordsworth, William, 86

Yudenitch, 317
Yusupoff, Prince, 163

Ziegler, Leopold, 258
Zukunft, 36, and *n.*, 39, 46, 52, 55, 90, 131, 144, 254, 262

CPSIA information can be obtained
at www.ICGtesting.com
Printed in the USA
LVHW081938290922
729515LV00018B/83